TRANSFORMING RUSSIA

For Erik

TRANSFORMING RUSSIA

From a Military to a Peace Economy

Tarja Cronberg

BLOOMSBURY ACADEMIC
LONDON • NEW YORK • OXFORD • NEW DELHI • SYDNEY

BLOOMSBURY ACADEMIC
Bloomsbury Publishing Plc
50 Bedford Square, London, WC1B 3DP, UK
1385 Broadway, New York, NY 10018, USA
29 Earlsfort Terrace, Dublin 2, Ireland

BLOOMSBURY, BLOOMSBURY ACADEMIC and the Diana logo
are trademarks of Bloomsbury Publishing Plc

First published in Great Britain by I.B. Tauris 2003
Paperback edition published by Bloomsbury Academic 2021

ISBN: HB: 978-1-8606-4903-5
PB: 978-1-3501-7858-8
ePDF: 978-0-7556-3340-1
eBook: 978-0-7556-3341-8

To find out more about our authors and books visit
www.bloomsbury.com and sign up for our newsletters.

Contents

Acknowledgements

To do empirical research on the other side of the globe requires good partners. My research into military technology and the arms industry in Perm in the Urals and in Los Angeles, California, would not have been possible without the support and co-operation of Yakov Vaysman, the head of the Ecological Institute of the Perm Technical University, Irina May, docent at the same place, and David Bernstein, Senior Research Fellow at Stanford University, Center for International Arms Control. I am truly grateful to all three for inspiration, support and invaluable assistance.

At its various stages this book has greatly benefitted from the comments and criticism of the following people: Ksenia Gonchar, Bonn International Center for Conversion, Ingunn Moser, Center for Technology, Innovation and Culture at Oslo University, Mark Elam, University of Gothenburg, Håkan Wiberg, Copenhagen Peace Research Institute, Niels Petter Gleditsch, International Peace Research Institute, Oslo, Elina Kahla, Alexander Institute, Helsinki, and Ljubica Jelusic, University of Ljubljana, and with her the whole EU COST action "Defense restructuring and conversion", which she chaired.

Grants have been made available by the Social Science Research Council in Denmark, which has funded the main part of the actual research work, and by Copenhagen Peace Research Institute, which has provided grants for research, international cooperation and language editing. The partners in Perm and at Stanford have financed seminars directly related to the dissemination of the research results.

When reflecting over the whole ten years of work, there is one person in particular who deserves the warmest thanks for her patience and encouragement in critical phases of the process, Kirsten Gammelgaard, from the Technical University of Denmark, who has provided much more then secretarial assistance during many years.

The final product would not have been possible without the help of my collegues at Copenhagen Peace Research Institute, particularly Anita Elleby and Mette Lykke Knudsen, who have been responsible for the camera ready copy, and Birte Laurberg, who has assisted in integrating the last comments.

Copenhagen, September 2002   Tarja Cronberg

Chapter 1

Introduction

In 1996 I published a book *Technological Powers in Transition: Defence Conversion in the United States and Russia 1991–1995*. This book, the result of five years of conversion studies, was a study of how defence enterprises in the Los Angeles area of the US and in the Perm area of the Russian Urals coped with reduced defence budgets after the Cold War. It examined whether or not military technologies developed for arms systems could be used in civilian applications: were they 'dual use'? It explored how individual enterprises tried to change their production profiles, how regions tried to create new types of innovation systems and how nations tried to rewrite their technology policies to reflect the new situation. By comparing the two superpowers, my colleagues and I expected to understand the conversion process in depth, both in a market economy and in a planned-economy context. Our comparison focused on similar types of production, i.e. aerospace and aviation. The two regions, Perm and Los Angeles, are both characterised by a concentration of production in these fields.

Conversion studies, which have had a renaissance and have flourished since the end of the Cold War, had already been initiated in the early 1960s and '70s. The early studies were called 'swords into ploughshares' or 'guns into butter'.[1] These metaphors included a moral imperative. If defence budgets were cut, a 'peace dividend' would be available and could be used in a more socially acceptable way. While swords would not literally be converted into ploughshares, the dollars saved from the defence budget could be allocated to other fields such as health care and education. Seymour Melman has calculated[2] that the defence dollars spent on education would give the most benefit in terms of jobs. As we know now, there has been no peace dividend. On the contrary, the bill for the destruction of the weapons is three to four times that of their construction. Not to mention the hundreds of thousands of workers who have become unemployed or the square miles of fields and military bases that are polluted.

But conversion is not only about the peace dividend and decreased military budgets. It is also about defence enterprises and their conversion to civilian or commercial production. In the United States, conversion on the enterprise level is defined as an individual company's ability to diversify, to increase its share of civilian or – as the term is used in the US – commercial production. Enterprises may achieve this in many ways. They may acquire non-defence enterprises and thus increase their share of non-defence production. They may sell their defence productions, which many US companies did after the Cold War, and thus reduce their dependence on defence production. Furthermore, defence production may be decreased on the enterprise level by simply shutting down a defence plant. This understanding of conversion as diversification[3] is consistent with the US system of market economy. Enterprises are independent actors. They sell, buy and shut down production units and thus define the businesses they want to be in.

Conversion in Russia, or rather in the former Soviet Union, was defined during the Gorbachev era as the retooling of existing defence plants. Existing resources, plants and know-how were to be converted to more commercial uses, preferably in the same plants. This retooling approach has been much criticised as an impossible avenue to commercial production due to the special characteristics of defence production. Defence production is often on a high technological level, with performance at any cost and production in small quantities. However, this retooling approach was built into the Soviet economic system. Enterprises were part of the State. They were not autonomous actors who could freely sell part of their production and buy others. The civilian economy was less developed, and on a low technological level. Since the defence sector had been the priority, it was seen as the key to the new profile of the country's production. Therefore the retooling approach was a 'natural' and taken for granted solution in the Soviet context.[4]

Retooling of defence plants was, for Gorbachev, a way to integrate Russia into the world economy. This may have been a natural expectation in a situation where the former Soviet defence industry had demonstrated its ability to compete with that of the Americans. On the other hand, it may also be dependent on the degree of militarisation of the economy. Shlykov[5] has called the Russian economy a 'structurally' militarised economy, as opposed to the 'usual' militarisation, which may be measured by defence budgets and military spending as proportions of the Gross Domestic Product. In a structurally militarised economy, the civilian economy cannot be separated from the military and no amount of cuts in the defence budgets will necessarily increase the size of the civilian economy or its effectiveness. Thus, the retooling approach, in spite of all its difficulties, may have been the only choice when initiating economic reforms.

According to the answer at hand, one could say that it is not possible to compare Russian and US defence conversion. The role of defence production was so different, the way defence production was built into the economic system was so intimate and its links to the civilian world so specific. However, we did compare the two. The results showed, not astonishingly, that the American conversion was more efficient: companies were restructuring, consolidating their activities and even increasing their performances on stock exchanges. Some companies specialised in defence production while others sold out and concentrated on commercial activities. People were laid off from plants that no longer had orders, and local and regional administrations got involved in trying to find replacements and retraining for jobs. The Russian conversion seemed to be more amateurish. Their fixation on the retooling approach without any restructuring of defence plants seemed to be a dead end. Even Russian sources deemed conversion efforts a failure.[6] We saw the Russian failure to convert, to create a production based on commercial and civilian products.

We interpreted what happened in a Western context, and studied it with Western concepts such as innovation economics and actor networks shaping technology. We described the regional innovation systems and criticised the fact that regions seemed to be unable to create institutional structures to support defence conversion. On the policy level, our results showed that while the Americans were turning to a dual-use technology policy, this approach would never be possible in Russia given the level of technologies in civilian fields. In conclusion, the Americans were making the conversion the 'right' way and the Russians were lagging behind. The military industries of Russia had not been able to throw away all the legacy of the Soviet Union and start producing goods for the civilian market. In the past ten years, they have not been able to create a production base adapted to the world market and a market economy.

But has the effort been unsuccessful? Although there is no peace dividend and very little retooling of the defence industries (although some good examples do exist) many things have changed. The economic system has changed. Reforms have been implemented. Military production has decreased. If conversion results are not measured by the increased proportion of civilian products from the defence enterprises, but rather by the total reduction of military production, Russian conversion has been extremely successful, as pointed out by Julian Cooper in his article 'Conversion is Dead, Long Live Conversion'.[7] Measured in these terms, American conversion has been less successful. Although the defence budget was reduced in the early 90s, American weapon exports have increased.

My conclusion concerning the Western-style conversion studies was that we have to study Russia in other terms, try to understand the changes taking place in a different context. Maybe comparative studies are not possible, not even in terms of something so material as technology. Maybe it is necessary to go deeper than just comparing innovations or organisational changes. Maybe, in order to understand Russia, we have to understand the social practices, the way people have interacted and the way technologies have been linked to these practices. The new sociology of technology claims not only that technology is society but also that in order to understand society we have to study technology. Technology and society are so intimately tied together that the two can no longer be separated. Understanding technological change is to understand social change. My general thesis in this book is, consequently, that by understanding the military technology of the former Soviet Union and the efforts to convert it into civilian uses in the post-communist Russia, we will also be able to understand the rebuilding of a Russian society, its reconstruction into a market economy and the political turmoil the country has been in since the end of the Cold War.

Renegotiating technology

Is it possible to understand a world different from our own? Is it possible to take a step in a direction which allows those being studied, and who are yet to be known, to speak for themselves without reinterpreting their understanding of the way things are, without imposing Western concepts on something where they may not necessarily fit? Shall we, when we learn to understand the other, also learn new things about ourselves?

It is not possible for a Western researcher like myself to represent the truth concerning the reality of the Russian military-industrial complex – nor of its potential for conversion. Instead, I shall try to open up the arena for Russian voices and their own interpretations of what has been going on since the end of the Cold War. The objective of this book is to understand how military technology becomes built into society, to understand how meanings and commitment around military production and the creation of defence technologies are constructed. This can be done in a situation where the invisible things around defence technologies become visible.

When technologies in arms systems are to be converted into commercial production, a number of hidden agendas become obvious. Was it only a question of defending the country? How did the people involved understand the kind of production they were involved in? The inertia in the transformation of weapon systems and military know-how to civilian production represents meanings, ideas, dreams and commitment built into the construction of weapon systems.

Although frustrated over the use of Western concepts and the insensitivity in the description of different worlds, I do not propose to dismiss the use of theoretical concepts altogether. On the contrary, I shall base this study on two types of theoretical resources: first, the social constructivist understanding of technology, where technology is seen as objects negotiated in actor networks and as results of social dynamics rather than material products defined by their own logic or by a specific social order. Secondly, the concept of a social world, in which basic social processes are studied as empirical questions in the tradition of the symbolic interactionism. Both of these theoretical resources have the quality of being non-normative, empirically open, relativist. They both focus on the making of relations and local practices.

The most important contribution of the social constructivist view of technology is its connection to the social. The concept of the 'seamless web',[8] where the technological is identical to the social, is well adapted to the study of military technology and its transformation to civilian products. The concept of the social world provides a tool for understanding the inertia of the conversion process through concepts such as awareness context, commitment and identity. But first a few words about each of these theoretical approaches.

In constructivist studies of technology, technologies are understood, not as autonomous nor as given by the social order, but rather as result of a negotiation process. Actors negotiate the meaning of technology, at some point reach an agreement, and technology is stabilised. Although there are differences between the different constructivist schools,[9] technologies are always seen as a result of social dynamics where arguments and counter-arguments, alliances and controversies create the context for the emergence of technological artefacts. Thus, advanced Cold War military technology was not a result of a technological trajectory, autonomous innovations or a technological logic. Military technology emerged during the Cold War as a heterogeneous process in which defence bureaucrats, industrial representatives, the army, scientists, engineers and the public participated in a complex network of actors creating alliances to support the emergence of the B2 bomber, the ABM shield or nuclear submarines.

Individual case studies, of which the best known is Donald MacKenzie's study[10] of missile accuracy, show how technology is created, not as an optimal solution to a certain problem, but rather as result of a messy process in which technological characteristics are negotiated. To support his thesis that technology is socially shaped, McKenzie shows how different solutions to the same problem emerge in the US and the Soviet Union.

Power, in the social constructivist understanding of technology, is the ability to keep technology stabilised. Alliances and actor networks that are able to define and stabilise technology have power over technology. This is not to be understood as structurally stable power. On the contrary, it is micro-power relating to arguments and meanings. When alliances are destabilised, when institutions and social dynamics supporting a particular kind of technology are destabilised, technology also becomes destabilised. Technology becomes renegotiable as new social relations support a new shape for the technology. Understood in this context, military technology is neither a result of the power in the military-industrial complex nor of any other structural actors. What looks like the power of the military is, in fact, the ability of certain actor networks to stabilise the understanding of technology, to 'black box' it, to use a constructivist term.[11]

The Cold War was an institution stabilising military technology. The striving for technological superiority among the superpowers was taken for granted; the military allocated the necessary resources and their arguments were given priority. The Cold War supported the military technology of the particular kind that is related to the competition for technological superiority among the superpowers. The end of the Cold War also destabilised the meaning and understanding of military technology, making it renegotiable. Power relations attached to the emergence of military innovations were disrupted, and the processes of technological development destabilised.

The constructivists are able to renegotiate technology at any time, as long as the technology and the social relations that support it are destabilised. This would seem to be an ideal starting point for renegotiations when military technology is to be transformed into civilian uses. Military technology has been destabilised by reduced defence budgets, new understanding of the enemy and a new world order. However, the stories told by the constructivists describe the emergence of technological artefacts, which are always new. The renegotiation processes studied have paid less attention to old artefacts. There are very few explanations as to how and why certain technologies become destabilised and how, if at all, they can be renegotiated. In fact, the end of the Cold War left a lot of submarines rusting in the ports of Murmansk and a number of missiles and tanks to be actively destroyed. What if the 'seamless web' of the social and the technological does not go away and what if a 'socio-technical ensemble'[12] seems to need more reconstruction rather than merely destabilisation of institutions and social relations? This book is about this reconstruction process.

Social worlds

Transforming Russia has been written as a corrective to my earlier books on defence conversion particularly in Russia. It is a move away from preconceived theoretical conceptualisations towards a more ethno-methodological approach. I have, since the publication of *Technological Powers in Transition*, been searching for theoretical approaches enabling me to stay in the realm of sociology but at the same time to address realities that are dissimilar to our own. If innovation economics is a discipline based on the Western industrial tradition and on conceptualisation of an enterprise and its role in promoting technological innovation, what kind of theoretical tools exist that could enable us to capture a different reality? A reality where the State has not only intervened everywhere, but has been co-constructed with everything else from the salaries of the defence workers to the very core of what innovations to 'create'.

Grounded theory developed by Anselm Strauss and Barney Glaser seems to fulfil the requirement of exploring unknown territory but with well-defined theoretical concepts.[13] According to Anselm Strauss a grounded theory is 'one that is inductively derived from the study of the phenomenon it represents'. That is, it is discovered, developed and provisionally verified through systematic data collection and analyses of data pertaining to that phenomenon. Therefore, data collection, analysis and theory stand in reciprocal relationship with each other.

One does not begin with a theory, then prove it. Rather, one begins with an area of study and what is relevant to that area.[14]

According to grounded theory, theory should be truthful to the everyday reality of the substantive area. Because it represents that reality, it should also be comprehensible and make sense to those who study it. The requirement of generality is met if the data upon which the theory is based are comprehensive and applicable to a variety of contexts, related to the phenomenon in question. In a way, grounded theory is a systematic qualitative research approach where certain procedures must be followed at the same time as openness and flexibility are necessary in order to adapt the procedures to new and unknown phenomena and situations.

In grounded theory, the basic social processes are empirical questions. For the interactionist tradition of Strauss, networks are not only open for all actors and actions, but rather more enduring and structurally oriented. Structural aspects are not unchanging, rather they are slower to change than other aspects of situations. For Strauss, structures are ultimately based on the commitments of individual actors to collective action – to work of some kind – state building, international capitalist development, social movement organisation, drug cartelling or sociological studies.[15]

Social worlds, the central concept of grounded theory, are distinct from formal organisation. Participation does not require membership and is based only on commitment. Social worlds are 'social wholes, which make meaning together, and act on the basis of those meanings'. The meanings of phenomena lie in their embeddedness in relationships, in universes of discourse. Work or collective action of some kind is the 'business' of a universe of discourse.[16] Social worlds are thus described as:

> Groups with shared commitments to certain activities, sharing resources of many kinds to achieve their goals, and building shared ideologies about how to go about their business. Social worlds form fundamental building blocks of collective action and are units of analysis in many inter-actionist studies of collective action. Social worlds are the principal affiliative mechanisms through which people organise social life.[17]

The social world as a concept is well adapted to the study of military technology. The individual and collective actors in the defence industry have made a commitment to work for their country. They have committed themselves to achieving technological superiority and to performing high-level scientific work. The networks in and around military technology were, in the process of conversion, not immediately accessible for new alliances and new patterns of enrolment in the commercial and civilian spheres. Rather, change was slower, even slower than expected as meanings attached to the work done, commitments made and experiences gained were shaping the situation. While not defined as structural, these aspects of the situation pose a challenge to understand why, and how military technologies change and how defence workers understand their work in society.

A number of defence-industry workers produced civilian products such as bicycles or washing machines. Many worked at the hospitals or day-care centres of defence-industry enterprises. Were they participating in the social world of the military? The concept of a social world allows for this ambiguity and heterogeneity. The critical question is the commitment of the participants. All Soviet citizens were enrolled in the discourse of the Cold War and in the defence of their country. In spite of this when describing the social world of the military technology, my empirical focus will be on scientists and engineers, i.e. those who worked for the creation of military innovations, tested them and produced them. I am not looking at the social world of the military, such as the army, although they certainly were the users of the end products of the defence industries and were even the controllers at the production units.

Crossing boundaries

The objective of this study is to focus on the links between the social world of military technology in Russia, and what could be called the 'social world of civilian technology'. The topic of investigation is the boundary, the renegotiations and the transformation of military technology to civilian production. The focus is on transformations between the military and the civilian, between products of war and products not intended for war, although the boundaries may be heterogeneous, porous and fluid.

An important concept in this context is the 'arena'. According to Clark,[18] an arena is formed when several social worlds focus on a given issue and are prepared to act in some way to come together. Many different collective actors are involved in arenas, various issues are debated, negotiated, fought out, forced and manipulated by representatives of the participating worlds and sub-worlds. All social worlds strive to establish and maintain boundaries between their world and the others, and to gain social legitimation for their own world. These processes involve the social construction of a particular world, and the very history of the world is commonly constructed and reconstructed in the process. From this it follows that military technology can be seen as an arena, a space where various issues related to technological development are debated, negotiated and fought out. It is the arena where different actors meet. In the arena of military technology, not only scientists, engineers and defence workers, but also the public and defence organisations of other countries meet.

Closely related to the concept of arena is the concept of boundary objects developed by Star and Giesemeer.[19] Boundary objects are things that exist at the junctures where various social worlds meet in an arena of mutual concern. These may be treaties among countries, software programmes for users or even concepts themselves. The basic social process is that the object is 'translated' in order to address the multiple needs or demands placed upon it by different social worlds that 'meet' around the boundary object. Thus reconstruction of, for example, a gas mask used in tanks to a filter used in water purification is such a translation in which the technological artefact is a boundary object. A contract to establish a joint venture to utilise military technology in a civilian field or satellite surveillance used in espionage translated for use in weather forecasts are also boundary objects. These boundary objects form links between the social world of the military technology and that of the civilian and commercial technologies.

The advantage of concepts of the social world and that of an arena is that they tolerate porous boundaries between and among various worlds because of the very openness of the conceptual framework.[20] Boundary objects between military and civilian technologies, which enable scientists to move from a military technology arena to a more commercial one, should promote conversion. As we know, boundaries between civilian and military fields have not been so porous, not so open and interpretively flexible as boundaries in many other fields. Classified information, secrecy surrounding production and the closeness of whole communities have been fences built around the social world of the military.

While constructivist studies of technology and grounded theory may differ in how they view structural conditions, my own conceptual framework is to combine study of the social world of military technology with the constructivist understanding of technology as a seamless web, where there is neither a social superstructure nor a technological core, but rather a situation where the technological is co-negotiated and co-stabilised with the social. A social world analysis means an empirically open approach where porous boundaries between different social worlds, floppy and messy arenas construct the heterogeneous reality in which negotiations about technology take place. Like the social constructivists, I am not making an effort to define technology. It cannot be defined as such, there is no technology out there. On each arena I shall talk about the technology in question, the technology which is being built in, entrenched and negotiated on this particular arena by the very actors of the social world in question. In this sense the social world theory and the constructivist studies of technology are epistemologically and ontologically consistent.

In the spirit of grounded theory, this book is about boundaries. It is about the boundary between how civilian and military lives are constructed in society and how the separation between the two is managed. It is about how military technology becomes separated from technologies outside the military and how this separation is maintained. More particularly, it is about the social world of Russian military technology, the way the military was built into everyday life in the former Soviet Union and the way it becomes deconstructed during the transformation to a market economy.

Following grounded theory I shall try to let the facts, actions and interactions by the individuals and organisations connected to the military to what formerly was called the Military-Industrial Complex speak for themselves. Instead of imposing concepts from innovation economics or technology theory, I shall build up a theory of boundary management, empirically based upon the reality of defence enterprises and defence workers in a far-out town in the Urals. The seamless web of the technological and the social is woven from different perspectives where, independent of the perspective chosen, the macro-economic structure of society is built into the small actions of everyday life. At the same time tensions of the Cold War remain woven into the way engineers and scientists look at the results of their production, such as artillery systems, ammunition or missile engines.

A theory about boundaries is never finished, boundaries change, are renegotiated and constantly redrawn. There is no sharp divide, not even during the Cold War. In the words of Donna Haraway I shall try to build upon diffraction visualising the borderlands between the military and the non-military, the military and the civilian or the military and the commercial. These divides are not institutional and organisational. We cannot draw a clear line between the military and a non-military enterprise, between military research and non-military research, or even between a defence engineer and a civilian engineer. What I can do is to demonstrate the boundary producing mechanisms that for example make it more attractive for female designers to continue to design artillery systems than to make calculations for baby food lines.

The contents

Chapters 2 and 3 establish the background to this study. Chapter 2 draws a broad picture of the Russian situation after the collapse of the Soviet Union. It looks at the changes in the state administrative system where the privatisation of the defence enterprises has taken place. It shows how the State still maintains a 'golden share' even though companies become privately owned. It shows the difficulties of this disentanglement of the mega-machine of military production, which also includes social services. In broad contours, the chapter outlines various new boundaries and the actors constructing them.

Chapter 3 focuses on the divide between military and civilian technologies. How does a technology meant for war differ from one produced for peace? In order to show the different ways of constructing this divide a comparison is made between the United States and Russia. As the objective of conversion is to transform military technologies into civilian ones, conversion is here defined as a boundary crossing. It implies crossing the gate-keeping mechanisms between the two types of technologies. Different mechanisms for gate-keeping functions are demonstrated both in the US and Russian context.

Chapter 4 deals with the physical boundaries of the military as constructed in cities dependent on defence industry. Perm in the Urals is both unique and typical of the cities built in the Urals to produce weapons in a structurally militarised economy. Defence industries with direct links to Politburo and the ministries in Moscow are being reconstructed into regional entities and new kinds of regional economies. The location, Perm, was not only a city of defence production, but also a region of prison camps and missile launching fields. The organisation of the everyday life of the city reflected the social responsibility of the military production units. Company neighbourhoods provided for culture activities, day-care centres, restaurants and even hospitals. Crossing the borders started at the end of the 1980s by opening the city of Perm to foreigners; later the boundary crossing moved to the enterprises and in 1992 even some of these were opened to visitors.

Chapter 5 describes, with the help of grounded theory, the ways the Perm enterprises crossed the borders to civilian production. It is not only a question of finding civilian products to produce, but also of creating a regional platform for co-operation and detachment from the state central government planning system. The Perm Auto example describes an effort from the 'inside-out' to reconstruct components in military production into a civilian product, a ranger car. Pumping gas with technology known from the design of artillery systems is an example from the 'outside-in' where a small company is established with direct networks to the heart of military enterprises' know-how.

Chapter 6 goes deeper into the local practices of military production and the crossing of the gap between civilian and military technologies. It is not only a question of technology, money or even will, but rather of pride, and a feeling of being a gatekeeper at the world's technological front. There is the desire to reconstruct the past, but only under certain conditions. The chapter describes the defence community's naturalisation of weapons as objects of work and the awareness context of the defence scientists and engineers.

Most of those I interviewed were men, i.e. defence managers and scientists from the Perm defence enterprises. In 1995, I had a chance to interview a group of women at a design bureau producing documents and calculations for artillery systems. Chapter 7 is a result of these talks and deals with the situation of women in a concrete location of the military-industrial complex. It looks at the way the women understood themselves as working for defence and the way they talked about the objects of their production, weapons and weapon systems. Further, the chapter explores the secret and invisible environment inside military production.

Chapter 8 follows up on the question of women and takes up the situation of women in the military-industrial complex both before and after the collapse of the Soviet Union. The emerging women's movement in the city of Perm is visited and the new employment practices of the defence enterprises in times of transition are discussed. In the words of the employment office, 'women represent a special problem'. The businesswomen's club in Perm is trying not only to help women become entrepreneurs but also gives psychological support.

Any description of the social world of Russian military technology would be incomplete without looking at the West as an actor. The links

were intimate as the Soviet military innovations were directly linked to
technological advances in the West. The difficulties in crossing the
Cold War divide between the West and the East are the topic of Chapter
9. The chapter reviews the way joint ventures on technology were seen
as a way to integrate Russia in the world economy.

Chapter 10 deals with the renegotiation of defence technologies in
the Russian context. The technological imperative built into these
negotiations is deconstructed by the example of pulsed power, a
military   technology   looking   for   civilian   applications.
Commercialisation of space is a field where aerospace and rocket
technologies are finding civilian uses at the same time as security is
being privatised. New more individual borders are being protected.

Welfare in warfare society is the topic of the last chapter. The
reconstruction of social worlds is a painful process, especially when
you do not have anything to believe in and everything was better
before. In this chapter I shall try to answer the two fundamental
questions of this book: Can we understand Russia and its
transformation by understanding the conversion of its Cold War
technologies? Are technologies flexible and are we able to renegotiate
the hard core of technologies when dramatic social change is taking
place and social institutions are fundamentally destabilised?

A view from somewhere

> Single visions produce worse illusions and double vision or
> many-headed monsters.[21]

> Looking is not a listing of adjectives or assigning of labels like
> race, sex and class. Location is not the concrete to the abstract
> of de-contextualisation. Location is the always-partial, always-
> finite, always-fraud, play of foreground and background, text
> and context constituting critical inquiry. Above all, location is
> not self-evident.[22]

Donna Haraway insists that the objects and subjects of knowledge-
producing practices must be located. During the course of my ten years
of studying Russian defence conversion, I have often had to think about
this question. What is my location in defence conversion in general and
in Russian conversion in particular.

When locating oneself, one is for some worlds and not for others.
This problem becomes even more painful as I started with a different

approach, that of innovation economics and social construction of technology and ended up with the more open-ended, empirically oriented social world theory. As concepts such as commitment, identity and awareness seemed to be more important than questions of enterprise strategies, core technologies or learning systems, I had to seek something else, a different place to be.

It sounds absurd to say that in my study of Russian military technology I have been co-constructed together with my object of study. It is not possible to freeze the arena, the Russian military-industrial complex, and make an authoritative true story about the changes having occurred during the ten-year period. If the object is not there, I have to write around it, tell a number of small stories to give it contours. Maybe this is also the crucial point in my criticism of the innovation economics and the social constructivist approach to studying technology. Here somebody is the authority, somebody knows how innovations emerge and how networks are to be described. My modest objective is only to describe some boundary crossings, describe how the military becomes built into the civilian and vice versa.

What I want to do, again using Donna Haraway's term, is to produce diffraction. Instead of critical reflexivity, she talks about finding a way 'to diffract critical inquiry in order to make difference patterns in a more worldly way. Reflection replaces the same elsewhere; diffraction patterns record the passage of difference, interaction and interference.'[23] Thus my objective is to produce patterns of diffraction in which those whose lives are involved are given a voice.

In 1990 when I first decided to apply for a research programme for military technology, I had made a number of studies on technology in everyday life, on methods for assessing technology and the information society. I worked as associate professor of technology assessment at the Unit of Technology Assessment in the Technical University of Denmark and was deeply involved in technology studies and technology management. As a member of the Danish Board of Technology, an organisation directly under the Danish Parliament, I had followed technology debates, not only on technology policy, but also on how to stimulate and maintain public debate and acceptance of technology. In all this work, military technology was a black spot; it was often referred to as the ultimate cause of the technologies of everyday life.

When in 1990–91 my colleagues and I decided to do a comparative study on the conversion of military technology in the US and the Soviet

Union, this for a researcher in technology assessment was the ultimate opportunity to understand how technology becomes entrenched into society. Conversion would make a number of things visible, not only concerning how military technologies are created and built into society, but also concerning the social construction of technology. As far as Soviet defence technology was concerned, I did not expect to do anything but to study documents, books that had been written on the topic and perhaps articles from Russian sources. Having previously worked for the UN, I spoke Russian and could therefore expect to make use of local sources.

Seen from the standpoint of our research programme, the collapse of the Soviet Union came at just the right time. I was participating in the conversion seminar 'on Conversion and the Environment' in Perm in the Urals, which was arranged by UNEP and the Oslo Peace Research Institute at the very time when the Soviet Union became history and the defence industrial ministries were abandoned. Not only did the government's reforms focus on reduced defence orders and conversion, but also there was a unique openness towards foreigners and new co-operation with the West. When I was in Perm, I decided to continue my studies there and to return in 1992. Between 1992 and 1997 I visited Perm several times a year to do interviews and to collect material. Since then, I have updated the study during visits in 1999 and the bibliography until 2000.

During the years 1991–97, I participated in a number of international conferences where I met Russian scientists and managers of defence enterprises. Of particular importance was the co-operation with the Centre for International Arms Control at Stanford University, which had research projects similar to ours. With the Stanford team, we exchanged information and participated in their workshops and seminars, which had large-scale Russian representation from cities and military sites other than Perm. Thus the US part of our study was conducted in close co-operation with Stanford University.

My relationship to military technology changed dramatically during this process. I started out from the peace economy perspective: money would be spent in a better way on health care and housing than on defence production. Sympathetic to the peace movement, I had never had time to participate and I thought I would make my contribution by trying to understand the conversion processes in the US and Russia. As a Western feminist, I also expected that the women working in the defence industries would be better served by more civilian production. I soon came to understand that the question of conversion was not so simple and straightforward. Welfare was in fact built into warfare. I came to understand why the Russian researchers and scientists were proud of their achievements and would not let go of their high-tech innovation culture. I came to understand why people went to work in a military enterprise even if they did not have anything to do and were not paid. Finally, I would like to quote two Russian reactions to our study.

In 1992, I wrote my first book about the early experiences in Perm: *Price of Peace: Military Conversion on the Enterprise Level in Russia*. The Technical University of Perm arranged a seminar to discuss both this study and our study of the Los Angeles area in the US. My colleagues and I thought it was also a good idea to discuss the American conversion process in Russia – and vice versa. Already at this time, November 1992, Russian attitudes towards the West had become more reserved. The expectations for quick conversion results had been reduced. I was curious to see what the Russians present at the seminar would think about an outsider presenting their experiences. The Russian reaction was rather unexpected. It was not the concrete results that were of interest, but rather 'it is interesting for us to read and understand the way you see us'. Seventy years of isolation had deprived the defence managers in Perm of the possibility of seeing with the eyes of an outsider.

In the summer of 1995, NATO arranged an advanced research seminar on Defence Conversion Strategies at Pitlochry in Scotland; and I was invited to present the results of our empirical studies on conversion in Perm. I was nervous because many of the participants were Russian. The US participants represented American business enterprises. The Russians who were present were mostly physicists and leaders of advanced research institutes. The European participants were, strikingly enough, mainly researchers. During my presentation the Russian participants started to question my quantitative data. In their view, military production had been reduced much more than my data from the Perm Regional Administration indicated. It made me nervous, but after the lecture many of the Americans came to me saying, 'Good work, Professor'. I took this as an indication that the way I had tried to integrate everyday life and other concerns into the study of technological transformation had contributed something new to the discussion.

However, the Russian reaction bothered me. After the heated debate at the presentation they were all silent. At a banquet two days later, I sat at a table together with the Russian physicists, military economists and high-level state officials. My neighbour, the leader of a research institute, turned to me and said: 'I underwrite everything you said about Russian conversion. It was a very good picture of what is going on.' And to my astonishment, he added: 'We have talked about it and we admire the way you go into the dirt of our country. You do not only study conversion as a clean process. You get your hands into the dirt of our country. You go deep into the Urals beyond Moscow and St Petersburg. It is very unusual, also for our own people.'

Notes

1 Melman (1986); Udis (1978).

2 Melman (1981).

3 According to Udis (1978), diversification implies an increase in the hetero-geneity of markets served by an individual military firm. According to *Future Relations between Defence and Civil Science and Technology* (1991), diversification refers to addition of *new* activities, while maintai-ning the companies' defence specialists and potential. Harbor (1990) writes that diversification in the 1970s and '80s was perceived as a more respectable word for conversion, particularly among those defence workers hostile to conversion.

4 For example, the weekly magazine *Conversion, Rica*, 20 February 1992 and Kortunov, Head of Directorate for Export Control and Conversion, Ministry of Foreign Affairs in a presentation by the Russian delegation at the NATO seminar on Defence Conversion in Brussels, 20–22 May 1992.

5 Shlykov (1995: 20) underlines the difference in defence industry relations to the economy as a whole in Russia and in the West: 'In a Western country, possessed of a strong defence industry – for example, the United States – the defence-industrial base is part of a much larger and usually efficient civilian economy. In Russia, which inherited its defence industry from the former Soviet Union, it is the very core and substance of the economy. The civilian part of it is merely an adjunct to the defence sector and so inefficient that in an open market economy it would have quickly died away.'

6 Ballentine (1991); Iziumov (1990).

7 Cooper (1995).

8 The term 'seamless web' was first introduced by the historian Thomas Hughes (1986).

9 The way these 'negotiations' are understood depends on the particulars of the constructivistic approach selected. One Anglo-Saxon tradition, often called the SCOT approach (Bijker, 1987; Bijker and Law, 1992) stresses the social dynamics between relevant social groups. These social groups

are constituted by their understanding of the problems, i.e. their 'technological frame'. As the selection process takes place between the relevant social groups, the interpretive flexibility of technology is gradually reduced. Technology is stabilised; finally, a consensus between the groups results in a closure, i.e. a solution to the problem. Another approach focuses on the history of technology; it looks at the way innovators create technology in heterogeneous networks (Hughes, 1989). A third approach stems from a French semiotic tradition concentrating on actor networks (Callon, 1987; LaTour, 1987, 1991). Actors build their scripts into technology. Technology itself becomes an actor in the process and is continuously renegotiated. As technology is constructed by the arguments of the participants, i.e. their ability to build in their particular script, power is constituted and reconstituted in the network as rhetoric strength.

10 MacKenzie (1990).
11 For an analysis of a social constructivist perspective on military technology, see Cronberg (1994).
12 A term Bijker (1992) used to describe the links between the social and the technical. Callon (1992) uses the term techno-economic network.
13 For the basics of grounded theory, see Strauss (1990: 23–33).
14 Strauss (1990: 23).
15 Ibid., p. 129, citing Strauss (1959, 1982b).
16 Ibid., p. 130.
17 Strauss and colleagues (1964); Strauss (1987); Becker (1974, 1986).
18 Strauss (1990: 133); Strauss (1978: 124).
19 Quoted after Clark (1991: 133).
20 Strauss (1990: 137).
21 Haraway (1991:154).
22 Haraway (1996: 440).
23 Haraway (1996: 429).

Chapter 2

A Seamless Military Web

A Soviet defence enterprise was like an amoeba, without any fixed boundaries. At one end there was the State, at the other was the private life of the individual employee. The whole defence complex was like a mega-machine the sensors of which reached from the State Military-Industrial Commission to the light bulb of the defence employee's dwelling. Everything and everyone was linked together: the members of the Politbureau, the employees of a design bureau and the doctors of the local Medicare.

The macro was so interwoven with the micro that any macroeconomic study of the defence industry is bound to miss the point. At the same time any micro-study of a local community would only represent part of the picture. In fact, the Soviet defence-industrial complex would seem to be an ideal case for the new sociology of technology. Here the macro- and micro-level analyses merge and the social is entrenched in the technical so that the only possible level of analysis is a socio-technical ensemble without boundaries.[1] This socio-technical amoeba reaches everywhere. Or perhaps the most adequate metaphor would be an octopus where nothing is outside its reach. In his analysis of life worlds and everyday life, Alfred Schutz[2] talks about the 'world within reach'. The world within reach is a concept where the individual is at point zero. Around him or her is a sphere that he or she may reach with his/her actions. This kind of life world analysis is not possible in the Soviet context. Or rather the world within reach reaches out to the whole society. The individual, the enterprise and the State form an integrable whole built into the Cold War.

The big story of the Cold War was also constructed into small details of the everyday life of the defence enterprise employees. Children played war games, and the technologically most challenging work was offered at the defence enterprises. The way the employees spent their vacations was determined by the State, and their illnesses were cured by the enterprise health care. The life stories of millions of employees were built into the structurally militarised economy of the Soviet State.

Was there a MIC?

The organic, interwoven nature of the Soviet system has raised the question as to whether or not we can talk about a military-industrial complex in the former Soviet Union. This term has in the West been used for the separation of powers among the political sphere, the army and the military industry. It describes a dynamic interaction among these three powers: separate, but co-operating. It implies a pluralistic interplay of interests undermined by the links between the armed forces, the industry and Congress, the so-called iron triangle.[3] According to Cooper, for the former Soviet Union this term may only be used in a distinct sense for the armament procurement system:

> In this sense it seems to me not to be an appropriate term for the Soviet Union since it implies too great a degree of pluralism – and implies pluralism as a norm – for the Soviet Union. The history of the Soviet state has been so much affected by questions of military power that it seems wrong to separate out a military-industrial complex within the state. This is not to say, however, that the Soviet military technological effort is not now driven to a greater or lesser extent by an internal dynamic, created in the course of international rivalry, but rooted now in the domestic power structure.[4]

In the same way we can ask whether we can talk about defence enterprises. For us in the West an enterprise is an autonomous production unit with an independent legal status. An enterprise markets its products and services, competes with other enterprises and finally, in due course, dies out when its products are no longer in demand. A Soviet defence enterprise was a merger between the State, which made all the decisions and marketed the products, a production enterprise interlinked to a number of research institutions and design bureaux, and a number of social services, which we in the West are accustomed to obtaining from the municipality or, for example, the tourist industry. The defence enterprises were interwoven parts of the State structure. In fact, they were the bottom line in a State structure that started with the Military-Industrial Commission, the Russian VPK with direct links to the military department of the State Planning Committee (Gosplan) and the Communist party. Under it were the nine defence industrial ministries, for example, the Ministry of the Aviation Industry dealing with aircraft, missiles and spacecraft and the Ministry of Medium

Machine Building, which dealt with nuclear warheads, reactors, high-energy lasers, and uranium mining and processing.

These ministries were then divided into branch structures and sub-units where research institutes, design bureaux and production enterprises dealing with, for example, certain kinds of aircraft came together to create new weapon designs. Finally, at the bottom were the Soviet Union's 1700 military production units and about 920 research and development organisations. About half of these enterprises had between 1000 and 5000 employees. A fourth had a staff of 5000–10,000, and most of the rest had more than 10,000 employees. Only a very few of the enterprises had less than 1000 employees.[5]

When American enterprises such as General Dynamics or Rockwell were faced with the challenge of reduced defence budgets and defence orders, they had problems. They either had to find new projects and convert some of their military units to civilian production or they had to shut down plants or perhaps sell these to other defence contractors. But they were able to make decisions as autonomous actors, to follow existing rules for how to do business and leave the social responsibility for layoffs to the local communities and state and federal governments.

When the Soviet defence enterprises faced reduced state orders, they did not know what to do. The State had made all the decisions for what to produce. They had to maintain their mobilisation capabilities[6] without any compensation from the State. They had a social responsibility for the employees' welfare, not only for their working life and pay, but also for social services. To disentangle this 'cat's cradle' and to make new boundaries and new rules of conduct was a much more difficult task than the one facing the American defence conversion. Everything had to be done at once. New boundaries had to be redrawn between the State and the enterprise, between the enterprise and the local government and between the different units within the huge vertical enterprises themselves – not to mention the boundary between work and the private life of the individual.

Military technology as a social construction

Donald MacKenzie claims that the most important single lesson of his book *Inventing Accuracy* is the fallacy of technological determinism. He studied missile guidance systems and showed that accuracy is not a 'technical fact' but is continuously created over decades in conjunction with changing strategic priorities. Technical solutions for missile guidance were different for the United States and for the Soviet Union. He concludes that technological change is social through and through. 'Take away the institutional structures that support the technological change of a particular shape and it ceases to seem "natural" – indeed it ceases altogether.'[7]

Constructivist approaches to technology, here represented by MacKenzie, challenge not only technological determinism but also social determinism. In accordance with social deterministic understanding, technological change within the military is due to the power of the military-industrial complex. Explanations for technological change are sought in the interests of those in power, institutional arrangements between the armed forces, the military-industrial enterprises and political interests.[8] Studies of international relations introduce internal and external factors in state behaviour as additional dimensions. Explanations emphasising the balance of power between countries see external factors as causes of technical change. The alternative is to focus on internal forces and bureaucratic politics. Evangelista[9] explains technological change within the military in the US as the result of a bureaucratic struggle to advance new weapon systems, of rivalry between the branches of the armed forces and between different groups including scientists. According to Evangelista, technological change in the former Soviet Union was initiated by external factors, primarily innovations in the United States.

In accordance with constructivist understanding of technological change, technological artefacts, including weapon systems, are a result of actors negotiating from different positions of power. Technology is the result of these negotiations, or rather its end product 'made durable'. A closure[10] represents an agreement between the actors, when a particular solution is seen as a solution to the problem. Technology is stabilised and taken for granted until the power relations change again. Then the 'black box' of technological artefacts is reopened for new negotiations among new actors with new problems.

Conversion of military technology to commercial uses represents the ultimate case of constructivism. There is no military technology 'out there' and technologies are only stable as long as the institutional relations where they are embedded are stable. Consequently, the key to conversion lies in destabilisation of the institutional relations surrounding the development and procurement of weapon systems. It is no longer a question of whether technologies, the technological objects, can be transformed from military to commercial use, but rather whether appropriate civilian or commercial institutional networks emerge to support this transformation.

The collapse of institutions

In June 1991 I visited Moscow for the first time as a researcher, in order to find out whether it would be possible to get in touch with defence enterprises and conduct interviews on defence conversion. As it was not possible to get in touch with the individual enterprises, I visited the Research Institute for Military Economics and Defence Conversion under the Military-Industrial Commission. There must have been some expectations in the air about the coming changes, as my request was not rejected at once. I was told that it might be possible to visit some of the enterprises, but I would have to submit a written application to the Military-Industrial Commission. The woman I interviewed was very polite. When I left her, I thought I would never again hear from them, written application or not. To my astonishment, later that day she called me at my hotel room. She asked me to have dinner with her in the evening. This invitation was, however, cancelled a few hours later without any explanation. This was my first and only contact with the Military-Industrial Commission and its subordinate research organisation. Next time I would come to Russia in November 1991 both the Military-Industrial Commission and the Defence Industrial Ministries had been abolished. Enterprises were trying to make contacts, particularly with foreigners on their own. No written applications were required.

At the end of 1991 the Soviet military-industrial complex was fundamentally destabilised. In fact, it collapsed into several defence complexes in the newly independent states, causing considerable confusion. Components were produced in one country, materials tested in another, rockets assembled in a third and launched from the fourth. Although the Russian defence complex was the largest with the most resources, it also underwent dramatic changes.

As the Soviet Union collapsed the Military-Industrial Commission and the nine defence industrial ministries belonging to the Soviet State were abolished. In the new Russia the defence enterprises were organised into a super Ministry of Industry, consisting of all industries, although there was a special department for defence enterprises and conversion. In late August 1992, a decision was made to dismantle even this Ministry of Industry and its departments. At the beginning of 1993, they were replaced by a State Committee for Industrial Policy and a number of subordinate industrial branch committees to co-ordinate and execute state programmes for industrial development. The State Committee for the Defence Industry, working in close co-operation with the Ministry of Defence, emerged as the highest government authority of Russia's military-industrial complex. However, it no longer governed the same planning authority over the defence enterprises as the defence-industrial ministries of the past had.[11]

Although the Military-Industrial Commission disappeared, fragments of it lived on in various agencies in Moscow. The Security Council of the Russian Federation took over more and more of the functions of the old Military-Industrial Commission. Gosplan's military departments became a department of the new Ministry of Economy. Julian Cooper (1993), who studied these organisations during the transformation, points out that many of these organisations employed the same people as before. Institutions were destabilised, but the individuals remained. However, not everybody was able to keep his place in the nomenclature. A number of bureaucrats had to leave and find new jobs.

In this process, parts of the old defence industrial ministries converted into semi-commercial associations or concerns. They offered their services, on a commercial or membership basis, to their former subordinate organisations. As these concerns and associations had once held a monopoly of contacts, for example, to foreign countries, there was some logic in this attempt at survival by the old government bureaucrats. In spite of the power of the Committee for Defence Industry and the role of these associations as intermediaries in defence-oriented networks, the power of the central government was drastically reduced. Most enterprise managers welcomed the opportunity to become more independent actors within the defence complex.

Table 2.1 Destabilised institutions and new networks (simplified)		
	1991	**After 1991**
State level	The Military-Industrial Commission (VPK) Defence Industrial Ministries	Russian Ministry of Industry (1992) → State Committee for the Defence Industry (1993) → Ministry of Economy → State Commission of Military – Industrial Affairs (1999) and also (since 2000) Ministry of Industry, Science and Technology
Regional	(No direct influence)	Regional and local administrations
Enterprise level	State enterprises	State enterprises, corpora-tized enterprises (state-owned, privatised); privati-sed enterprises (Employee-/manager owned, later even outside owners, possible golden share for the state); new commercial struc-tures/joint stock companies
Finance	State	State; banks; outside inves-tors (also foreign investors, companies); financial-industrial groups

A new autonomy

The collapse of the ministerial bureaucracy in 1992 briefly left a power vacuum in the military-industrial complex. In constructivist terms, the black box of the Soviet military technology was opened. Institutions were destabilised and old norms and rules abolished. In this process the former Soviet Union's 1700 production units and the 920 research and design organisations found themselves with a new kind of autonomy. Basically, they were expected to start production for the market, both military and civilian, as the defence budget was dramatically cut from 1991 to 1992. According to Cooper:[12]

> I believe that the Gaidar government quite deliberately cut procurement so sharply, partly obviously to balance the budget, but also because there was such widespread feeling that this was the only way actually to shock the defence enterprises into action, to make them realise that the old days had ended that they had to adapt to a new climate, a more demilitarised economy, and that the defence plants had to take action to civilise the activities some way or other.

The defence enterprises were expected to take independent action, to create new relations in the emerging market and to plan at least their civilian production independently. Although the Gorbachev programme for conversion[13] had already prepared the enterprises for the idea, most companies were unprepared for the radical cuts in financing and the shock therapy they experienced in 1992. Faced with the new situation, the enterprise managers could select one or a combination of several courses of action.

As most of the enterprises already had civilian production, they could try to increase this proportion as much as possible. Enterprises with potential export markets could try to establish independent contracts for weapon export or press the government for export activities. Conversion was a third alternative. Managers could seek to establish new production lines in civilian fields. Furthermore, enterprises could cope in an ad hoc manner by renting out facilities, and renting or selling equipment and raw materials. A common but rather unexpected strategy was to continue military production without state orders and to deliver the products *as if* they had been ordered.

The destabilisation of state institutions also meant that the enterprises had to reorient their networks in order to secure supplies, establish markets and secure financing in the future. In 1992 the Russian League of Entrepreneurs and Industrialists made a survey[14] of the new and emerging economic ties between enterprises. The survey covered a range of enterprises (not only military), of which 82% were state owned, 7.7% had been turned into shareholding companies, 6.3% belonged to workers' collectives and 1.4% to local councils. The dominant way to establish ties was through independent searching. This reflected the Russian managers' new autonomy from a restricted, secrecy-plagued environment. A third of the new client relations 'came by themselves'. It was quite obvious in 1992 that there was both a lack of knowledge on how to find partners and a great deal of activity in trying to establish new relations.

Not only were bureaucratic ties cut, but also the linear links between research, design and production were broken. In the Soviet system of innovations, research institutes did basic research, which was transformed by the design bureaux to applied science and technology in the form of documentation, which in turn created the basis for production in the enterprises. Very few enterprises had their own research, development and design capabilities. However, faced with the shock budget cuts in 1992, enterprises turned away from the established contacts with the design bureaux and research institutes and started product development and the elaboration of in-house conversion ideas.

As if the government wanted to strengthen its message to the defence enterprises, privatisation plans that had first been envisioned to include only the defence enterprises in the later phases (after 1994) were already pushed forward and initiated in 1993. Privatisation in general, and privatisation of the defence enterprises in particular, has been a controversial issue.

First there was the issue of which enterprises could be privatised and which could not. In August 1993 Yeltsin signed a decree which exempted 474 of the 1700 defence enterprises from privatisation. These enterprises would not even be made into stockholding companies. They would belong, as strategic units, to the State. A few of the Perm production units belonged to these 474, among them a chemical industry making ammunition. The next level of state control was 'option one' for privatisation, according to which the State retained major control (51%) of the shares of the company although it was made into a shareholding company. In Perm, a company making explosives was privatised according to this model. The next level of privatisation was 'option two', where the majority of the shares were sold to the employees against vouchers and a part given to the management. Here the State retained a minority package. In Perm in an aviation design bureau making mechanical and electrical steering units, the employees together with the management took over the majority of the shares. Finally, there was a third option where a group of employees could make a commitment to carry out privatisation and in return receive 20% of the shares. In Perm a former military enterprise that made gas masks, but which in 1992 converted to all-civilian production of water purification filters and medical equipment, was privatised according to this model.

Secondly, there was the issue of continued State influence in order to guarantee the vital defence interests of the State. The State certainly did withdraw from the management of companies. Boards of directors appointed by the general assembly of the shareholders had by 1997 taken over power in the majority of the privatised defence enterprises. According to my interviews with some of the higher level employees, there has been a worry that the management of the enterprises would get too much power. They were awarded a large part of the shares and would – and in fact have – become a major factor in decision-making. There was also a desire to exclude external shareholders who would be more interested in profit than in the maintenance of the company. In spite of this resistance, the State Property Fund has kept some shares and the remaining parts of the shares in all the models have been auctioned off. In fact, the management is often the party voting for the State's share of the package.

In spite of the formal state withdrawal, there is still a very strong mutual dependency between the State and the privatised enterprises. The companies still, in the beginning of the 90s, hope for state aid and the State still to a great extent pays the salaries. None of the defence enterprises in Perm had gone bankrupt by 1999, although some were said to be in a state that could best be described as bankruptcy. In the privatisation programme passed as a law in September 1994, the idea of a 'golden share' was introduced. This was a minority ownership position reserved for the State, which gave the State the power of veto over any major reconfiguration in an enterprise. In practice, this meant that the State Committee for Management of Property and the State Committee for Defence Industry had to approve of any major changes in the defence enterprises.

In spite of these remaining links, the boundary between the State and the enterprises has become more fluid. For most of the defence enterprises it is a question of the state veto power on the one hand, and state aid on the other. The State is still a guarantor of survival and in return has a say in the affairs of the enterprise.

By 1997 most of the Perm defence enterprises were either privatised or in the process of privatisation. Investment was not the issue. Most of the employees invested in the company they worked in without much enthusiasm or lots of pondering about where to spend their voucher[15] money. The management of the companies gained considerable influence. This was something that most of the high-level officials I have interviewed, both in Perm and in Moscow, considered the right thing to do. This way the managers would be tied to the company and become more engaged in its affairs, a thought not unlike Western management practices. On the other hand, the boards of directors have acted and made some changes. The 'old generation' director of the Perm Motor Works, one of the major defence companies in Perm, which make engines for missiles and aeroplanes, was dismissed and replaced by a younger, newly educated manager. However, conflicts are also in the making. In the next round of privatisation workers are losing their say and the 'new Russians' – managers, bankers and even criminals – are taking over. The government is still relied upon to pay the bills while the new investors secure the profit.

The commercial split-up

In the days of the Soviet Union not only the defence industrial complex but also the enterprise itself was an organic whole. A defence enterprise was by no means a clearly defined concept. A company in the Western sense is an entity with rules that regulate economic transactions, ownership and obligations to owners. Even privatised, the Russian defence enterprises are dependent on the State. They have social responsibilities not known in the West, and they are embedded in a system of informal networks, a heritage from the Soviet Union. Although relationships between enterprises and the state – as well as between enterprises – are changing, the role of government as owner, supplier and client is still fluid. The new owners in privatised companies are only slowly finding their role.

The Russian defence enterprises were 'organic' in two ways. First, working in a supply economy they were integrated vertically. As access to resources was the basic problem – even the military could not always guarantee access – the defence enterprises had their own power plants, their own tooling departments and their own workshops for casting of sheet metal and instrumentation. They were trying to control the raw material supplies and had very few sub-contractors. This is a dramatic contrast to the structure of the American defence industry. The US defence-industrial-complex is dominated by a relatively few large firms, known as prime contractors. These prime contractors receive contracts from the Department of Defence and sub-contract these to other firms. In the US roughly half the value of prime contracts is in the US sub-contracted to other firms.[16] Sub-contracting in the Russian defence industry on the initiative of the enterprise is not a common practice. The division of labour was previously organised by the ministries and decided upon in the hierarchical structures combining different industries, research institutes and design bureaux in smaller or larger agglomerates.

Organic in a second sense, the Soviet enterprises had both civilian and military production. This is not unusual as many of the Western (namely, US) weapon-producers also have civilian activities. In the West, however, civilian activities are carried out in separate plants and divisions. As a Soviet heritage the Russian defence enterprises already had large civilian production capabilities, which were not separate but were integrated into military production.

Civilian production had a long history in Soviet defence enterprises. Already in March 1971, Brezhnev announced that 42% of the volume of the production of the defence industry served civilian purposes.[17] This proportion seems to have been relatively stable during the past two decades, judging by the fact that Gorbachev, when announcing his conversion initiative in 1988, put the military-to-civilian ratio of the defence complex's production at 60:40.

One hundred percent of the Soviet's television sets, radios, video recorders, cameras and motor scooters were produced by defence enterprises. A third of the washing machines and vacuum cleaners and about half of the refrigerators also originated from defence enterprises. The defence industry produced tractors and bicycles, not to mention civilian aircraft and ships. Industrial equipment such as industrial robots, metal-cutting equipment, optical equipment and lasers also came from military enterprises. The electronic industry of the defence complex was the producer of computers.[18] Civilian industries have been transferred to the military-industrial complex in order to increase their output. So, for example, the Ministry of Machine-building for Light and Food Industry and Household Appliances was dismantled in March 1988, and 220 of its plants transferred to defence industrial ministries.[19] While this was not conversion, it certainly increased the non-defence output of the defence complex. The timing of this transfer coincided with the planned reductions in the military budgets to be announced by Gorbachev in December 1988.

Before the Soviet collapse, the responsibility for civilian production rested with one of the deputy ministers in each of the defence ministries concerned. When the enterprises were transferred to the Russian Ministry of Industry, no large restructuring and separation of the military from the civilian production seems to have taken place.

The defence enterprises have thus faced multiple challenges. Not only did they have to deal with the collapse of the state institutions and the division of labour maintained by it, but they also had to face internal restructuring in order to be able to survive. For the first time the companies had to create market departments. This was often done by renaming the old planning departments. Later, as privatisation proceeded, many established law departments to deal with the complex question of ownership, shareholding and legal entities.

Production as a vertically integrated organic mega-machine had to be torn into smaller parts although there was strong opposition within the companies, particularly in the earlier years (1992–94). Many feared that this would destroy the technological base or the technological chain of the company. The State did not promote restructuring; and consequently, only in the later phases of the transition have divisions, profit centres and independent units emerged in the company structure. In many cases a simultaneous process of creating holding companies and small 'spin-off' units has taken place. Enterprises continuing military production have had to separate the production for state defence orders and export of weapons and weapon systems from other activities. Although the State had a monopoly on weapon export during the years 1992–97 the companies have increasingly negotiated their own weapon export deals. Weapon exports still have to be approved by the State.

Restructuring not only into smaller but also into bigger and more effective units has been on the agenda. In 1993–94 there was talk about Financial-Industrial Groups consisting of larger conglomerates of industries, research institutes and design bureaux combined with financial institutions such as banks and investors. The idea was to guarantee financing for the restructuring process at the same time as the enterprises would become more commercially oriented. Nothing, however, happened and the government designed in 1997 a new reconstruction plan for the military industries. Here the idea was to retain a core of effective enterprises to cater for military needs, to concentrate State orders to these. In 1998, the government and the regional leaders obviously carried out a number of regional negotiations. The plan was that the government would finance retraining of personnel thus dismissed and promote mergers to concentrate production on fewer units. Obviously, the regions have succeeded in lobbying for their case as nothing has happened.

TsAGI

As an example of the complicated process of how to deconstruct a defence enterprise, I have chosen TsAGI, one of the more famous defence research institutes in Moscow. TsAGI is a special example of a former defence organisation. The State still retains power over the main activities at the same time as small, more or less commercial companies, have spun off from the main organisation.

TsAGI was formed in 1918 as the Central Aerodynamic Research Institute in Moscow and later moved to Zhukovskii outside Moscow. Before the Second World War it had spun off new institutes such as the All Union Institute of Aviation Materials, the Central Institute of Aviation Motors and the Tupolev Design Bureau. TsAGI was involved in the design and testing of major Soviet military and commercial airplanes, helicopters and spacecraft. Its facilities included wind tunnels and chambers for testing turmoil strength. Previously, a subordinate of the Ministry of Aviation Industry, TsAGI is now under the Committee for the Defence Industry and the Ministry of Science. It has later become one of the State's Science Centres. The aim of these centres is to protect the high-tech capabilities of the defence-industrial complex.

Early in the transition process, already in 1992, TsAGI established contacts with the Centre of International Security and Arms Control at Stanford University in the US and has since then worked together with their experts on issues such as privatisation and diversification.

Before 1989, 70% of the orders TsAGI received from the State were for defence. The defence orders fell dramatically and were practically down to zero in 1993. Foreign orders grew rapidly and in 1993 made up 40% of TsAGI's budget. Civil orders from the Russian state stabilised at 50% of TsAGI's budget. As a research institute with one of the most advanced capacities in the world for aviation testing, TsAGI started to reorganise its activities. Several small enterprises were formed to exploit possibilities for diversification and reducing the dependency on defence orders.

Because TsAGI lacked production facilities, its aircraft designs were sent through the Committee of Defence Industry to major aerospace design bureaux, and links with these were maintained. In 1993 TsAGI had 64 contracts and 118 special projects with 30 companies in 20 countries. With a department of international affairs, it has been able to market technologies and provide legal services. Furthermore, a Russian-owned subsidiary in Seattle was formed (TsAGI International) to provide protection for intellectual property in the US and to learn international laws pertaining to intellectual property rights. TsAGI's international partners now include Boing, General Dynamics and McDonnell Douglas, and it is working with British Aerospace to develop a space plane.

Successful in its international operations and able to use its core technologies in a market economy, TsAGI has had to redraw the boundaries between its different facilities and assets in order to exploit them commercially. The TsAGI State Science Centre, which comprises the basic facilities, is wholly owned by the State and is not privatised. In 1994, TsAGI had more than 30 subsidiaries, with varying degrees of autonomy, ranging from state-owned enterprises, closed joint-stock companies and partnerships with limited liabilities. Subsidiaries utilised state-owned equipment, state technology and state know-how, but entered into contracts with non-state customers. According to Bernstein,[20] there were three categories of activities: one for marketing existing core capabilities 100% owned by the State, another for commercialising core technology uses 50% owned by the State, and a third category for earning profits (for example, in a shoe factory) where state ownership would be variable, even as low as 5%.

TsAGI is only one example of how the seamless web of the State and the enterprise, here a research institute, is becoming loose and how new boundaries are being redrawn around testing facilities, international operations and wholly new productions. In this process, complex negotiations are taking place to determine who has the right to the core technologies of the company, who owns its facilities and testing equipment and who has the right to exploit them commercially. All this has taken place in a chaotic business environment with changing tax laws and without legislation on property rights and established banking rules. While TsAGI, due to its especially advanced capabilities in a specific area, has been successful in exploiting foreign contracts, in particular, I shall later come back to less advanced and lucrative examples from the Urals.

Undoing the social

A defence enterprise in the Soviet Union was not only for production of weapons or military materials. It also produced social goods. An enterprise took care of the employees' vacation plans, health, education, cultural and sports activities. I once interviewed a woman who said, 'They used to call us from the office and asked if you wanted to go on vacation to the Black Sea or to the Baltic States.' The employees lived in housing, which, although owned by the State, was maintained by the enterprise. Some of the larger companies had housing areas of several tens of thousands of apartments where not only the employees' families but also the companies' retired personnel or even their friends lived. Vacation homes were owned by the enterprises in different recreational areas of the Soviet Union. Some of the larger companies had their own medical facilities employing doctors, supplying ambulance services etc. In my interviews, the defence enterprise managers and employees saw these social facilities as the way things were. It was natural, they were not problematic. None of the persons ever referred to a desire not to live in a company dwelling or not to use the recreational areas of the enterprise.

The social sphere or the social assets (as they are called in Russia) of the Russian defence enterprises varied, but included child care, health care, access to leisure and recreation facilities, for example, sports fields, housing, vacation resorts and sometimes even consumer services, such as laundries or hairdressers. A number of enterprises owned collective farms and sold food to the employees at reduced prices. These social assets were present in all Russian enterprises. However, evidence suggests that corporate social facilities have been concentrated proportionally more in areas dominated by defence enterprises and in one-company towns.[21] The Soviet defence enterprises did not have an investment fund or other financial reserves. What they had were the social assets. This was the property of the company, its main economic asset.

When faced with reduced defence orders and economic troubles in 1992, the defence enterprises started dismantling their social assets. Vacation homes and day-care centres were closed down. In the first phase, they were not sold, only closed. In early 1992–93 there was no municipal or regional structure to take over the social facilities such as health care and day-care. Therefore, many enterprises continued to carry on with their social activities, at least for a transition period. In 1997, most of the social facilities such as day-care centres and medical centres have been turned over to municipalities. A great deal of housing has been privatised and given or sold to the tenants. Most vacation homes have been sold to private interests. Some companies still choose to run day-care centres and to pay part of the costs for their employees.

Grey zones between the enterprise's responsibility and the municipality's responsibility still exist, and a number of transition and local solutions have been implemented. Payments have been introduced and burdens are increasingly placed on families. The family, the local administration and the enterprise now share, in a new way, what previously was the enterprise's social sphere. In spite of this, the link the individual feels to society is still based on the enterprise, as I shall show in later chapters.

Notes

1 Referring to the term used by Bijker (1992).
2 Luckman and Schutz (1974).
3 Adams (1984) has labelled the interaction between the Pentagon, defence firms in the US and the Congress the 'Iron Triangle'.
4 Cooper (1982: 288).
5 Anthony (1994: 87).
6 Soviet defence enterprises had to maintain excess capacity, so-called mobilisation capabilities of raw materials, space, personnel and other resources. After the collapse of the Soviet Union, there was no change in this policy. The question of mobilisation capacities was a sacred cow in the Soviet Union. Internationally, they were first discussed at the NATO Conference on Conversion in May 1992. The 1992 law on conversion stated 'in the basis of agreements and using defence allocated funds, conversion enterprises will assure creation, maintenance and development of mobilisation capacities' (Anthony, 1994: 78). The law applies to all defence enterprises of the former defence complex, also those choosing not to bid for government contracts. For the companies under privatisation, mobilisation capacities are subject to negotiations between the state and the privatising enterprise. The question is controversial on many accounts. There is an incompatibility of goals for increases in civilian production and the maintenance of these capacities. The privatised enterprises may have to retain standard units for militarisation purposes, which entitles government intervention. The state is supposed to pay for these capacities, but many of the interviewed enterprise managers expressed their scepticism about whether this will actually be the case.
7 MacKenzie (1990: 384).
8 Senghaas (1990: 23).

9 Evangelista (1988).

10 'Closure' is a term used by Wiebe Bijker in the SCOT (Social Construction of Technology) approach to technological change (Bijker, 1995).

11 The military industry has continued its search for a place also after the completion of the main empirical part of this study in 1997. In 1997, the control of the defence industry has moved to the Ministry of Economy. In 1999, the State Commission on Military-Industrial Affairs was established as a main coordinating body for the industry. At the same time five branch specific agencies (Aerospace, Ammunition, Control Systems, Conventional Weapons, Ship Building) were created. A step, which could be seen, as a return to the old structure with the Military-Industrial Commission with the nine defence ministries of the Soviet Union. However, in mid-2000 the state control over the industry underwent even further changes. The defence industry was placed under the joint control of the newly established Ministry of Industry, Science and Technology and the five agencies coordinated by the State Commission on Military-Industrial Affairs (Gonchar, 2000).

12 Cooper (1993: 37).

13 In his speech at the UN General Assembly on 7 December 1988, President Gorbachev committed himself to unilateral conversion of the military economy in the USSR. A 14.2% reduction in military expenditures was to be implemented, including 19.5% cuts in procurement of arms and military equipment. Conversion was to be started in more than 420 enterprises and 200 research institutes and design bureaux of the military industrial complex.

14 The results of the survey are here quoted from the weekly magazine *Conversion*, published by RICA in Moscow on 11 June 1992.

15 Vouchers were distributed to all citizens at the outset of privatisation as a symbol for the people's ownership of the means of production.

16 Cronberg (1996: 25).

17 Alexander (1990: 32) points out that it was never clear just what the 42% consisted of. His best guess (according to him) would be that only production (and not services) of the Ministry of Defence Industry, just one of the nine ministries, were included.

18 Amann and Cooper (1986).

19 According to Alexander (1990: 20), the disbanded Ministry possessed 260 factories, but only 220 were transferred. The other 40 may have discontinued their activities.

20 Bernstein, 1997

21 Perlmutter (1994: 184).

Chapter 3

Golden Technologies

When wars have finished, weapon-producing industries are turned over to civilian production. Resources spent on military production are rechannelled to consumption. After the Second World War, conversion of industrial plants was accomplished smoothly. It was largely a question of reconversion, returning to the production from before the war. This could also have been the case after the Cold War. After the collapse of the Soviet Union military defence budgets were reduced both in the US and in Russia. Defence enterprises received less orders and were faced by the challenge of trying to turn their production into civilian uses.

This time reconversion, crossing the boundary from the military to the civilian, was not so easy. The distance between the military and the civilian had grown after the Second World War, as the US military became the most significant driving force of technological development in the world. Not only as a sponsor of R&D but also as a consumer of high technology, the military provided low-risk conditions for the development of technologies such as radar, electronics, computers and aerospace which were readily available for exploitation in the civilian sector. After the Second World War, many of the scientists and engineers returned from the wartime R&D effort to work in the civilian sector. Directly after the war the military R&D was regarded as an important contributor to economic growth through commercial spin-off.[1]

The picture, however, changes in the 1970s and '80s. The military requirements no longer coincide with the likely needs of commercial users. This is due to the more complex nature of the military technology, its special product development environment and the general dynamics of the military-industrial complex itself. Innovation in the military becomes scrutinised and leads only to incremental improvements. Kaldor[2] calls it 'a baroque arsenal', as for example submarines become faster and faster, quieter, bigger and with longer ranges instead of becoming simpler and more efficient. At the same time the military industry becomes more dependent on commercial technology, such as computers. So there is a continuously changing but complex relationship between the military and the civilian technologies.[3]

While the relationship between the two kinds of technologies has changed, what makes military technology different from civilian technologies? Many have tried to define the border between these two. A British study of 'Future Relations between Defence and Civil Science and Technology' makes a distinction between high and low R&D intensity. Defence products contain more research and development. American literature on conversion looks at civilian technologies as essentially commercial. By this definition military technology becomes 'non-commercial'. As a rule, several criteria are used in combination. Military technology exists when work is done for the Defence Ministry; research and development results are incorporated in military weapon systems; a Defence Ministry holds the property rights and/or work is classified for military reasons.

There seems to be no technological distinction between military and civilian technologies. There are neither technologies solely for war, nor technologies only used in consumption. The boundary is always socially constructed and contingent. Sometimes advanced materials may be military technology, sometimes not. To be able to separate technologies intended for war from non-war technologies we have to explore this boundary. We have to understand how it is constructed in order to understand how border crossings become possible. This chapter is about how the difference is made. Focus is on the social construction of military technology in Russia, but in order to show the contingent nature of this border I shall shortly refer to the US case.

An institutional boundary

In the US, the definition of military technology is institutional. Military technology is technology produced in accordance with rules defined by the Department of Defence.[4] In the US the Department of Defence (DoD) defines not only technical specifications for military products, but also the cost-accounting systems and the quality-control procedures to be followed by military enterprises. Furthermore, the Department of Defence also acquires the property rights, i.e. the right to transfer knowledge and know-how to competing firms. This fact has led to a situation where a number of civilian enterprises refrain from military work.[5]

This institutional definition of military technology also integrates a number of civilian technologies into what is considered 'military'. The DoD has at times drafted specifications for cookies, toilet seats and other consumer products. The definition between what is considered military and what is civilian is one of specifications and procedures rather than one of technological know how or objects. The boundary of what is considered military and what is civilian is continuously negotiated, as products become 'military' when they are included in the military specifications.

The practice of defining as military those technologies that correspond to DoD specifications leads to two industrial and technology bases in the United States,[6] one for the military and one for the civilian. The linking mechanism, spin-off, was based on the assumption that technologies developed for the military, automatically or at least without any state intervention, diffused to the civilian sphere. This notion has increasingly been contested, and integration of the two industrial and technological bases is on the agenda.

The very strong influence from the Department of Defence in the US upon the structure and function of the defence industry makes it relevant to define this industry from its decisive relationship to this single customer relationship rather than by its products:[7]

> The nature of this governmental customer is the single most important determinant of the characteristics of the industry, because the DOD's monopsony power permits it to set directly the specifications of the products sold in the market and the rules under which business in transacted. This is not to argue that the private defence firms have no market power, but only that they exercise their power in the context of the rules set by the government.

Contrary to market transactions, jobs from the DoD are acquired on the basis of bidding for government contracts or allocated directly to firms within the military-industrial complex. More than 65% of all defence contracts are routinely awarded without competitive bidding.[8]

The Pentagon's procurement of defence goods is regulated by the Government's procurement regulations, which are both defined and implemented by the Pentagon. These behavioural rules are defined in the *Armed Services Procurement Regulations* and *The Defence Procurement Handbook* that comprised 100–125 pages when they were introduced in 1947. By 1973 they had expanded to 3,000 pages.

The Pentagon's procurement regulations not only indicate product specifications but also often affect in detail the production organisation and the product development process. Often the Pentagon allocates their people to the production plant to monitor the development and production process closely. The firms' own room for influencing the production and hence the defence technological development consequently becomes rather limited. Further, the demanded accounting procedures influence the organisation of defence production. As a consequence of these regulations, firms involved in both defence and civilian production often have to split up their production into two separate units each with their own book-keeping.[9]

Findings and innovations under a DoD contract belong to the DoD, and the inventing firms are, as a point of departure, not allowed to exploit these in their commercial production. The strictly regulated environment for defence production, involving intense testing combined with very restricted use of the findings for commercial purposes and a very bureaucratic book-keeping system, all contribute to an erosion of the contractors' commercial competitiveness, and consequently hamper their ability to penetrate the commercial markets when faced with reduced defence orders.

After the Cold War, procurement reform was put on the agenda. In 1992 the US Defence Conversion Commission, which presented its final report, *Adjusting to the Draw-down, 1992*, recommended that efforts to foster commercial-military integration be strengthened, expanded and accelerated considerably. The Commission suggested the transfer of technology originally developed for defence from federal laboratories to commercial activities. It promoted the idea of dual-use technologies and that the Department of Defence should work closely with Congress and other Federal agencies, in order to reduce or eliminate those regulations, which prevented greater commercial-military integration. Furthermore, the commission proposes that

> the Secretary of Defence should require that DoD use commercial specifications, standards and buying practices for all procurement actions except those for which he or she has approved military-unique practices on the basis of a demonstrated, compelling need (p. 24).

This, however, means fundamental rethinking not only the procurement system, but the American political system as a whole:[10]

> Because the barriers between DoD (and its contractors) and the commercial sector are deeply rooted in the American political system, closer integration will require a fundamental rethinking

of competing policy objectives. Greater integration would mean relaxed procurement requirements and greater discretionary authority for procurement officials – both of which are likely to be politically contentious. If such changes occur, they will reflect the recognition that DoD's isolation now threatens its technological edge, as it did not when defence technology was superior to anything the commercial sector could provide.

Spin-off becomes 'dual-use'

The integration of commercial and civilian technologies through procurement reform put focus on the assumed bridging mechanism, the spin-off. In the US just after the war, military R&D was seen as an important factor for economic growth. Early military and space programmes helped the US electronic industry to achieve research and production superiority over its competitors through the early 1970s. The military requirements – for example, for miniaturisation and lower power consumption – coincided almost exactly with the likely needs of commercial uses in the computer industry. On the other hand, the opposite was the case with the numerical control (NC) in the machine-tool industry. According to Stowsky,[11] the military guaranteed lucrative contracts to machine-tool and control manufacturers but created at the same time a limited and highly specialised market for NC-tools through its procurement policies. As consequence, it took a long time before the original idea of numerical control was embodied in practical all-purpose machines. The picture on spin-off is thus heterogeneous and dependent on technology and industry. Some may have profited from the spin-off mechanism, others not.

At the end of the Cold War, the spin-off's impact on economic growth has been increasingly questioned. In their famous study *Beyond Spin-off*, Alic *et al.* demonstrate through case studies the relative ineffectiveness of a spin-off effect. While they do not claim that it did not exist, its economic value is debatable. Furthermore, they argue that spin-off was an inefficient way to link government efforts to commercial performance although the public was recruited in support of this understanding:

The important point about the spin-off paradigm is not that it was a half truth at best, but that the unusual circumstances of the post-war-world did not force the Americans to question it.

Few asked whether the spin-off was an efficient way to link government efforts to commercial performance.[12]

The authors see the commercial sector taking the lead in many fields. Consequently, military technology is no longer necessarily more high-tech nor does it have a larger R&D content. However, it is not easy to introduce commercial technologies into military products, not only due to the complexity of the procurement process and military specification, but also because of the fact that the Department of Defence acquires property rights.

After the Cold War, the US bridge between the two technologies has been reconstructed. The rhetoric at the beginning of the 1990s is no longer about the spin-off, where R&D is first built into the military technology and from these products diffuses into commercial production. The American rhetoric is about dual use. While the spin-off bridge meant putting all the money first into military R&D and technology, dual use assumes that a common R&D and technology base may be established for *both* military and commercial technologies at the outset. Certain generic or critical technologies are to be researched without distinguishing whether the use will be in the military or civilian field. Examples are satellite technologies, sensors or high-strength composite materials. Satellite surveillance may be used to detect enemy movements but can also be used to gather weather information. Sensors are used in missile guidance systems as well as in medical equipment. Advanced composite materials are built into aircraft both for military and for commercial purposes.

The 'dual-use' bridge is by no means new. Gummett and Reppy[13] have pointed out that between 'pure' military and 'pure' civilian technology there is a vast group of dual-purpose technologies. Dual purpose here indicates that the same technology can be utilised for both military and commercial applications. However, dual purpose here covers a wide range of concepts. In spite of the obvious similarity between military and civilian airplanes, the products often have to meet very different requirements for example in engine performance, landing characteristics and life expectancy. Often the most important dual-use aspect is not related to products and their use but rather to technological knowledge.[14] Other studies have concluded that dual-use technologies are more likely to be found in generic materials, electronic and information technologies and in component manufacturing, rather than in the higher realms of sub-system manufacturers.[15] Also already by the 1970s and '80s large-scale technology development programmes had essentially been dual use, such as the high-speed integrated circuits problem programme and the strategic computer program.[16]

While one could claim that at a certain level all technologies are dual use, at some points the military and commercial applications do diverge. Engines for a military airplane have a shorter life span, operate under harsher conditions and are exposed to extreme strain. Commercial engines, on the other hand, are required to have a longer lifetime and meet strict safety standards. What is new in the US rhetoric on dual use after the end of the Cold War is the common R&D base before the requirements diverge. Whether or not this bridge enables us to cross the divide between the military and the civilian requirements is an open question.

Let us now look at the Russian divide or rather how the distinction between the military and civilian technologies was made in the Soviet Union. In spite of the barriers to commercialisation created by the US Department of Defence procurement practices authors, for example Stowsky, underline that compared with the former Soviet military-industrial complex the United States defence industry lived in a true symbiosis with civilian research and procurement.

From gold to steel

In the Soviet Union all technology was government owned. In five-year plans the government defined what technologies were to be developed and used. Appropriate activities were thereafter taken by the research institutes, design bureaux and production enterprises. All technologies were defined by ministerial procedures and specifications. Technical documentation was drafted and approved by the State. Testing was carried out in state laboratories. Procurement rules may have been different but the whole procurement system was similar for military and civilian technology.

Military and civilian production units were separate in the US due to the special control requirements of the Department of Defence. In the Soviet Union they were often combined and only in the later stages of production, in assembly, does a specialisation occur. Contrary to the US separation, civilian technologies and productions have been consciously transferred into military enterprises.

The objective of this transfer of civilian production into military industry was not to create technological spin-offs but to raise the quality of the management of the civilian production. The military's image of high-quality and high-discipline production was to be transferred to the civilian production characterised by low quality and mismanagement. This integration also led to a de facto integration in the plants. Civilian and military productions were carried out in the same plants and controlled by the same groups of people. The secrecy attached to military production was not only limited to military technologies but to all production in the military-industrial complex, including the production of washing machines, videos and the like. Whole industrial plants, even cities were closed off, although specific facilities required special permission to enter.

When asked about the basic difference between military and civilian technologies the enterprise managers I have interviewed in Russia without exception underlined the question of *access* and that of *price*. Military technologies were of 'gold', civilian production of 'steel' to cite a frequently quoted expression. Gold here is symbolic. It stands for abundant resources, priority in supplies, access to products of high quality. Consequently, when trying to transcend the gap between military and civilian technologies, the Russian engineers and scientists working on conversion faced a different set of problems from their American colleagues. They were to convert gold into steel or to get gold accepted in civilian production.

This divide reflects the military sector's role. It had the highest priority in society. The Military-Industrial Commission with representatives both from the Politbureau, Academy of Sciences and the Defence Departments had the highest power and authority in the country to allocate resources. Nine military ministries channelled the resources further to around 1700 enterprises, which completed the tasks of weapon developments and production. These enterprises, including research institutes and design bureaux, were allocated the best raw materials. The best brains were reserved for weapon development and working in the military sector implied a number of privileges including higher salaries. So for example when components were produced in a factory, the best were stamped 'good for military use', while the rest went to civilian uses.

Quality control also differed between the civilian and the military sectors. In the latter, designs and prototypes were carefully finished and tested. The technical documentation was checked and the personal responsibility of the chief engineer in the design bureau enforced. Barriers to the transfer of know how were bridged by giving institutions the power to co-ordinate efforts or by setting up special agencies for weapon development programmes (ballistic missiles, nuclear weapons).[17]

American literature on conversion from the 1970s and '80s[18] also refers to this gap, to the 'performance at any cost' approach of the military and the failures in utilising military technologies in civilian spheres due to lack of market thinking and cost optimisation. However, this problem was much more dramatic in the Soviet Union. It also defines the conversion problem. It is one of transformation from the high-tech, high-cost and high-status sector to the low-tech, low-quality and low-prestige sector. Furthermore, this technological transformation is to take place in a context where the economic system is being transformed to that of a market economy and where changing prices of raw materials, energy and other resources are creating a chaotic situation.

Conversion histories

In his speech at the UN General Assembly on 7 December 1988, President Gorbachev committed himself to a unilateral conversion of the military economy in the USSR. A reduction of 14.2% in military expenditures was to be implemented including 19.5% cuts in arms and military equipment procurement. Conversion was to be started in more than 420 enterprises, 200 research institutes and design bureaux of the military-industrial complex. Historic as his speech was, this was by no means the first conversion experience of the USSR.

Conversion has been carried out both after the massive demobilisation of the armed forces after the civil war in 1918–20 and after the Second World War in 1945–47. While this in both cases was a major economic undertaking, it did not present a major problem. After the Second World War conversion was accomplished relatively smoothly since it was largely a question of reconversion, that is of return to the original production of the enterprises. The first peacetime conversion was undertaken in the 1950s on the initiative of Nikita Khrushchev. The conversion, which continued until 1964, involved the reduction of the armed forces by two million servicemen, reduced the Soviet military budget and scrapped certain types of military hardware.[19]

The goals for conversion were clearly stated by Gorbachev. Instead of the 60:40 ratio of military to civil production within the defence complex, this ratio would be turned upside down, i.e. 40:60 by 1995.

This quantitative goal allowed for a broad interpretation of the conversion issue. Potentially, military procurement could be reduced without any increase of civilian production. Furthermore, it could cover increases in existing civilian production within the defence complex without any changes in its military procurement. Or it could cover additional transfer of civilian industries into the defence complex. However, the intentions were clear. Military procurement was to be reduced and the resources earlier spent in development of the military industry would be reused in civilian production. According to Mikhail Malei (president Yeltsin's advisor on conversion) conversion was from the very beginning seen as a technical retooling or reorientation of military productions.[20]

The reasons for focusing on the retooling and reuse of technology know-how and methods are many. The main discourse, however, sees the military industry as a national resource. Since the Soviet defence industry had the highest quality of any industry in the country and had access to the best engineers and managers as well as scarce materials and a functional support infrastructure, these resources could not be scrapped away. Defence conversion becomes a strategic imperative and 'it would be extremely undesirable, if not criminal, to dissipate this potential'.[21]

As opposed to conversion experiences from other countries, the conversion of the defence industry in the former Soviet Union and in Russia has been connected with overall economic reforms. Consequently, it is obvious that the notion of conversion has also undergone changes dependent on how and what kind of economic reforms the government has tried to implement. Common to all phases of the Russian conversion process since Gorbachev's statement at the UN has, however, been the following rhetoric:

- the maintenance of the nation's technological base *in* the defence complex;
- focus on conversion of the technological capabilities to *high-tech*[22] products in the civilian sector rather than everyday consumer goods;
- reorganisation of the defence industry's production capabilities *within* the present the industrial structure, i.e. a company-by-company or plant-by-plant conversion.

The conversion effort of 1988–90 failed right from the start. Critics of the Gorbachev conversion policy claim that the conversion programme had already collapsed by 1989 as the military-industrial lobby tried to save their branches by new defence orders. The formal programme, although unpublished, was also an object of severe criticism by many leading economists. Iurii Iaremenko, director of the Institute of Economy and Prediction of Scientific and Technological Progress, pointed out that it was designed to support the old forms of the economy. He pointed out three main faults in the programme:[23]

1. lack of incentives to redirect the scientific production and technological potentials of the military-industrial complex to civil purposes because of the low prestige and secondary role of civilian production;

2. being only a part of the output of the military enterprises, civilian products were bound to bear the expenses of military production, thus contributing to price rises and inflation;

3. lack of market orientation of the civilian production within the military-industrial complex.

According to the official view, a number of things were accomplished during the first 18 months of conversion. The military budget was reduced, in 1989–90 by more than 10 billion roubles. Conversion was at least reportedly, being started in more than 420 enterprises and in 200 research institutes and design bureaux. In 1991, more than 400,000 people in the defence sector were assumed to begin work for civilian production. However, the real achievements were more limited. By the end of 1989 out of the planned 120 new types of civilian goods the defence industries had managed to start producing just 23. Only 15% of the new products were estimated as meeting international quality standards. It is often assumed that in a planned economy, conversion could be carried out efficiently. This is not the case for this first conversion period. Various reasons for the failure of the programme have been listed by Iziumov.[24]

- lack of serious preparatory and research work prior to taking the political decision to initiate conversion; the decision to start conversion came as a surprise to many of the plant managers;
- orders were passed down from above, often unmatched by funds and raw materials and taking little account of the technical possibilities of the enterprises involved;

- empowering the Military-Industrial Commission with the leadership of conversion in fact was contrary to its corporate interests;
- lack of financial resources for conversion;
- absence of a legal basis for conversion and later privatisation.

Men'schikov[25] points out that the word conversion during this time (1990–91) was in daily use in the country. But the accent was more on difficulties and problems than on priorities and potentials. Capital expenditure for restructuring military factories was not available. It was dangerous to destroy centres of military R&D, because they could be needed at any time. Keeping up armaments production was necessary for having the capacity ready when called upon. He points out that conversion was not possible under such argumentation. He even claims that the sabotage of the conversion in 1988–90 was a crucial factor that helped ruin the Soviet economy.

In this situation it is not unexpected that weapons export is proposed as a solution. Already in the spring of 1992 Yeltsin declared that weapon sales were essential to obtain foreign currency for conversion and his adviser Mikhail Malei expressed:[26]

> For a long time the military industrial complex has been absorbing large sums from the state budget. Now the task is to make the military industrial complex a source of budget revenue. If the military industrial complex is not ready to export non-military products, it should start earning hard currency for the state by exporting weaponry.

Military production is not argued for here on security grounds but on economic grounds. The task is to integrate Russia into the world economy.

In spite of this, arms exports from the former Soviet Union continued to decline in 1992 although less steeply than in 1989–91. According to Gennadii Ianpol'skii, General Director of the Defence Industry Department of the Ministry of Industry (September 1992), exports accounted for 30% of the sales by the Russian defence industry in 1991 and 7.2% of sales in the first half of 1992. Estimates indicate that Russia exported arms for 23 billion in 1989 and for 7.8 billion in 1991. The sales for 1992 were around 3 billion.[27]

Reasons for this failure are many. Earlier the incomes generated by export sales have not been questioned as prices have been held artificially low due to the privileged position of the defence sector for raw materials and supplies. Stopping arms production and selling raw materials might be a more economic way of earning the funds necessary for conversion. Export incomes often came from totalitarian regimes and were in the form of credits rather than actual payments. Finally, there was the question of whether arms sales would have a negative impact on world opinion, and divert potential support to the conversion process in Russia.

A persistent divide

The Gorbachev experiment to renegotiate military technologies within the Soviet Union failed. The Russian explanations quoted above explained this as being due to lack of incentives although the way the question was approached was typical of the Soviet system. It was conversion by command. Orders were passed down from above and, as pointed out by Iziumov, the possibilities of the enterprises were not taken into account. On the other hand, this again was the way production was established in the Soviet Union, by an order from the top. Putting the blame on the civilian production within the defence enterprises seems rather strange as this again applied to the whole of the civilian production not only the part located in the defence enterprises. Rather explanations why the early experiment was unsuccessful could be sought in the nature of the divide. Privileges related to the military were not abolished and defence technologies were still of gold although the order was to make these into steel.

Nor did the weapons export track produce any quick answers for the economy, although some individual enterprises have performed quite well. In 1991–92 two government proposals had already failed. It was necessary for the enterprises and regions to start to work from the bottom-up. It was necessary to do so, not in a supply economy, but in an emerging market economy where the products had to be sold in open competition with others. In spite of these changes the conversion discourse remains the same. Changes are to take place within the existing enterprises; conversion should be high-tech to high-tech in order to be able to safeguard the national resources built into military production and technology.

Notes

1 Future Relations between Defence and Civil Science and Technology (1991).
2 Kaldor (1982).
3 The sources that have assessed that the military and the civilian technologies have grown further and further apart include Future Relations Between Defence and Civil Science and Technology (1991); Kaldor (1992); van Opstall (1991). On the other hand, the military's need for a more commercial technology is underlined in Future Relations Between Defence and Civil Science and Technology (1991); Gansler (1988); Defilloto (1990).
4 In van Opstal (1991) the differences between civilian and military production are further elaborated.
5.See for example Future Relations between Defence and Civilian Science and Technology.
6 'A defence industry and technology base is the combination of people, institutions, technological know-how and facilities used to design, develop, manufacture and maintain the weapons and supporting defence equipment needed to meet the US national security objectives.' The civilian or commercial base is the one responsible for the same outside this domain (OTA, 1991: 39).
7 Reppy (1983: 25).
8 See e.g. Stowsky (1986).
9 Cronberg and Aeroe (1995).
10 Alic et al. (1992: 163).
11 Stowsky (1986: 21).
12 Alic et al. (1992: 10).
13 Gummett and Reppy (1988).
14 Smith (1990).
15 Future Relations Between Defence and Civil Science and Technology (1991); Walker (1988).
16 Smith (1990); Stowsky (1986).
17 Evangelista (1988).
18 See for example Melman (1983, 1986, 1988); Lynch (1987). For a review of the literature see Cronberg and Haugbølle Hansen (1992).
19 Iziumov (1990).
20 Conversion, Rica, 20 February 1992.
21 Kortunov, Head of Directorate for Export Control and Conversion, Ministry of Foreign Affairs in a presentation by the Russian delegation at the NATO seminar on Defence Conversion in Brussels, 20–22 May 1992.
22 The word 'high-tech' is used without further clarification.
23 Iaremenko, Sovershenno Sekretno, No. 8 (1990).
24 Iziumov (1990: 12): for example, some factories of the military aviation industry instead of concentrating forces on producing and designing badly

needed passenger planes started designing machinery for tanning tomatoes or processing pasta.

25 Experiences of Soviet Conversion, 1992.
26 In Conversion, Rica, 19 May 1992.
27 SIPRI Yearbook (1993: 447–9).

Chapter 4

'En by i Rusland'

'*En by i Rusland*' is a Danish metaphor for something incomprehensible, something far away, unreachable – something you give up on. Translated, it means 'a town in Russia'. For me, Perm was a town in Russia: a city of one million in the middle of Russia on the European side of the Urals, south of Komi and north of the Bashkir region. The distance from Moscow to Perm is greater than the distance from Copenhagen to Moscow. It takes 28 hours by train to get to Perm, a distance of 1500 miles to be flown in less than two hours. The city, located in a region with the same name and about the size of France, was in the old days a gateway to Siberia.

I came to Perm for the first time in November 1991. The Soviet Union had collapsed a few days before and I was to attend a conference on 'Conversion and the Environment'. The conference, organised by the Norwegian Peace Research Institute in Oslo (PRIO) and the United Nation's Environmental Programme (UNEP), should have been held in Moscow. But at that time the Moscow hotels refused to take roubles. UNEP wanted to pay in roubles. The conference had to be relocated to a 'rouble zone'. The newly opened city of Perm was selected.

We, a handful of foreign participants met in Moscow. None of us had even heard of Perm. Rumours circulated that it would be difficult to get there due to snowstorms in November. Therefore, we would be flown in by military plane. When we arrived at the airport, we found out that there were scheduled flights to Perm several times a day. When we arrived in the city, we were met by 'normal' Russian hospitality, a conference organised in a 'normal' Soviet way and an abundance of food, disproving all rumours of hunger in the area. The conference took place in a defence design bureau specialising in artillery systems. We were the first foreigners to visit its premises, which were surrounded by barbed wire and strict security checks.

The Siberian gateway

In the old days, transportation was along rivers from St Petersburg to Siberia. In these days Perm was a strategic point, a centre for transportation between the Kazan way and the Siberian way. Up the

Kama River flowing down to the Caspian Sea, transportation was by river and then transferred to transport on land. The river station is still one of the most beautiful buildings in Perm. At this time there was no military industry in Perm, in fact, no industry at all.

Peter the Great started the modernisation of Russia and needed an army and military equipment. He sent one of his experts, Tatishchev to Perm where there was copper, steel, forests and coal. The first copper-melting plant was built in Perm in 1723. This was the start of Perm, at the time a little village named Iegoshicha, a small river flowing into the Kama River.

In 1780 the industrial development started. Catherine II wanted to conquer Siberia and sent an order to create a city, Perm. Perm came from the Finnish-related word *perama* meaning a country or land far away. The city was created in 1781. Industries were established, everything could be produced in the region. There was a saltmine selling salt even abroad. There was steel and metals as well as power. Boats were produced in Perm in spite of its location in the middle of the continent. A canon producing plant, Motovilikha, produced canons, in Russian *pushka*, and equipped the Russian army with these. Chemical industries were based on the saltmine producing sulphate acid. Based on German technology aniline and nitrobenzol were also being produced for military purposes. Subsequently, the chemical industry was, alongside the production of canons, to become the industrial basis for military industries in Perm.

While the revolution in 1917–18 left Perm largely untouched, the military industry started to flourish. During the First World War Germany had invaded the Don basin and Japan advanced in the Far East. These two theatres of war, one on the European and one on the Asian side, led to a decision that military industry should be placed in places far away from both of these. A decision was made by Stalin to establish a military-industrial zone including Sverdlovsk, Cheliabinsk, Izhevsk and Perm in the Urals. These cities were to become military-industrial production centres. In this zone both coal, oil, gas, wood, metals and chemical industries were available.

Subsequently, a large-scale development programme was established for the Ural Zone for military purposes. In Perm a metallurgic combinate produced high-quality steel, a large chemical combinate was established close to the saltmine and the existing plants were diversified to ammunition and explosives. A certain division of work developed in the Ural cities. While Sverdlovsk and Cheliabinsk produced tanks and Izhevsk kalashnikovs, Perm became the centre of explosives and canons. When aviation developed after the First World War an industry was built in Perm for the production of engines.

At the outbreak of the Second World War the Urals was a fundamental region of the country for defence purposes. During the Second World War industrial plants were evacuated from Ukraine, Moscow and Central Russia, some of which arrived in Perm. Histories are told in Perm how machines were packed from these evacuated areas, arrived in Perm, were put on the ground and started to produce weapons even before buildings were built. This was the time when the machine-building industry was established in Perm and the aviation industrial base was further developed. New metals, titanium and magnesium were in demand and available in the Perm region. Guidance systems for aviation were developed at the same time as scientific institutes were established for the industrial needs in the city.

The first conversion in Perm took place after the Second World War. Industrial plants were closed down as the orders for the army were reduced. Instead of intensive explosive production the chemical industry of Perm started to produce paints and linoleum and other surface materials. More workers were available for civilian production, and industries related to both radio and telephone emerged in Perm. However, the military industries continued to produce, although not to the same extent.

During the Cold War and the arms race Perm became a centre for the development of new weapon systems and the modernisation of the old ones. The competition for space needed new technologies, such as jet engines for missiles. A number of engineers and experts were needed and the Perm Polytechnic, established in the 1950s, started to mass-produce engineers for tasks defined by the military industries. Weapons and defence equipment were not only produced for the Soviet army, but also for China and the countries in the Warsaw Pact. Close ties were developed between all these countries. However, because Stalin did not allow the development and production of complex weapon development to take place in other countries, research and development activities were concentrated in Russia.

Although the problem of conversion was first posed in radical dimensions by the Gorbachev era and at the end of the Cold War, already during Khrushchev time conversion was on the agenda. He proposed a cut-down in the army and reduction in military production. His strategy was to give priority to development of submarines and strategic missile-carrying aircraft. During his time the atomic defence of the country was built and new kinds of missiles developed. For Perm, this meant further development of engines, new kinds of artillery systems and development of composite materials and related technologies.

In a way Perm is unique. It is a product of its history where a number of ethnic groups have moved or been moved. By moving a Baltic university to the city before the Revolution an intellectual climate was created. It is a product of its location where before the Revolution there were a number of rich persons donating university buildings and hospitals. At this time it was a region exporting bread, butter and honey. Its particular location far from the theatres of war combined with the wealth of raw materials made it a place for the Cold War's arms race: a war that created the Perm of today with both its problems and potential.

A militarised community

The Perm region has 3 million people, of whom 1 million live in the city of Perm. In January 1991, the year of the collapse of the Soviet Union, the total workforce was 1.5 million, of which a third worked in industry.[1] Almost half of these people worked in the defence industry and about 90,000 worked directly with production of weapons. The rest were employed in civilian productions of the defence enterprises or in their service sector (day-care centres, holiday resorts etc.). Of the region's 23 military enterprises, 20 were located in the city of Perm.

The size of these enterprises varied from 'design bureaux' with some one hundred employees to huge 'science production associations' employing tens of thousands of workers.[2] An indication of the degree of militarisation of the economy of the city and the region is shown by the fact that the ten largest defence enterprises accounted for 50% of the industrial employment of the city. The industrial enterprises of the region as a whole were related to machine building, metallurgy, the chemical industry, mining, forestry, and oil and natural gas.

A special characteristic of the military enterprises in the Perm region was their dependence on end producers. The enterprises produced aircraft engines, guidance systems, rocket engines, composite materials and other parts. There were only a few producers of end products. The largest of these was the Motovilikha plant, the former Lenin Machine Building Plant, which produced howitzers, heavy armoured vehicles and rocket launchers. Other large-scale production enterprises include the Perm Motor Works – formerly the Sverdlov Motor Building – which made jet engines, and the Kirov Chemical Plant which produced ammunition, rocket fuel and explosives. The region's research institutes worked mainly on advanced materials and powder metallurgy. For the most part, the research and development capabilities related to the region's industries were located outside Perm, in Moscow or St Petersburg. Perm design bureaux, for applied research and pilot production, developed artillery systems, engine designs and guidance systems. Two main types of technology networks were present in Perm, one related to aircraft engine construction and design, the other to artillery systems and end products from this know-how, for example, rocket launchers.

The research institutes of the region were closely tied to the production units. So, for example, the PAKB design bureau produced steering systems for Perm Motor Works which, in turn, was closely related to the design bureau Aviadvigatel', which was also located in Perm. Iskra, a design bureau in the field of space research, supplied rocket engine designs for Perm Motor Works and worked closely with the Kirov chemical plant in producing fuel.

The civilian production of the defence enterprises in Perm included bicycles, tractors, trailers, cultivators and household appliances. Before 1991, the proportion of civilian production in the defence enterprises ranged from 5% to 40%, depending on the enterprise. For example, in 1992 the five aviation industry enterprises in the region had a total of 29,000 employees. Of these, 12,000 worked directly with military production and 18,000 with civilian production. Consequently, the Perm defence enterprises had, as was common in the country, both a civilian and military production, although the resource divide was in place. The civilian and military productions were not necessarily related in technology. So for example, the Motovilikha plant producing artillery systems also produced washing machines and mixers. The Perm Motor Works, producing aircraft engines, also produced tractors and cultivators. Velta, the defence electronics plant, produced bicycles and trailers. Sometimes civilian and military plants were separate, sometimes integrated. The assembly, due to particular secrecy requirements, was always closed off from the civilian production.

Perm also has a number of educational institutions. Among them is the old university, a branch for the Russian Academy of Sciences, a military academy and a polytechnic institute established to produce the engineers the defence industries needed. Around 60,000 engineers have been trained in Perm, many of whom specialised in very narrow military disciplines, such as aircraft engines or artillery systems. There is a close contact between the polytechnic institute, now the Technical University, and the defence industries of the region. Even today the enterprises establish disciplines in the Technical University that support their product development and production processes.

Enterprise neighbourhoods

Perm lies on the banks of the Kama River, a tributary of the Volga. One of its most beautiful buildings is the River Boat Station, a yellow building located on the river bank. The river is polluted – also by the defence industries – although in the early spring you can see hundreds of fishermen sitting on the ice. The campus of Perm Technical University is located on the right side of the river as is the former Lenin Machine Building Plant, now called Motovilikha Plant. Most of the city is located on the left bank, with housing neighbourhoods organised around the defence enterprises.

In the centre, surrounded by open parks are two huge multi-storey administrative buildings, one for the region and one for the city. One of these used to be the building for the party. Behind these administrative buildings is the Hotel Ural and a central department store. The obligatory Karl Marx Prospect passes through the centre of the city. Office buildings on this street, formerly belonging to the state administration, have now been turned into banks. At the end of the main street is a neighbourhood in green, which reflect the Second World War Stalin architecture. Here the Perm Motor Works neighbourhood begins with 30,000 housing units belonging to the enterprise. In the centre there is a cultural house, sports fields and, further down the road, factories and workshops surrounded by barbed wire. Leaving this neighbourhood, you can enter the neighbourhood of radio electronics with a similar structure. Further on, there is a similar area around a telecommunication plant. The same pattern continues with a chemical-plant neighbourhood, an oil-refining neighbourhood etc.

The research institutes and design bureaux are spread around the city in smaller facilities with fewer housing units and recreational facilities. Some of them are located on the premises of Perm Technical University, although separated from these facilities by barbed wire and special controls. Although most of the defence-related research institutes and large design bureaux were in the Moscow and St Petersburg area, Perm had its own niche in engines, fuel, chemicals and advanced composite materials. The university campus is located in the middle of the forest a few kilometres from the city. Most of the institutes are related to machine building, aviation or space exploration. A military academy in the centre of the city educates officers and specialists for the army. Furthermore, the Urals Branch of the Russian Academy of Science also has activities in Perm.

As the Perm region was rich in oil and minerals, there is an oil-producing neighbourhood, the neighbourhood of the Permneftorgsintez, a huge neighbourhood with tens of thousands of dwellings built around oil-producing plants. This neighbourhood was known to be hazardous for health. Most of the children have asthma, bronchitis and other lung problems. It has been discussed whether Perm should be proclaimed a dangerous environment to live in, but as my host, a professor in ecology at the Perm Technical University, said, 'Why worry the people?' There was no alternative. On my way by train from Perm to Moscow, I once travelled with the chief of environmental control for this plant. He had with him cucumbers, which had been grown in the greenhouse on the site of Perm Neftorganosintez. According to him, they were grown ecologically.

You can travel to Perm by train; it takes 23 hours in a comfortable Russian train. Russians have a train culture. They are used to travelling long distances and know how to relax and pass time. You can also fly to Perm airport. As a centre for aeroplane engines, design and production, the airport is also used as a testing facility. Test planes fly above the city, and military planes take off to patrol the North Pole.

The northern part of the region is covered with forests, although there is very little forestry or wood-processing industry. During the Soviet time the area was considered to be unfavourable for agriculture. Agriculture and food production is almost non-existent, although increasing.

Perm 36

Any description of Perm would be incomplete without mentioning the prison camps. At the seminar on 'Conversion and the Environment', my host-to-be, Prof. Vaysman of the Ecological Institute of the Perm Technological University, opened the seminar by saying, 'The people of Perm are the best. They are descendants of those who came here to prison camps. Many of them worked to develop the weapons that are now produced here.'

Already during the Tsar time 'unpleasant' people were sent not only to Siberia, but also to Perm. Perm was a place people were sent to because of political reasons, among them many members of intelligentsia and writers, but also people with technical skills. The Tsar sent Poles during the Polish revolution and Poles still form a minority in Perm. According to Prof. Vaysman, Stalin sent people to Perm who were intelligent, democratic in their mind and therefore 'genetically interesting'. He sent Volga Germans, some of whom have now left for Germany, to Perm. He also sent a number of persons from the Baltic states, Ukraine, Jews and 'kulaks' (farmers) from the countryside. All these 'dangerous' people became the fundament for the Perm industrial development. Particularly due to Stalin's fight against cosmopolitanism, Jews, Germans and other minorities who were refused working places in other parts of the Soviet Union came to Perm. Also a number of well-known chief designers for the space programme, such as Korolev, sat in the prison camps in Perm. Rumours tell that Tupolev, the designer of the Tupolev aircraft, also spent some time in the Perm prison camps. These innovators, scientists and engineers, were transported from the working places to the industrial plants and after the day's work returned to the camps.

I never asked to visit a prison camp, but the following is an excerpt from an article in *International Herald Tribune* under the title 'The Ghosts of Russia's Past':

> The only sign of life amid the cluster of blackened, rotting wooden shacks is one that portends death: a freshly painted green guard tower that once loomed above the inmates of Perm 36, the most notorious labour camp for political prisoners in the Soviet Union.
>
> [...]
>
> Perm 36 was closed in December 1987. The last remaining 10 political prisoners were released from nearby Perm 35 in 1992 by President Boris Yeltsin – the year after the Soviet Union collapsed.
>
> [...]
>
> And it is to roll away the thickening mist of mystery and amnesia about the Gulag that a few local academics are trying to reconstruct Perm 36, much of which was razed by bulldozers in 1989. They want to restore its lumber mill, cellblocks and barbed-wire fences as a living museum of Soviet depression.

[...]

'I'm a historian, so I know how quickly memory vanishes', said Viktor Shmyrov, 50, professor of medieval history in Perm, who is leading the restoration effort. 'When I saw how the camp was disappearing, I thought that it had to be saved for history.'

[...]

The effort to restore Perm 36 has unleashed painful undercurrents. The region's governor is a supporter and allocated some money from his budget for the restoration. Local Communists are vehemently opposed.

[...]

The local Perm chapter of Memorial, a historical society dedicated to victims of Communist oppression, is co-sponsoring the effort. The reclusive Mr. Solzhenitsyn agreed to serve on the museum's board. But even among survivors, there is a reticence about dwelling on their suffering.[3]

There are still today a number of prisons in the region. I asked one of the professors of the Perm University about the Perm mafia. His answer was that as Perm was the site of prisons, there were a lot of criminals in the region on their way in and out of the system. Some may have skipped. Consequently, Perm might have a higher criminal activity than other regions in Russia.

Perm, however, also has a reputation for decent people. Prof. Vaysman told his story. He is a Jew from Ukraine. He wanted to become a journalist in Kiev, but this was not possible for Jews after the war. So one of his teachers told him that he should leave Ukraine and go to Perm, where the people were decent. He left at the age of 18, and became a doctor in Perm. For many years he worked with the environmental problems of Perm's military enterprises, was a member of the Communist Party and a family man with two sons. Now he is the head of the Ecological Institute of Perm Technical University.

The conversion numbers

Conversion has been on the agenda of the Perm defence enterprises ever since Gorbachev took the initiative in 1988. In at least one of the enterprises of the defence complex, a composite-materials research institute, received an order to start producing needles for medical syringes as part of the Gorbachev conversion programme. When the state defence orders from 1991 to 1992 were reduced to about one-third of that of the year before, all defence enterprises in the region tried to increase their civilian production. Defence workers were transferred to civilian departments of the enterprises. For example, in the mechanical industry the number of workers working for military production was halved from 1991 to 1992. At the same time, the civilian workforce of the industry grew by the same number.

Ideas for new civilian products were put forth in 1992–94, in particular, to potential Western investors. Expectations were high for contacts to Western enterprises as a source of financing. As these optimistic expectations did not materialise, the economic situation has gradually deteriorated. Although the Perm enterprises have, in co-operation with the regional administration, designed regional conversion plans, no large-scale funding has been forthcoming from the government or other sources.

The numbers for the first five years of transformation to a market economy and for conversion efforts are the following. Given the production index of 100 in 1990 (in stable roubles), the military production had by the end of 1994 been reduced to only 11% of the 1990 level. Civilian production had risen slightly for investment goods and been relatively stable for consumer products. The data includes only civilian production within the military industry, which to start with was below 40% in most of the Perm enterprises. Consequently, civilian production has by no means been able to compensate for the dramatic losses of military production.[4] The stability of consumer goods production may be explained by the fact that some of the consumer goods produced by Perm enterprises such as shampoo, knives and forks or tractors and bicycles were able to maintain their markets even when threatened by foreign competition. But new products such as microwave ovens and other consumer goods developed by the Perm defence enterprises were not able, in the overall picture, to affect the production of consumer goods.[5]

The most amazing figures are those for employment. Although military production was during the period 1990–94 reduced to around 11% and the production of investment goods shows only a slight increase, employment decreased by only 30%. Many formal reasons can be found for this. The prestige of Soviet enterprise managers depended on the number of workers they employed. Furthermore, it

was prohibited by law to dismiss employees. The mobilisation
capabilities, i.e. the ability of the enterprise in crisis situations to
expand production, also entailed human capabilities making it
impossible to dismiss employees, at least crucial experts and workers.
However, my interviews with the defence managers also mirror a real
social concern. The managers do not actually want to get rid of
employees. Not only do they lack incentives to do this, but they are also
aware of the importance of the enterprise as a link to society. In 1991–
94, unemployment was not a normal phenomenon. To dismiss workers
was not an acceptable practice. The accepted thing was to keep your
employees.[6]

Only a few years ago, Perm was a closed city. No manager of a
military enterprise had ever been in the West. If the enterprise exported
weapons, the ministry in Moscow took care of the export. Their main
source of information on foreign technological innovations was the
KGB and the defence industrial ministries. In response to foreign
advancements, the ministry and the VPK ordered innovation of weapon
technologies. During the Soviet period, military enterprises had no
client contacts of their own, nor did they participate in marketing
activities. Very few scientists had been at international conferences.
What Soviet scientists and engineers knew about their products,
weapon systems and military equipment was that they were 'world
class'.

Business discourses

In 1991, Russian firms had, as a rule, no experience in doing business
with Western partners, nor any experience of working under market
conditions. Serious Western firms that made early efforts to establish
co-operation met a number of barriers. They faced tremendous
difficulties in a country where access to both physical and intellectual
property was not defined. The business environment was chaotic and
the way of doing business very different from that in the West. These
problems were felt in Perm even more so than in Moscow or St Petersburg. Away from the mainstream travel routes of international visitors,
Perm, as of early 1992, had only been visited by a couple of
delegations, one of Japanese industrialists and the other of American
bankers. Occasional visitors had made personal contacts.

The UN/PRIO Conference on 'Conversion and the Environment'
was one of the very first international conferences ever to be held in

Perm (November 1991). At this conference, the general atmosphere was one of 'everything is possible'. Now that the Soviet Union was no longer the enemy, the West would come and help to establish – the goal was vague at this point – 'a better life'. Russia would no longer have to spend the bulk of its resources on the military. The military would convert with the help of Western companies. The Russian participants underlined, however, that they were to be considered partners and not foreign-aid recipients.

In March 1992, the defence enterprises of Perm found themselves in an institutional vacuum. The formal structures of the planned economy no longer existed. The defence branch ministries and the VPK had been abolished. The new military doctrine, conversion and privatisation laws had neither been passed nor implemented. Although the enterprises acquired an autonomy they had never known before, room to manoeuvre was still limited. Not only were old restrictions such as mobilisation requirements still in place, but also their own internal structures, norms and practices inherited from the past created limitations. In spite of the collapse of ministerial structures, in 1992 the enterprises were an integral part of the state.

In March 1992 when I interviewed defence enterprise managers, the interest was focused on Western investments and technology. Managers consented to be interviewed in exchange for being able to explain technical proposals for foreign investments. These were proposals with technical characteristics describing the technical capabilities of the enterprises. Proposals for civilian production were put forth based on a 'technology push' approach without any consideration of the clients or the market. The 'market' simply needed better technology.

In 1992 there was also a weapons-export reaction to reduced defence budgets. This was also present in Perm. Some of the managers, rather than converting to civilian production, tried the export route – although this was by no means a dominant or even a common strategy in 1992–93. Only the Motovilikha Plant was actively promoting exports of its products (howitzers, rocket launchers, heavily armoured vehicles). The company argued publicly for the right of military enterprises to establish independent contacts with weapon exporters and foreign clients. According to one article,[7] the company's conversion need over a five-year period was estimated to be 29.9 million roubles at 1992 prices. Conversion opportunities appeared to exist in equipment for oil extraction, the coal industry and metallurgy.

As the government was not financing conversion, the only choice, according to the top manager, was to export weapons. During the first quarter of 1992, the enterprise had not received any government orders. Through a Bulgarian non-governmental intermediary, the company had acquired the possibility of exporting its products to a third country:

> He [the director] holds that the best way out of the critical situation is the direct supply of arms to foreign firms. In his opinion, the conditions for the contacts must be determined by the management of the enterprise, and all currency after reduction of the mandatory sales-related costs and taxes to the government should be received by the factories. Quick action is necessary – if the government, which has the monopoly on weapon exports, hesitates in solving the problems, it will soon turn out that there is nothing to sell.[8]

In November 1992 there was a radical change of atmosphere. Western joint ventures and technological aid did not solve the conversion problem. Furthermore, based on their own resources there were very few examples of successful conversion. The defence managers started to look – not for Western investments or technologies – but for market assistance. Many were also eager to learn how to develop a business plan and how to do market studies. By this time, many of the defence enterprises in Perm had completed their defence orders from the year before; some were producing without any orders and there was a general effort to increase civilian production.

In spite of all these efforts to find co-operation with the West, to increase civilian production or to export weapons, the production in the Perm industry fell during 1992–95. 'Lack of financing' was the defence managers' and the scientists'/engineers' explanation for why they had not succeeded. The West did not want to help. They did not have adequate technological capabilities for civilian product development and mass production. Capabilities for doing feasibility studies and market assessments were only just being developed. Still, in 1993–95 hopes for Western joint ventures survived. Privatisation of the military enterprises was also viewed optimistically. In order to understand the ins and outs of these early discussions on conversion we can look at it through the eyes of one the managers, Iurii Dudkin, from the Perm Unit Design Bureau, PAKB.

Iurii Dudkin

The first time I meet Iurii Dudkin (ID) is in March 1992. I have arranged for an interview through my contact, Professor Vaysman at Perm Technical University, a friend of ID's. He is the head designer and director of a design bureau making guidance systems for aircraft engines. The design bureau was founded in 1943, during the war, as the Ural branch of a design bureau in Moscow. In 1947 it became an independent design bureau and is today one of the few in its particular field.

I am excited about the visit. It is my third interview and the first one to take place on the premises. The design bureau has just received permission to open its doors to visitors, also foreigners. The barbed wires are being dismantled and we enter the building through the characteristic rotating carrousels with a controlling reception. Once inside, having shown my passport and filled in the papers, the director takes me down to the basement. He points out that much of their facilities are underground in order to be protected during wartime. I am the first foreign visitor to be let in. We enter a conference room where some of the guidance systems are demonstrated in models.

The work the design bureaux did was both for the civilian and for the military aviation ministries. In March 1992 ID is still fulfilling the old orders. He has not received any new orders from the ministry. He points out that now it is the enterprises that should order. The problem is that they do not have money and are ordering without money. In 1991 the ratio of military to civilian production in his design bureau was one to three. Now it is one to two. The change is due to rising prices, not to increased military orders.

ID points out that his technological potential is very high for both civilian and military uses. However, due to the advanced nature of their work it is difficult to find orders. He is thinking about diversification and wants to produce large quantities of cheaper and competitive goods. While the electronic and high mechanical guidance systems may not be dual-use, i.e. able to find civilian applications, he is more optimistic about the company's micro-electronic technology. The design bureau is vertically integrated and is actually making printed circuits. TV and radio production, computers and programming, even washing machines, are the alternatives in his mind. Although his firm does not have experience in mass production, he is optimistic about the use of military technology for civilian purposes, due to its higher quality. This could give potential advantages for civilian uses, for example, in fuel consumption.

Of the company's 2400 employees, half are working in production. Design bureaux like his have pilot production plants. Of the rest, 800 are designers, 80 in middle management and 50 in top management. The rest are drivers, maintenance personnel etc. The company has its own housing areas, a vacation home and day-care centres. In March 1992, these have become a burden due to the lack of money. In addition, the level of salaries is deteriorating. Previously, the military was one of the highest paying employers, but today (1992) he is only able to pay, on average, 1500 roubles at a time where he should be able to pay 5–6000 roubles in order to compete for qualified personnel. A number of his employees have left the company and entered small enterprises. He is considering subdividing his company into smaller units in order to use the workforce and machines more effectively. His idea is a 'second job'. A person with high qualifications may be willing to work 3–4 hours more each day and thus increase his/her salary. The second job could be done in a co-operative company, using existing facilities, instruments and qualifications.

When I meet ID the next time in late 1992, he is in the middle of a privatisation process. This time we are not able to meet in his design bureau, but meet at Professor Vaysman's house, where I am staying. Privatisation of PAKB is to take place according to Model Two, in which 51% of the shares are bought by the working collective. The workers can choose whether or not to buy. The rest of the shares remain with the State Committee for Property. Later, 25% of these can be bought by the company and the rest will be sold at an auction. He has not yet received the final permission to privatise. This depends on how many of the workers will agree to buy shares. He himself has also collected vouchers from his wife's office, as she works at a budget bureau. People working in such places are not interested in buying shares in their working places, he says.

ID is not expecting dramatic changes after privatisation. The main advantage is that he can refuse government orders if they are not advantageous enough. This right has not existed before. It might also become easier to solve the eternal organisational problems. The labour unions are pressing. They are not interested in the companies' profit, but rather in people having work and a stable income. Earlier it was difficult to send people home. They got a salary, but did not do any work. Now this might be easier.

To my question about what will happen after privatisation if the company goes bankrupt, ID answers that he does not know. There is no legislation and there are no examples. The defence enterprises have accumulated debts. Perm Motor Works owes PAKB 5 million roubles. There is a debate as to whether or not the government should write off the defence enterprises' accumulated debts. According to ID, the debt write-off should not include the government, as he has not received money from them yet. ID has no confidence in the banking system as it takes a long time for money to come from Omsk to Perm, and money disappears on the way.

He feels that the people do not need privatisation. What they look forward to is being able to go to work every day in peace and get a stable salary. A salary, that is not, as today, unstable and subject to inflation. People want a place to work, a job on which you can also count on still having the next day. According to him, the enterprises symbolise patriotism and give people something to believe in.

ID is worried about aviation. There are reductions not only in defence but also in civil aviation. The world market is saturated and prices are low. He has tried to export, but has not been successful. As he cannot compete in the West, he is thinking about selling services to Western aviation companies. He has had some subcontracts to foreign companies in areas outside his core business and has dropped the idea of producing consumer products. Washing machines and sewing machines would not be competitive. There is also the problem of making an end product. His only choice would be to make special machines that could be built one by one. However, he is thinking about the production of metal doors. They were cheaper before. Now they are very expensive, and it is difficult to get the metal. He has also experimented with a Japanese water boiler. The prices were too high. He has experimented with alarm systems. There has been a large regional project for new alarm systems for the police. However, it was too complicated and he dropped the idea.

At this time, there is discussion about agriculture, both nationally and in Perm. Consequently, ID has looked at equipment for agriculture, for example, ventilator motors and dryers. He is also interested in refrigerators and refrigerating aggregates, maybe even whole refrigeration rooms – only in special products, however, not in mass production. He turns to me and asks if I can arrange contacts with Danish producers of agricultural machinery.

When I meet Iurii Dudkin in June 1994, the design bureau is organised under the Committee for Military Industry, under the special department for aviation. Although the organisation is similar to that of the former ministry and its sub-departments, he emphasises that they have no power. There are very few defence orders and the design bureau is now working 10% for the military and 90% in the civilian field. Privatisation is still going on and is not yet completed. He feels that he has a new autonomy as he now negotiates both prices and designs. There are no longer any proposals from the top down. On the contrary, he is now being asked from the top about what kind of weapon systems to develop.

At this time, the design bureau is negotiating with an American firm, United Technologies/Pratt & Whitney about a joint venture. Its subsidiary, Hamilton Standard, has similar production to PAKB. The idea is to develop a joint venture in Perm, based 95% on the Russian design bureau's technology. The remaining 5% is US technology from Hamilton Standard. According to ID, Pratt & Whitney selected his system instead of their own due to the price. Pratt & Whitney would make motors in Russia and assemble them in St Petersburg. Most of the components would be produced in Russia. American engineers cost $25 an hour while a Russian engineer costs $50 a week, he says. The joint venture is only about civilian aviation. 'We might also have gone together in defence aviation,' ID stresses, 'but the Americans are still afraid.' Negotiations are complicated. A joint venture, where both partners have tried to price their know-how and to get to know each other, needs time.

ID points out that he has his view of the future. An American joint venture might represent a long-term solution for conversion, while the Chinese are the solution in the short term. The company is working for the Chinese in order to be able to pay salaries to the workers. The problem with Chinese contracts is that only half the price is paid in money, the rest is barter, i.e. the price is paid in goods. Furthermore, Chinese products are losing popularity on the Perm market. The previously very popular consumer products are of poor quality. For the work they do, the design bureau gets computers from China. There is also a Russian project to make aircraft engines into gas pumping stations. This is a large joint project with a number of Perm enterprises, including Aviadvigatel', the design bureau Iskra and Perm Motor Works. The order to develop the design comes from Gasprom.

ID has now learned marketing. He has been to a course in Hungary, where there were only Hungarian teachers who spoke only Hungarian. He has also been in Oklahoma in the USA where the teachers spoke only English. There were no interpreters. He could not understand anything, but he was interested in learning how Americans lived. By now, he has dropped the ideas of mass production altogether. It would have been too expensive and household appliances required mass production technologies, which in turn would require massive financing. The buying power of the population was going down. The rich do not buy sewing machines. He has returned to his core technologies rather than speculating in household appliances and mass production.

The design bureau now has 1700 employees, half of whom are women. Hundreds come each day and ask for work. He can only take one or two. He is trying to maintain his specialists, and he is worried about the young who do not choose this field any more. He has therefore made a contract with Perm Technical University and paid 2 million roubles for the education of specially qualified young engineers.

A miracle of survival

Each time I have come to Perm I have expected a catastrophe. Western and even Russian forecasts have been gloomy. People were expected not to survive the first cold winter – this was the message of the Western media in 1992. Two-thirds of the population in Russia lived under a minimum wage level, according to the UNICEF estimate a year later. Massive unemployment with millions of unemployed has been forecast innumerable times during these years. Millions of defence workers were expected to be out of work, creating social unrest and threatening the little political stability that remained. Scientists were expected to seek work in countries like Iran and Libya and risk the security of the world by working for dictator and terrorist regimes.

None of this has happened. Each time I have travelled to Perm I have been fearful. My family has warned me of crime, hunger and cold. I myself have been doubtful, feeling sick and weak before departure. But each time I have come to Perm my fears have vanished. A number of dramatic changes have taken place.

While in 1991 the food was Russian, foreign foods had invaded the markets. Also in Perm, Snickers became the symbol of the 'food revolution' while 'Uncle Ben', the rice trademark, grew to be a friend in Russian kitchens. Vegetables from the Netherlands flooded the market in Perm in June 1994. Even roses were imported from there at a time when Russian gardens were full of them.

Each time I have come to Perm the defence industries have been deeper into the crisis. Each time there has been a little less production and more people dismissed. Each time Western ways of doing business

(business plans, cost-benefit analysis, market research etc.) have been better and better known. Each time there has been not only less and less faith in Western support, but also less and less faith in the ability of national leaders to deal with the crisis.

There has been no massive unemployment in Perm. With the exception of a few strikes, protests against the lack of state subsidies, the situation has been stable. Everyday life has gone on as usual. People have gone to work in the morning. The children have gone to school. In Russian homes, the kinds of big meals are served – at least for guests – that make you feel that you'll never be able to eat again. People survive, but the optimistic tone of 1992 has gone. The dreams attached to the market economy have faded away. Life was better before. The Brezhnev time seems, compared to the Yeltsin time, for many, and particularly for army personnel and the retired, to be a paradise. Everyone had enough to eat. Employees in the military industries could travel on holiday wherever they wanted, although only within the Soviet Union. Children were taken care of in the day-care centres. Food and other goods were distributed through the enterprise. But there were also problems. You had to stand in queues, and you had to buy what was available.

No matter how much chaos, political instability, daily struggles and reduced living standards, the society has shown minimal social unrest. I experienced this every time I returned to Perm. Factories were only working part time and delays in salary payments were up to six months. But there was no social unrest, no violence, no demonstrations. Only in 1997, upon arriving in Moscow, at a time when I had given up on the Russians ever protesting against the worsening conditions in the military enterprises and in the country in general, were there signs of the opposite.

The date was 17 March 1997. This was the day for which the Profsoiuz, the trade unions, had announced strikes all over the country. Millions of people were expected to participate and to protest against delays in salary payments, against reduced living standards, against unemployment. On my way to Moscow from the airport a taxi-driver told me that at ten o'clock the city centre would be closed. Nobody was advised to go out and taxis would not be driving in the city. 'The people are angry,' he said. 'They are mad. There will be violence, it will be like Albania.' I hurried to my meeting, finished it as quickly as possible and returned to my hotel. In the evening when I looked at the TV news, I learned that there had been demonstrations all over the country.

100,000 demonstrators had protested in Moscow. But the protest had been without any violence. It was a civilised, orderly protest by people who were worried about their pay. They did not ask for the government to go. They did not ask for the return of the old regime. They did not ask for higher pay. They only asked for the money, the government owed them for the past six months of work.

Notes

1 The data presented here are from diverse sources (Cronberg *et al.*, 1996).
2 The 'technological chain' consisted of research institutes, design bureaus and production enterprises. Sometimes these were combined to ease the transfer of technology to 'science production associations' (Parrott, 1983: 287–90).
3 *International Herald Tribune*, Thursday, 30 October 1997.
4 The data originate from the Perm Regional Administration. Corresponding figures have not been published for the latter part of the 90ies. See Appendix for more detailed analysis.
5 Statistic for the civilian output for the Perm defence industries is not available for the late 90s. However, in Appendix an estimate is made for the civilian output of the defence complex. In Perm the relation of military to civilian production was estimated to be 10:90 (see Appendix).
6 Simon Clarke (1996, 1998, 1999) has analysed the Russian labour market and the Russian enterprise. His conclusion is that the managers wanted to maintain the best qualified people. While this, of course, is true my interviews indicate also a broader social concern.
7 In *Kommercant*, No. 12, 16–23 March 1992.
8 Quoted from an interview by *Kommercant*, No. 12, 15–23 March 1992.

Chapter 5

Trying Transformations

The microwave oven is a classic case of a military spin-off. The first microwave oven, Radarange, developed by the US defence contractor, Raytheon, evolved from military know-how into a commercial success. However, the process was neither easy nor cost-free. The story is told in *Beyond Spin-off*:[1]

> One day late in 1945, Percy Spencer, a Raytheon engineer of unusual ability (138 patents), placed a bag of popcorn in front of the wave-guide driven by the magnetron from a military radar set. The grains began to pop inside the bag. The following day, Spencer exploded an egg over a group of assembled onlookers, who were nevertheless impressed. Laurence Marshall, then Raytheon's president, became very enthusiastic about the possibility of a microwave oven for restaurants. Many problems, such as radiation safety, had to be solved. But by 1947, Raytheon introduced a restaurant oven. The home appliance market promised to be far larger, but Raytheon managers knew they would have to reduce costs greatly to sell the Radarange even as a luxury product, much less a mass-market item. They would also need distribution and marketing channels. In 1965, Raytheon undertook development of a much smaller, less expensive Radarange for home use. In the same year, by serendipitous good fortune, Raytheon merged with the Amana Refrigeration Corporation, which solved the problem of consumer-product design knowledge and provided a ready-made sales and distribution network. The home oven could not meet its cost target unless Raytheon could manufacture the magnetron for $35 each, whereas the actual cost when manufacturing began was $125. Tom Philips, Raytheon's president at the time, agreed to a corporate subsidy of the $90 difference for one year. In effect, the corporation subsidized the early technological learning so it could introduce its home Radarange at a realistic price. In 1967, Raytheon launched the product with great fanfare at a Chicago home appliance show,

and sales exceeded the forecast of 50,000 units a year. The microwave oven was a great commercial success. By 1970, the year inventor Percy Spencer died at the age of 76, commercial businesses accounted for half of Raytheon's revenue.

The lessons to be learnt from this are many. It was the innovation of one man. It took almost 20 years to develop a commercial household appliance. The first Radarange models were industrial products with high costs and low volumes. Raytheon acquired another company in order to exploit product design, sales and distribution capabilities. As pointed out in *Beyond Spin-off*, investment, good management and patience were needed to commercialise defence technology.

Russian defence enterprises, including those in Perm, expected the transfer of defence technology to take place overnight. Americans would supply investment and technology and they would provide their defence know-how to start the production of household appliances, luxury yachts and high-strength crutches immediately. While very few dollars, and no technology, flowed to Russia in 1992–94, some of the early conversion experiences and examples tell more about the Soviet military complex and the plan economy than about the potential for spin-offs.

The microwave oven was commercialised in the US in the 1960s. In the 1990s Russian homes had no microwave ovens. In fact, they had very little technology at all. Microwave ovens and dishwashers were unknown. Washing machines did exist, although mostly in very simple designs. Sewing machines were in demand as the Soviet women sewed their own clothes. However, the State had discontinued production during the past five-year plans as industrial production of clothes was supposed to fulfil the demand of Soviet families for clothes. Given this lack of household appliances and consumer technology, what would be more natural, in conversion, than to start making microwave ovens?

This was also what happened. In 1992 when I interviewed three of the defence enterprise managers in Perm, they told me they were planning to produce microwave ovens. Market assessments were not needed as it was obvious to everyone that Russian homes did not have these ovens. All three managers were sure that they were the only potential producer of these ovens in Perm. One of them mentioned that there were only two other producers in Russia. One of them thought he was the only one in the country. At this time the regional administration quoted that there were 103 producers, or potential projects of microwave ovens, in the country.

One of the Perm producers produced microwave ovens for $150. According to him, he made 15,000 of them a year, and would be able to increase production by 6,000 without capital investment and could then produce 100,000 microwave ovens a year. The manager emphasised that the quality of his ovens was better than other models. They had a rotating dish and good product security. On the other hand, he was looking for a joint venture with a foreign company in order to improve the oven design, the heat durability and the control functions. At the time, late 1992, the company sold ovens directly from the plant (there were two shops on the premises) and had a number of sales agents outside the region.

A year and a half later, in June 1994, when I visited homes in Perm, some had already bought a microwave oven, though not from the Lenin Machine Building Plant, from Mashinostroitel or from any other of the military entreprises. No, these microwave ovens came from Philips, Siemens or Electrolux. Visiting the families, I was to read instructions in English, German or Swedish.

The Russian microwave ovens from defence enterprises could not compete with Western products, which were both cheaper and of better quality. Having opened the borders, Russian consumers were able to experience quality Western products, which made the conversion to civilian commercial consumer products very difficult. Many of the managers I interviewed were complaining of quality problems. A military company, having produced trailers since 1974, was complaining of technical problems with galvanised coatings. The product was not on 'the world level'. He wanted to modernise the galvanised-coating technology, but to start design and development as a joint venture would require an investment of about a million dollars (in late 1992).

These barriers reflect a poorly developed consumer market in the past. There was no design experience or qualifications. Consumer production was seen during the Soviet era as inferior in comparison with military production. Expansion of existing consumer production, although theoretically a possibility in Russian defence enterprises, which already produced videos, bicycles and washing machines, was hampered by lack of mass production know-how, experience and technologies. Consequently, large-scale investments would have to be made to modernise technology and reorganise production.

Furthermore, there was the question of price. In a planned economy, prices were set centrally and did not necessarily even reflect the production costs. Some researchers have even argued[2] that in the Soviet defence enterprises civilian production carried some of the overhead costs for the military's products. In one of the companies I interviewed, a consumer division had been established in order to pay for certain investments also covering some of the military equipment. Thus commercial products from the defence enterprises were expensive to start off with. This price also included the costs of mobilisation capacities which the companies had to maintain themselves. Not only defence but also civilian production paid for the extra space, equipment and other facilities.

At the beginning of 1992, enterprises were able to start to price their own products. This was a confusing process. Add to this the problem of how to define a market price in a country without a market and in a country with continuously changing taxation laws and you have a chaotic system where it is difficult not only to price products but also to make a profit. I remember once sitting in a meeting-room together with a defence enterprise manager and his chiefs of financing and planning departments, both women. We were discussing the question of price for water-purification filters and suddenly the chief of the planning department, turned to me and asked, 'Would you tell us how to set the market price? Would double the price of the costs be enough?'

A problem closely related to this was the Russian insistence that high technology was needed in the civilian sector. Russian defence managers were proud of their technology. They had, in their own view, the world's best technology, were a technological superpower and had at great cost reached parity with the United States. On the other hand, they saw the lack of technology in the civilian sector producing products of low quality. A simple conclusion in this situation was that the civilian industry needed defence technology. Advanced glass fibre and container technology of a defence enterprise was immediately seen as useful for making glass fibre pipes for the chemical industry. The quality of the pipes in the chemical industry was poor, and basically there was a need for better pipes. The problem was that the chemical industry at the time was not able to pay for these high-quality pipes. The problem of a customer not being able to pay for a better product seems to have been completely new to the defence enterprise managers. A manager of a chemical ammunition plant, which also produced coatings and now was converting to artificial surface materials, was facing the same problem. His customers found the products to be too expensive and he was angry at the situation. He exclaimed to me: 'I know they need them. But they are not willing to pay.' In a supply economy where quality has always been a problem, it is, of course, incomprehensible that the available quality products are not being paid for.

Finally, there are some totally absurd examples of conversion. In the early years, around 1991, rumours were circulating that Russian defence enterprises had started to produce titanium spades. Every time a conversion researcher, including myself, heard of this example there was laughter. This was, we thought, the ultimate absurdity of the defence industrial way of thinking. The defence enterprises had access to raw materials, also titanium. When converting, they would simply think that spades were needed and that titanium would be a tough, strong and light material for spades. However, I had to rethink my laughter when in 1995 a Russian military economist pointed out to me that it was completely rational to make titanium spades. In these years the export of titanium was prohibited, while the export of spades was not.

Regional discourses

Defence industries were, in the past, part of the State structures. They were directly controlled by a ministry. They had nothing to do with the region. In fact, as secrecy surrounded military production, the regional administration did not even know the type of resources and facilities existing in the region. In 1991, when the Soviet Union collapsed, not only the enterprises but also the regions found themselves with new responsibilities. The key to the future welfare of the region lay in the ability of the region's defence enterprises to convert to civilian production.

In March 1992 Yeltsin and the Supreme Council of the Russian Federation approved a law on conversion. The law defines conversion as

> A partial or complete reorientation of production capacities, science and technology potential and labour resources released from the military activities of defence and defence-related enterprises, associations and organisations to civilian need.[3]

This law sets some of the basic principles for Russian conversion, such as the focus on high technologies combined with social protection programmes. Although military enterprises did receive conversion funds, these were mainly used for salaries and infrastructure. At least in the Perm area, no visible effects of this early conversion programme were seen.

A new federal programme for military conversion was drafted in 1993. Here the main goal was to support preservation of the professional, industrial and technological potential of the defence complex alongside the import substitution of energy-saving investments and techniques. Special programmes were drafted for the aircraft industry, shipbuilding, fuel processing, forestry industry, housing, road construction etc. Again the programme remained without visible effects.

The national programmes were reflected in regional programmes. The first regional programme was prepared in November 1991 in Perm. This was the first initial co-operation among military-industrial firms ever to take place on the regional level. The regional administration had conducted an inquiry among the firms exploring their interest in partnership and joint ventures. The goal of the first plan was to compensate for economic losses experienced by the region's defence complex and to maintain and exploit their scientific and production potential. A new regional conversion plan was designed for 1992 and 1993, consisting this time of a total of 180 proposals and requiring financing estimated at 30 million roubles (estimated 170 million US $ at the time).

The discourse this time was not only about preserving the technology of the defence enterprises or using military technology in civilian production 'in order to make it cheaper'. Here adaptation of defence enterprises to market conditions was also considered as well as development of the region's production infrastructure. Again the social sphere was given high priority as well as consumer goods and food production for the local consumer market.

A third regional conversion plan has been drafted in the Perm region for the period 1996–2000. There are two important differences compared to the earlier plans. First, although the plan was drafted in relation to a federal plan on conversion, there was no longer any hope of federal money to finance conversion. In fact, in 1996 the Perm region did not receive any funds from the federal administration for conversion. The second difference is that there is less stress on maintaining the technical and scientific capabilities of the defence industries or transferring the high-tech capabilities of the military industry to the civilian sphere. The focus now is on working places, and a quantitative goal of 7,000 working places is set in the plan. Some of the earlier projects would continue. These include jet engines transformed into pumping stations for gas as well as the development of heating equipment, communication systems, bicycle production, multiple-coloured packaging and production for ecological security, particularly for water purification. What is also new is that there is a focus on local and regional co-operation to create networks between the companies, which previously had been isolated and had relations only with their sectoral ministries. In Perm a Conversion Fund was established which allocated come regional funds for feasibility studies. Its more important function was as a meeting place for the military-industrial leaders.

The total cost of the programme was envisioned at 135,900,000 US$ and was expected to create an income and production for 1,284,000,000 US$. When visiting the Perm administration in April 1997 and asking for permission to see the programme, I was shown the programme, but no longer given a copy of it. This was not a return to the old secrecy; on the contrary, everybody was willing to tell me about the programme. The issue was now that companies did not want information that was very detailed to be openly distributed. It was a return to secrecy, but not because of state control but because of competition. Company information would have to be guarded. If the information should be distributed permission would have to be asked from the companies, not from the KGB.

These plans illustrate the 'conversion work' needed to cross the boundaries from military technology to civilian applications. The rhetoric changes from (1) the preservation of high-tech capabilities through (2) making civilian production cheaper to (3) the creation of working places. It took five years to see conversion not only as a question of 'financing' and 'technology', but as one of jobs and welfare. The tools are the same as during the Soviet period, i.e. plans. But the starting point is different; the enterprises now define their own ideas and capabilities. They are no longer recipients of orders from above as in the Gorbachev plan for conversion. Another difference is that all costs are calculated in dollars. The 'technological superpower' is using the monetary unit of its former enemy to calculate the cost of converting its military technology into civilian uses.

These programmes clearly demonstrated some of the problems as well as the potential for regional conversion. First, the regional administration learned about the enterprises and their facilities. Next, their need to establish regional networks to replace former ministerial networks was acknowledged. Very little funding has been available, although a number of regional funding schemes have been drafted. One of the latest proposals was to channel 80% of the surplus derived from the privatisation of enterprises to the conversion programmes. These funds have been channelled to the State budget instead.

In order to understand the 'conversion work' in the Perm region in the social world context, I shall now review two concrete examples. The first is the Perm Auto, a project in the regional plan in 1992. It was partly funded by the regional administration. The next is a small business created by a few individuals without any funding, but based on defence know-how.

The Perm Auto

Already in 1992 I had heard of plans to develop a Perm Auto. At the conversion seminar that we had arranged in 1992 to talk about our project for the defence enterprise industry in Perm, the head of the regional administration in his speech indicated that there was a good possibility that the region might embark on car production. A number of components were already produced in the area; according to him, more than half of the Moskvich components came from Perm. When the regional conversion plan was compiled in 1992, the idea arose of producing the car. The project was supported by the Regional Conversion Fund, with a credit of 300 million roubles from the regional administration. Car production was seen as an example of regional synergy. Perm Auto would be a four-wheel drive jeep with a fibreglass frame, to be developed by the region's industries having knowledge of composite materials. The motor would be the same as the Moskvich Orbita. No work would be put into developing a motor in the region.

Velta, formally the Perm October Revolution Machine Building Plant, which produced defence electronics, bicycles, motorcycles, household appliances, trailers and other commercial products, also produced wheels and spare parts for the Moskvich from 1965 to 1992–93. Then the Udmurtia enterprise decided to switch to other suppliers. As a result, Velta had a substantial capacity for component production but no orders. At the same time, an enterprise in Tatarstan was contemplating starting production of a Ranger car on licence from the UK. The car would merely be assembled in Russia, using parts from the UK. Currency problems put an end to these plans. The president of Velta and the Tatarstan firm decided to develop a car that would be assembled at Velta.

Velta organised a separate joint-stock company in which it would participate along with the company from Tatarstan and other companies in the region. By 1995 twenty jeeps had been assembled. The jeep had been tested at a Moscow institute and, according to the production manager, the test results were not negative. The plan was to produce 100 jeeps in 1995, the year I interviewed the manager about these plans.

There was no shortage of problems. The jeep was targeted for the working man and needed to be cheaper than other cars on the market. Production costs were high. The frame came from Tatarstan, the motor from Ufa and the seats from a third region. In fact, the Perm area produced no more than 30% of the parts, the manager concedes. He points out that Velta had no previous experience in automotive assembly and lacked qualified workers to do the job. The prototypes were assembled manually, and there were no plans for acquiring the funds for mass production or the know-how to implement it. Technically, the jeep had a rear-wheel drive, but it was expected to have a four-wheel drive in future.

The manager was optimistic about solving these problems. In 1995 he was negotiating with a foundation for production of a car for the disabled. While the jeep was not being distributed yet, he was convinced that he could sell it for the price he had planned. One competitive feature was a frame that did not age like metal. Besides there was a regional need for a four-wheel drive jeep. Furthermore, according to him, there were no competitors in this market. The expectation was that if a larger number of components were produced in-house, the jeep would be competitive.

When I visited Perm in March 1997, the Perm Auto project had been abolished. No more than 20 jeeps had been assembled and a representative of the regional administration told me that it was not a bad car. However, the problems of marketing and of serial production had been insurmountable.

The Perm auto is an ideal type of Russian conversion. It is more advanced than the simple technology push from high-tech in the defence sector to low tech in the civilian field or for making 'gold into steel'. Here there was, in fact, production know-how for the civilian market. Velta had produced components. Furthermore, there was some idea of the market. There was a need for a jeep-type car that could drive in harsh conditions. But there was no plan for how to establish an automated factory where cars could be assembled. Another Henry Ford – together with considerable investment – would have been needed to establish industrial production of cars instead of the manual assembly used at Velta. Furthermore, there was a lack of know-how regarding car assembly, it was not merely the sum of its components. This know-how was not available at Velta and, in spite of the fact that several of the companies had worked together to establish a joint stock company, the manager was alone with his production. Foreign cars did take over the market for four-wheel-drive jeeps in the region.

Pumping with guns

In Perm, one of the defence networks was related to artillery systems. The network centre was the largest enterprise in the region, Motovilikha, which produced howitzers and rocket launchers. Its civilian production also included equipment for the oil industry. Temp, one of the design bureaux in Perm, specialised in the design of artillery systems and worked closely with Motovilikha. Furthermore, there was a Technical-Scientific Institute engaged in tooling and experimental production.

Malyi biznes is the Russian word for a small enterprise. Rather than conversion of the defence industry, *malyi biznes* represents the capitalist idea of how new businesses emerge. Already in 1991–92 the establishment of small businesses was seen as the way to a market economy. Such businesses received a number of tax benefits and other support from the Gaidar government. Spin-offs of small enterprises were also established within the larger companies in order to exploit a commercial idea and, as has often been the case, to semi-privatise some of the assets of the enterprise. Very few actual production companies emerged in the early years of economic reforms. Most *malyi bizneses* were companies for trade and distribution, often companies only on paper. When small businesses in production did emerge, they were based on the resources of existing companies, design bureaux and research institutes, and rented some of their facilities and equipment. Small businesses often consisted of only an office in some block of flats or research institute.

Elkam Neftekhimia, which produces pumping systems for natural gas, was in 1997 a success story about a small business based on defence know-how. The mother company is Elkam, a company established for the creation of innovations and small businesses.

I met the director at a party in early 1995. At that time, he explained to me how, during the Soviet period, he had been employed in an enterprise that repaired equipment for the oil industry. When the company was restructured, he decided to start his own. His idea was to utilise the fine tolerances of the artillery systems in the oil industry. In

1992, he bought the technical documents from the military in order to apply them in the civilian sector. In Azerbaijan this technology had been used for some time, so he combined his know-how with the experience from Azerbaijan. In early 1995, I had visited the Technical-Scientific Institute, which was working on tolerances and durability of the artillery tubes. According to the engineers the problem was exactly the same as in pumping oil and gas. In April 1997, I was to visit the directors of Elkam Neftekhimia to document their success story in conversion.

The multi-storey building on the outskirts of Perm was one I had visited a number of times before. It housed the offices of the Regional Conversion Fund, an organisation working with the region's defence enterprises, mainly on feasibility studies and technical economic documentation. This was also the building where the Technical-Scientific Institute of Perm was located. Now, obviously Elkam Neftekhimia had also acquired office space here.

At the usual control post with the rotating bars, I was, to my astonishment, not let in. I had visited the building several times before in 1992–95 and had had no problems getting in just by showing my passport. However, now I had to leave my passport and wait for the papers. I waited in a hall and had ample time to observe the workers of the Technical-Scientific Institute leaving for lunch. It was as if nothing had changed in these five years. These were not the well-dressed women I saw in the streets, nor the attractive young business men and bankers. These were women over forty in their winter boots and worn-out winter coats. The Technical-Scientific Institute had no doubt become a place for those who could not leave. After a while the woman came back and told me that the problem of my entry into the building could be solved later when the director would be there. In the meantime, I could go and see the production. I was astonished. Times had truly changed. One could enter production without papers, but entry into the offices of a small business required special permission.

The production unit was in another building. Elkam Neftekhimia had rented space to start production of tubes for oil pumping. To get to this space, we first had to pass through a huge machine hall where the machines were standing still. There was nobody in sight although in the furthest corner of the factory there was some activity. New equipment had been installed, an Austrian machine for making the tubes. The workers, two of them, were very proud to show me the latest in machine building, a CNC-machinery with a laser measurement unit.

We talked for a while about the tolerances, looked at the instruments and discussed their plans for future production.

The scene around us was very symbolic of post-Soviet Russia. The hundreds of machines from the Soviet time, which surrounded us, were like a technology graveyard. Machines from the 1960s and '70s lay idle. The workers had left the scene. The scientific-technological revolution seemed to have come to a standstill. I remembered all the proud stories of the development of the production forces, of how technology in the hands of the dictatorship of the proletariat would lead to a world of freedom. Now there were only two workers left. These stood in a corner and were enthusiastically admiring lasers and computers, objects of technology produced by the enemy. I sent an apologetic thought to Marx and all the Marxist technology researchers of the Danish university system.

Later I could enter the offices of Elkam Neftekhimia. Behind a table the two directors, one for Elkam Neftekhimia and one for Elkam, received me. They were busy and would have only 25 minutes. They explained their business idea. The starting point was the directors' background in the repairing equipment for the oil industry. This had been combined with the defence technology developed by the Technical-Scientific Institute. Instead of working – as before – for the Motovilikha Plant, the institute was now using its know-how and experience to produce pumps. Oil pumping equipment was previously made in Baku in Azerbaijan and the tubes were bought from abroad. Now they produced the tubes in Russia and 50,000 of them had been sold in Russia. At the moment, two were being installed in Texas.

Elkam had been formed as a holding company with the idea of nourishing *malyi bizneses* and creating new production units. Elkam Neftekhimia exploited the idea of oil and gas pumps and was a company where financiers, technology, space for production and know-how came together in one organisation. A start capital of 30 million US dollars came from Russian sources. The company was a shareholding company, in which the Technical-Scientific Institute, the Perm factory Mashstroi, Elkam and an out-of-town company, Elraz, together owned 80% of the shares. The employees of the Technical-Scientific Institute had supplied the know-how and owned some of the shares. They were responsible for the research work and were the owners of the patents.

I asked how this was possible. The director of Elkam pointed out that the heads of the Institute's scientists and engineers supplied the know-how of Russia. Some of this was now on the market and could be sold. To make sure that the link to the Technical-Scientific Institute was there, the two directors had bought 20% of the Institute's shares when it was privatised.

I asked about the influence of the State in a research institute having critical know-how about artillery systems and production of the tubes for it. One of the directors answered that the State still had a 'golden share' in the Technical-Scientific Institute. But they both emphasised that this had no practical meaning. The State had no shares, only a veto right. The State was represented on the Board of Directors, but it did not disturb normal work. The task of the representatives of the State was to make sure that the qualifications would not disappear and would be available in wartime, if needed. Elkam Neftekhimia paid for research work, technology was further developed and qualifications could be maintained. This was an advantage both for the military industry and for the State.

My follow-up question was about what actually had been converted and whether the activities were based on military technology. The directors carefully explained to me that the problems were the same. The elements of the know-how were the same, the brains from the Technical-Scientific Institute were the same. New research results had been obtained and the production of pumps and pump tubes was based on a completely new technology. Six Russian patents were pending. They used the facilities of the Technical-Scientific Institute, but only space. The machinery for production of pumps was completely new.

When I asked why the Technical-Scientific Institute had not developed this pumping technology before, the answer was: 'We worked for the military industry, no one ever put forth the task to us.'

Using grounded theory

We can look at these transformations with the help of grounded theory concepts such as arenas, work needed to cross the boundaries and awareness. In the two examples arenas are constructed in different ways, boundary crossings are experimented with different degrees of success and technology itself is renegotiated into a new context.

In the Perm Auto example the region finds out that a great number of car components are already produced in the defence enterprises. Furthermore, military technology could be used to produce the remaining components and the frame itself. The efforts of making these into an aggregate, a car, are not successful. A whole car is more than some of its parts, and the 'component push' approach fails to produce the desired results. This bridging effort makes visible the lack of commercial culture and experience in how long it takes to transform military know-how to civilian products. After all, the microwave oven of Raytheon took almost 20 years to become a domestic household appliance.

The second example, the turning of artillery systems and related know-how into gas-pumping stations was more successful. Focus is not only on the fact that the main actor had experience from the civilian field, in repair of oil equipment from the oil industry. Equally important is the type of arena created for building the bridge between military and civilian technologies. A new arena is created here. It is a small business outside the framework of a defence industry. It has close links to the defence enterprises, particularly the Technical-Scientific Institute where the technology has been originally developed. Know-how is exchanged for shares in a negotiation where the institute, Elkam and even the State win. The State secures military high-tech know-how capabilities, Elkam makes a profit and engineers of the institute are paid their salaries.

One of the main points of criticism, particularly raised by Western conversion researchers and defence industry experts, is the fact that the retooling of the Soviet defence industries into civilian and commercial uses was to take place within the framework of the enterprise as it was. While the retooling approach was one of approaching the civilian–military divide from the inside to the outside, the Elkam example provides the opposite direction. From outside this company approaches the social world of military technology networking into its know-how system and later even to ownership. The link between the defence and civilian technologies is provided thus by a combination of experience, of approach, ownership structure and shares as well as know-how.

According to the social constructivist view on technology, technologies are destabilised when all institutions disappear and new ones emerge. As power is only a result of a negotiation process – a time-limited closure where actors agree to maintain a certain view on technology – the disappearance of these agreements also implies renegotiations of technological artefacts and their meanings. In the case of Perm Auto components produced by the military industries in Perm, both civilian and military, were renegotiated to become a civilian ranger car. The actor network involved basically one of the major defence enterprises in Perm, which was also the arena for assembling the car. Both the State through the central ministries of Moscow and also the regional administration were involved in financing. A network of the Perm defence industries were involved in component production and contacts were made to a Tatarstan company. Motors would be bought from the outside.

The automobile was tested and found not to be a bad car. A combination of factors can explain why the negotiations were not successful. Foreign cars entered the market. Maybe the most important actors were the foreign car producers as well as the State making this import possible. Assembly know-how through actors from the automobile industry was missing and the arena is totally inside the defence enterprises' own technological framework. Viewed in retrospect this actor network lacked representatives in the automobile industry as well as in potential customer organisations.

Negotiations are more successful in the Elkam gas-pumping case. Ownership of the military industry changes. Even research institutes are privatised and transfer knowledge to the civilian field. Here an actor network is formed where the initiative is from a private entrepreneur with experience from the industry. Through contacts in the military enterprise making artillery systems, a network is formed where specific know-how, i.e. tolerances for artillery systems, are renegotiated into know-how for gas-pumping stations. An Italian producer of new machinery is enrolled. Stations are being sold to Azerbaijan and tests are made in Texas. The State is involved with the golden share, a right to veto any transfer of know-how. A negotiation agreement is made where the State is guaranteed the further development of its defence technologies at the same time as a private entrepreneur is exploiting it in the oil industry.

Researchers who have studied the transfer of military technology into civilian fields, such as for example Walker,[4] have pointed out that the lower you are on the escalator from materials and components to weapon systems the easier it is to transfer technology into civilian fields. We have seen in this chapter that components are more difficult to renegotiate than whole artillery systems; produced, however, not with the help of the old technology of the artillery producing plant, but with an Austrian CNC-machinery. Although there may be some hardness in technology, the renegotiations indicate that the ability to create new arenas and to make civilian actor networks is more important than the technological complexity of the product to be transformed.

Transforming Russia

Notes

1 *Beyond Spin-off* describes a number of cases where military technologies have been used for civilian purposes and classifies some of the processes involved. For the story of the microwave oven, see Alic *et al.* (1992: 58–9).
2 Cooper (1986: 46) offers a possible interpretation in that enterprises of the defence industry organise civilian production in such a way as to minimise costs through the economics of scale and high level of mechanisation. In this way they are able to meet the cost targets specified in military contracts by the transfer of overhead costs to the civilian activity.
3 The presentation of the 1992 Conversion Law is quoted from the SIPRI Yearbook (1993: 362–3).
4 Walker *et al.* (1987).

Chapter 6

Communities of Pride

Soviet workers were lazy. There was no motivation to work. Everybody was guaranteed work and housing. Wage differences were small. Qualified workers earned more than university professors. Entrepreneurship was not promoted. Private entrepreneurship was consciously suppressed. In fact, Soviet history is also a history of the destruction of initiative and entrepreneurial individuals such as farmers, engineers and progressive managers.[1] Those are some of our Western clichés of a grey, monotonous everyday life, a life without challenges and individual careers. A life where those most conforming to the discipline of the Party and those most likely to undermine the initiative of others were the winners.

Little attention has been paid to the fact that the defence enterprises were different. A large part of the Soviet economy did work, but according to a different logic. A number of incentives were built into work in the military-industrial complex. The pay was better.[2] Young people were recruited in competitions. Only the very best were selected. Scientists, engineers and workers within the defence industry received housing and other social benefits much faster than others – and better quality benefits. As we have seen before, the social world of the individual was largely controlled by the enterprise. Consequently, it was easy for the research institutions, design bureaux and enterprises to transfer these benefits to their employees. They in turn were given high priority by the State.

Incentives were not only built into pay and social benefits. There were also incentives built into the work and challenging tasks. The best equipment, often bought from the West, was accessible in the defence R&D facilities. The best raw materials were available in the defence departments of military enterprises. Scientific journals were copied for the military research establishments, while universities and other research institutes were starved for books. The KGB made available information about American innovation and military achievements. Although access to Western technology was denied the Soviet Union by the COCOM[3] rules, the military could always find ways to get access to the latest Western technology. One of the paradoxes of the

COCOM rules was that, while its intention was to prohibit the military's access to advanced technology, in fact, it mainly prohibited the civilian sector's access to high technology and was a barrier to its modernisation.

In the military-industrial complex, carrots were, however, combined with sticks. Incentives were combined with sanctions which, in turn, were both related to performance and secrecy. The chief engineer, head of a design bureau, was always personally responsible for the success of his designs. He was also responsible for applications of the transformation of designs into production. The managers of production enterprises were personally responsible for maintaining the mobilisation capabilities. Sanctions consisted of penalties, loss of job or even prison.

Communities of practice

Communities of practice[4] are, in grounded theory, collectives having 'conventions of use' about materials, standards, measurements and the like. These conventions are respected by the members of the community and they are stable for the members, although they may change in time. For the members these conventions order the world; for others outside, the world may seem chaotic. If you know you are supposed to stop at a red light, you abide by the conventions of the traffic community. If you learn how to play a violin, you gradually become a member of the community of violin players.

Everybody is a member of several communities of practice at the same time. Membership is multi-layered, and maybe both casual and committed. Being a woman makes you a member of one kind of community, being an African woman of another. Both are non-optional and lifelong. Being a member of a scientific community is more a question of choice although it may also last a lifetime. People may also move from an illegitimate peripheral participation to full membership.

What is characteristic for a community of practice is its relation to objects. Activity is always mediated by objects and material arrangements.[5] Objects become naturalised, taken for granted and lose their situated nature. The members forget the object's meaning and the actions that go into recreating its meaning. Membership in a community of practice may, according to Leigh Star, be described as the experience of encountering objects and increasingly being in a naturalised relationship with them.

The military-industrial complex of the Soviet Union was a community of practice. Although heterogeneous and multi-layered the members shared certain conventions, ways of working and had a naturalised relationship to certain objects, particularly the objects that were the result of their work. Already the way of choosing the members, as particularly privileged with number of benefits not accessible to others, or accessible at a later date (such as an apartment, a car) must as such have made a difference between those inside and those outside. The reputation of these workers as an especially disciplined group is another dividing line between members and non-members. Access to the best raw materials, foreign equipment and articles and books has also separated this group from others.

As a community of practice, the military-industrial complex in the Soviet Union provided work in a disciplined community together with others with equal qualifications. It was a community of practice where the normal rules of the supply economy did not apply, at least not fully. Abundant resources were available, equipment was bought abroad and books were accessible. It was a community of practice that worked on the forefront of technology focusing and competing with the enemy. Consequently, it was also a community of practice where competition prevailed, and the goals were defined by the achievements of the enemy. Also between institutions and design bureaux working for aviation, competition for best design was actually promoted. Many of the clichés of the Soviet system – undisciplined workforce, lack of competition, and supply economy – did not apply for the communities of practice of the military enterprises.

Communities of practice and the naturalisation of the related objects are the focus of study in this and the next chapter. In this chapter, the basic ways of working, or as Susan Leigh Star calls it, the articulation work, is looked at in terms of how scientists, here male scientists, maintained their world view as members of defence communities of the Soviet Union, and how this world view was crumbling as a result of the changes taking place. The next chapter is devoted to the way women naturalised the objects and how they saw these communities of practice.

Mobilisation for a sacrifice

The Soviet economy as a whole has been characterised as a mobilisation economy.[6] The population has been mobilised not only in wartime, but also in peacetime to achieve production goals, to fight alcoholism or to tame nature in Siberia. Mobilisation has been the way to 'do things'. Campaigns to achieve a goal have been a fact of everyday life. Kosals[7] claims in his book *Why Russian Industry Does Not Work* that Russian workers do not work effectively in the normal flow of things. They are inactive and lazy. But when they are mobilised to work, they can move mountains.

In defence enterprises we find the best-motivated part of the workforce, the most talented and most disciplined employees. They were not only mobilised for the economy or for technological progress. They were also, and perhaps foremost, mobilised for a national task. Their task was to defend the country against the enemy, to prevent the horrors of the Second World War, when 25 million Russians lost their lives, from reoccurring. They have solved this task and are today extremely proud of their achievements. Today there is no mobilisation. Why?

Although there have been a number of conversion initiatives, conversion has never been defined as a national task. There has been no mobilisation for the creation of new commercial enterprises, nor for increasing the welfare of the people. During Gorbachev's time there was a programme for conversion, which ordered some of the defence enterprises to convert. Later, during Yeltsin's time there have been a number of conversion programmes, which have included empty statements about priorities and projects to be financed. There has been no financing for this economic project and no mobilisation. There may be several reasons for the lack of mobilisation.

In a plan economy it is easier to mobilise people for campaigns. Resources are channelled and agitation is supported. State-owned press and media can be aligned to create an atmosphere where mobilisation is actively maintained. Mobilisation in a market economy, particularly one that is in a state of chaotic transition, is not as easy. What is the national task? To integrate Russia into the world economy? To do this with sacrifices in the individual household's level of living? Is the task to support some people to get rich so that the market economy can start investing in new innovations and productions?

A case in point is the privatisation of industry. There was very little enthusiasm among the workers to become owners of their own companies by investing their vouchers. Very few people in Russia actually understood what was going on when vouchers were distributed to the workers as a symbol that they owned the means of production. There were no crash programmes or mobilisation to introduce a Russian concept of ownership, nor any Western understanding of private ownership. Given that there had been 70 years of propaganda against ownership, it is hard to imagine how an ideological mobilisation could have been carried out in a few months. And, there was no effort in this direction.

When mobilised for a national task the Soviet scientists and engineers were mobilised for high technology, to solve complex technical problems under extreme conditions. Conversion of these high-tech products to commercially viable and marketable products, or making 'gold into steel', has not been an attractive task. Development of missile technology or a new fighter required advanced technical know-how and huge projects mobilising thousands of scientists to solve the problem. The production of knives and forks, tractors or baby-food lines has not involved complex technological processes mobilising the defence scientists and engineers for sacrifice.

Civilian objects, although sometimes produced within the same enterprise, have not been naturalised in the same way as the objects of war. The objects of war were for the defence of the country and the pride of the scientists. The objects of civilian production were naturalised in another way. They were the objects of little technological challenge, objects of lesser priority and objects without pride. They were not stamped 'good for military use'. As we have seen in Chapter 3 the divide between the military and civilian technologies and production was one of access to resources.

When conversion was put on the agenda scientists and engineers were committed. Some of the scientists and engineers were looking for a new task, one they and their nation could be proud of. They were again looking for something that would match their natural way of working, one where mobilisation, crash programmes and high level of resource allocation would apply.

Creation of a market economy might have been such a task. In many of my interviews the scientists underline that the way Russian leaders have approached market reforms has not been through large-scale mobilisation for national survival. A high-level manager of a scientific research institute pointed out to me that the way Gaidar and the others have approached the rebuilding of Russia after the collapse of the Soviet Union has been wrong.

> Had they instead loved the people and called the nation to build
> a new Russia, people would have had something to work for.
> They would have had an idea of the future and they would have
> been ready to make sacrifices.

Many of the employees of defence enterprises confirm this view. They call for the managers to mobilise.

> If they had just called the people of the factory and said: Now we have to build this working place. Everybody would have been willing to make a sacrifice.

Mobilisation and having something to believe in plays a decisive role in the communities of practice in the defence industry. You need something to believe in, to be proud of and then you are able to move mountains. Stalin knew how to mobilise, Gaidar did not.

People wanted something to work for both on the level of a nation building and on the level of the working place. The question here is whether it had been easier to cross the border from a plan economy to a market economy if the old ways of working had been used in the transition process. Could the idea of a new 'market Russia' have been the one mobilised people for sacrifice? Had a new working place, functioning in the capitalist way, been able to mobilise the social dynamics of the workers? While there is no answer to these questions it is obvious that this is the way the Soviet system worked. There was a clear break in the way things were done in the military communities of practice. The conversion task was not built up in the same way in order to allow for an easier border-crossing.

The technological race

> It was the nature of our bureaucratic system. Even if we created new things, and new ways of doing things, our bureaucratic system told us to do the same things the Americans did. But to do it better or cheaper.[8]

Soviet scientists and engineers did not, as a rule, initiate technological innovations or new weapon designs. They were mobilised from the top. High-level decision-makers used mission-oriented campaigns as a reaction to technological advances in the US. Engineers and scientists were mobilised to solve a problem rather than stimulated to create new technological ideas and proposals. The Soviet process of weapon design was one of 'demand-pull' rather than of 'technology push'.

Evangelista[9] has compared the military innovation systems in the US and Russia. According to him, due to the abundance of resources and minimal central control, technical ideas for new weapons tended to flourish in the United States. During the Cold War initiative for new weapon systems and weapons was widely diffused and the university laboratories, non-profit research institutes, industrial suppliers and arms services all participated in this process. Private firms were willing to undertake research at their own expense and higher political authorities were reluctant to restrict R&D programmes, even when the prospect of success was uncertain.

Political support for a technological innovation was mobilised by the scientists and the military-industrial R&D community. In order to build a favourable consensus these innovations incorporated all technical features, the promoters thought were desired by potential supporters. This resulted in weapons of great sophistication, maybe greater than was desirable for a given military mission. In the US system, there was an inability to limit technical options. Rivalry between the military services – the army, airforce and the navy – contributed to change. In the end, congressional support for military innovation was often gained by arguing for employment opportunities and referring to an external threat, that of the Soviet Union.

While the internal dynamics dominated the work on technological innovation in the US military communities of practice, external factors dominated the Soviet system of weapons innovation. Holloway[10] characterises the Soviet R&D system in the postwar period as an uninnovative system where the revolutionary technological changes came from its potential enemies. When important innovations occurred in other countries, this created a response in the Soviet Union. Design bureaux were ordered to produce breakthroughs to counteract foreign technological surprise. Priorities were established at the top and after the approval the necessary resources were rechannelled. Innovation in policy was accompanied by innovation in technology. For example, a policy adopted by Stalin, for air defence against high-altitude strategic bombers, resulted in the development of high-altitude interceptor aircraft. Contrary to the United States where military engineers and scientists were able to promote new ideas, Soviet scientists who advocated new ideas were imprisoned or even executed.[11]

Promotion of a particular innovation was referred to as the mobilisation phase. High-level authorities endorsed new priorities in order to overcome the systemic inertia towards change. Crash programmes for the development of new weapon systems were created and a network of research institutes, design bureaux and production units were enrolled to carry out for example the rocket development programme. For a strong central government it was possible to transcend organisational and technological barriers by referring to external threats. This is maybe one of the keys to understanding why military production was superior in quality, even when the military and civilian products were produced side by side in the same facilities.

Wrong ideology

> The Americans say they won the Cold War. This is possible. We had the wrong ideology. We tried to build a world with communism and to develop a dialogue about it. All our money was spent for that. I am basically for conversion. But the problem is that the people no longer have an ideology. The people have lost their belief in work. You come to work, but you do not get paid. Today (in June) people are getting their salary for the month of March. Who is able to maintain a belief in work under such conditions? There is no ideology any more. Somebody believes in God. Some say God will come. My God is inside me.

This quotation is from the director of the Perm Regional Conversion Fund, a former manager of a design bureau. He is trying to implement the regional conversion programme in Perm, trying to make networks among defence enterprises, to do technical and economic studies about conversion and initiating concrete co-operation among enterprise managers and scientists. He is disillusioned, not because there is very little money for conversion in the region, but because there is no more ideology. He is worried about people losing faith in work. He is not worried about how work is done in a market economy, nor about competition, but about the fact that people who before believed in work no longer do so.

When the Soviet Union collapsed many other worlds collapsed. The communist ideology was lost. It was, in the words of the Conversion Fund director, the wrong ideology. At the same time the belief in what before had been the achievement of the Soviet system, its technological pride, was lost. The military communities of practice also lost their faith in the future. The engineers and scientists who had believed they were the world's best in their own field had to accept that the task they had worked for was no longer there. Not only had the task disappeared, the ruins of the technological race were not even able to support the ideology of work, nor to get your monthly pay cheque.

The question of whether socialism or capitalism was able to create more advanced technology has been disputed in the former Soviet Union time and time again. The proof of who is winning has always been sought in military technology – not in civil innovation, however advanced. In reality more and more of the Soviet intellectuals were in the past forced to acknowledge that technological development is also taking place in the West, and at an accelerated pace. The controversy over this issue led to a continuous debate between what has been called the traditionalists and non-traditionalists.[12]

The traditionalist claim has been that socialism is superior in technological innovation and change. Even if this is an inherent characteristic of the system technological innovation should, nevertheless, be promoted. The traditionalist focus is on indigenous technology. There is no need for a world division of labour in science and technical development. There is no concern over the fact that Soviet engineers and scientists may be working on problems already solved in the West. The traditionalists argued for a military build-up and for military technology. Goods for production were given priority before consumer goods. Diffusion of military technology into the civilian sphere was generally opposed.

The non-traditionalists were less predetermined about Western technological capabilities. They allowed room for doubt and claimed that the technological development in the West should be studied. Co-operation should be initiated. The non-traditionalists were promoters of arms control and underlined that military technology should give spin-offs to civilian production.

The debate between these two groups has been a balance act and periods of non-traditionalist dominance can be detected both during the Khrushchev and Brezhnev eras. The power balance between the traditionalists and non-traditionalists may be measured by the number of scientists who visited the West in any given year.[13] The more visits the stronger the position of the non-traditionalists. The traditionalists have feared defected Soviet scientists in the West and espionage. At the opposite side of the coin has been the desire to get access to Western technology. The traditionalists have argued that the Soviet Union will become dependent on the West. The non-traditionalist counter-argument has been that this dependence is mutual (both parties develop a dependence on technology and of each other) and creates conditions for a more peaceful co-existence. However, the non-traditionalists have had problems with their argument, as the West has required political concessions as a payment for relaxation of restrictions on technology transfer. At the end of the Cold War this debate between the traditionalists and the non-traditionalists has come to an end.

Regardless of which side Soviet scientists and engineers have placed themselves, they have had to accept that in many, if not most, fields in the end Western technology was superior to their own.

Design cultures

Morrison and Little[14] have compared the distinct characteristics in terms of values and ideologies of the US and Soviet Union weapon-design cultures. Drawing a distinction between the task environment in which a weapon exists and the institutional environment which supports it, they conclude that US weapon culture is technology and profit-driven, while the corresponding culture in the USSR was more task-oriented.

This is an interesting difference. The US weapon culture is seen as a technology push, technological qualities are built into products, even when simpler solutions could be used in order to satisfy potential supporters. Actor networks and alliances were built through a technology push argument. The opposite is true of the Soviet Union. As pointed out by Evangelista, the Soviet approach to innovation was initiated by technological advances abroad, particularly in the US. And although the Soviet military industry was separated from the civilian sector by access to resources, resources have still been in short supply compared with the US.

Automation and sophistication were, according to Morrison and Little, key qualities of the Western weapon-development. Designs embodied autonomous and intelligent mines, torpedoes or 'intelligent' antitank missiles and autonomous reconnaissance vehicles and knowledge-based tactical assistance systems. The Soviet weapon designs were characterised as heavily manpower equipped, cheaper, less sophisticated and more reliable. While acknowledging the potential economic efficiency of intelligent weapons, the authors question their functionality under conditions that are less than optimal for their performance. In the Western mode of thinking, weapon performance is something that stands in isolation. A weapon's effectiveness depends on its technology alone, not on the environment in which it finds itself. This results in sophistication and technological complexity rather than functionality. Commenting on Soviet design culture, the authors underline the following:

> While the Soviets have traditionally considered technology as important, for them it is relevant to military matters only in so far as it can help achieve particular tactical or strategic goals. In

the West there is an implicit assumption that, if it can be made, it should be, and implemented as well. By contrast, Soviet planners have often ignored technological potentialities unless they offer a means by which their military objectives can be assisted. The MIG-25, for instance, as we have already seen, involved design compromises that were virtually unthinkable in the West, in order to achieve a specific mission – the neutralising of the proposed B7 supersonic bombers.[15]

The robustness and simplicity of Soviet weapons design is seen by Morrison and Little as the result of a deliberate design policy in order to achieve a military task. Instead of developing new technology, the Soviets refined existing designs, which allowed production runs to continue with minimal disruption. Larger production runs were possible at lower unit costs and simplified maintenance.

Design actors

The Soviet scientist worked in a mobilisation economy where the design culture was determined by the supply conditions and task-orientation The design cycle and its actors have been described by Amman and Cooper.[16]

Major decisions about research and development work in relation to weapon systems rested with the Politbureau. Fundamental discussions were carried out in scientific councils where representatives of the scientific community, the defence ministries and its research establishment and those of the Academy of Sciences participated together with the members of the Military-Industrial Commission. Research was then carried out by one of the nine ministries in its research establishments. Here military requirements were defined, each of the nine defence-industrial ministries having under its control central research institutes doing applied research and a network of design bureaux to design and develop new products. The latter also had some pilot production and testing facilities to form the link between research and production. Research institutes and design bureaux were financed largely from the state budget, but there was also contract work. The work was planned directly and supervised by the ministries' technical administration, which also co-ordinated the plans for the product administration when introducing new technology. Technical documentation was co-ordinated by the ministries' scientific and technical councils who also made recommendations about research and development policy and reviewed design proposals to see whether they were up to the 'world standard'.

There was a linear innovation chain where the research institutes of a particular ministry gave research reports to the same ministries, design bureaux, which in turn designed and developed new weapons and new production processes. Some of the weapon design bureaux were responsible for the overall weapon system, others worked on sub-systems such as airplane engines or rocket motors. When a design was chosen for production a contract was concluded between the Ministry of Defence and the Industrial Defence Ministry. A production plant was chosen and the design bureaux could set up a branch at the production plant in order to ease the transition to production. The Ministry of Defence also had a control function located at the production plant to check that the technical recommendation was followed.

Amman and Cooper point out that applied research was institutionally separated from design. Although the design bureaux were powerful their work was closely regulated by the research institute guidelines for design and the armed forces control system. Basic research in return was carried out by the Academy of Sciences and other civil research institutions, which participated in the scientific councils. In some cases the Academy of Sciences had their own design bureaux and research institutions working for the military.

The mode of communication in this innovation system was through documents. The defence-industrial ministry, through its technical administration, issued the requirements and specifications for new weapons. The basic document in weapon development was the Tactical-Technical Instruction (Taktiko-Tekhnicheskaia Instruktsiia) prepared by the technical administration. The documents were agreed upon between the ministry's technical administration and the design bureau and confirmed at a higher level within the Ministry of Defence and probably also by the Military-Industrial Commission. When the design was approved for production a document called Technical Conditions (Tekhnichskie ysloviia) was prepared as a basis for production. Also this document was approved by the Ministry of Defence. This was then the basis for quality control exercised by the military representatives of the technical administration in the enterprises themselves.

To the world's best standards

The quality definition of technological development was a peculiarity of the Soviet defence-industrial complex. The metaphor was 'the world level', 'the world standard' to 'the world's best standards'. Design proposals reviewed by the scientific and technological councils of the defence industry and ministries had only one quality indicator. Weapons and related products should meet the world level.

I met the 'world level' both in documentation and in interviews. State programmes for conversion emphasised that not only should the conversion efforts maintain the core of scientific and technological potential of the defence industries but also 'work in the directions in which world level results have been scored and where achievements from promising a big commercial success are expected'.[17] Managers and chief engineers constantly emphasised to me that their enterprises were able to convert on the 'world level' and meet 'world standards'.

Given the shortage of other meaningful information, the 'world level' has been used to calculate the quality of the machine or the output profile of an industry. This rhetoric suggests that there is a well-defined technological 'frontier' that clearly indicates the route to be followed in machinery design and production. In practice, this 'world level' has been constructed by US achievement and technical performance, available in international documents. However, as a general objective it lacks meaning particularly if the 'world level' is to be renegotiated into commercial products.

> In any sector of production, best practice consists of a continuum of technologies selected according to the circumstances attending their use. Many may be found operating, to one degree or another, at the same time in different production locales. In addition, even if a technological 'frontier' can be identified through objective means, the question of the dynamic path one takes to achieve this level is not easy to resolve and will surely depend upon local circumstances.[18]

The Soviet scientists and engineers tried to achieve the world level, and in the Cold War weapon production actually succeeded. This goal has survived in conversion programmes and has defined the tasks for how military technology is to be converted to civilian uses. But while the design communities of the Soviet Union had information about the world level for weapon systems and were able to identify American achievements, the Russian civilian technology has been underdeveloped. In the early years of conversion (1992–93), there was virtually no information about the technical qualities of 'world level' washing machines, microwave ovens or trailers. Bewildered at the loss of orientation, it was taken for granted that the transfer of military technology to civilian production would give obvious and self-evident advantages. After all, the pipes of the chemical industry would be of better quality if made by military know-how for glass-fibre containers. In negotiations about technological joint ventures and technology transfer Russians are still extremely sensitive to the world level. They want the best and the latest, regardless of how and where the technological objects are to be used.

The desire for Western high technology in civilian production, the high-tech to high-tech conversion and the task to save the technological base of the country (see Chapter 10) have became a straitjacket in the conversion process. Or, as pointed out by Popper, who studied the modernisation of the Soviet industry:

> The Soviet Union does not need high-technology. Nor, for that matter, does any other economy. What it needs instead are those technologies that will render the industrial capital stock highly predicted and efficient. High technology is important, but not necessarily all important in achieving this goal. Yet, the code word has become the standard for determining success in machine-building.[19]

In the military sector, the world level was defined by American documentation, by reverse engineering and by intelligence activities. Targets for mobilisation have been clear and the achievement of goals easy to test. The opposite was true of the civilian sector. In conversion, the problem is to determine the world level in consumer products. This has not been studied and no new goals have been identified. Consequently, ways of working in the military industry could not be transformed to the civilian sector.

Competition was the key to the international Cold War scene. In the military industry, it also existed within the military-industrial complex itself. Competition or 'parallelism' as it was called in the Soviet Union, was a controversial issue. Ideologically, competition was doomed to lead to technological and economic stagnation.[20] Real freedom could only come from central planning. Central planning gave the perspective while competition would lead to personal misfortune. In spite of this ideological atmosphere, competition was allowed, even promoted, at least among research institutes and design bureaux. This was a more efficient way to achieve foreign military achievements and was particularly true in aircraft design. Consequently, in well-defined fields a choice has existed of designs for production. But even here the engineers and scientists within the Soviet military complex worked without open internal competition against the shadow enemy of 'the world level'.

In order to understand how this community of practice worked and how difficult the transformation of a scientific community has been, I shall present a person I have interviewed at regular intervals in Perm: Vladimir Antsiferov, the director of the Technical Centre of Powder Metallurgy in Perm.

Vladimir Antsiferov

Vladimir Antsiferov (VA) is educated as an engineer from the Perm Technical University and has completed post-graduate work and received a doctorate in Moscow Institute of Steel and Alloys whereafter he returned to work at Perm Technical University. Here he has created a faculty and institute of a new type conducting not only fundamental research in metallurgy and materials technology. The developed materials find use in space. The scientists of the institute created the filter for the Soviet space shuttle Buran and have developed filters and other porous components with high permeability and a long lifespan based on nickel, titanium, chromium and iron. The institute is famous for its pioneering work on continuous rapidly cooled titanium fibres, the calibration of which is now in progress.

I visited the institute for the first time in 1992. It was located in a picturesque pine forest near the student's campus of Perm Technical University. VA meets me in his office, a spacious room with a number of certificates and prizes on the wall. VA himself is a scientist to his fingertips, devoted to materials technology. He looks at me attentively, trying to understand what I am here for. I try to present my case – Danish researcher interested in conversion and wishing to learn about his experience.

VA tells me that the high technologies developed in the institute can be used in civil industries. The problem is that it is not favourable for the large Russian enterprises to introduce these high technologies. They are not used to working with high-tech and significant expenses are required. This is the problem, for example, with advanced vacuum technologies. In his words:

> We are interested in conversion of production, in new commissions in order to save creative potential, qualified people and to raise salaries for them. The employees have received the State premium, premium of government of the USSR and ministries of education, which reflect the high valuation of their work and confirmed their significant contribution to science.

In 1992 the institute worked on conversion in two ways; first, the creation of the small enterprises: five enterprises were based in the Perm area to develop equipment and to introduce new high technologies without large investments; and secondly, development of co-operation with foreign countries. VA had sold a pilot production to Japan. But he had not received any money because of inexact registration of the documents. In Japan you need to deliver two signatures instead of only one, he says. Furthermore, the institute had received five grants of Chicago University. Activities were also underway to sell patents, according to him, both individual and institute patents.

At the end of my visit, I had a chance to see an exhibition of the institute's converted technologies. VA showed, among other things, a rabbit made by slip technology. It was a prototype model for manufacturing polyvinyl toys. He pointed out that the toy market was underdeveloped in Russia and that they tried to meet these needs.

The next time I meet VA is in June 1994. The situation is more frustrating. According to him, there is no technology policy. The government is unable to define priorities. 'They share butter with everybody, but there is very little butter.' There is no one to take the responsibility for saying yes or no. Everybody has difficulties. The government is afraid of social unrest. First, there is a need for courage, and secondly a need to guarantee the people their social welfare.

VA is disappointed in the West. Everybody expected the West would come and co-operate. But it turns out that nothing happens. China gets a priority-country status to the West, but Russia does not. VA is not satisfied with the humanitarian help that has been sent from the West. 'The money', he says, 'goes first to the pockets of Western bureaucrats, and secondly to the Russian bureaucrats. Ordinary individuals do not see this help.'

He underlines that there is a need for help, billions of dollars, or even at a level of the help granted to China, but not only for humanitarian purposes. Instead of giving humanitarian aid, the West should support companies and institutes similar to his, where 100,000 US$ for development of production would guarantee social welfare and stability. This money would not mean anything to the West, but would have great importance for Perm and Russia. The individual person sees very little of the Western humanitarian help.

The institute has survived in spite of the crisis. A new residential building was constructed and the salaries have been paid to the employees. The personnel has been reduced and maintained only in fields where there was a potential. VA is the co-ordinator of the governmental three-year programme in powder metallurgy, which was completed, but is expected to proceed in a new three-year programme. Although conversion is well under way, he maintains, it is a psychological problem. He thought in the beginning that it would not be necessary to convert. 'Now there is no one who is in doubt. Everybody can understand it,' he underlines.

New contacts are established as customers are visiting the institute. Chemical industries as well as machine building are interested in co-operation. It requires much effort to reach a certain degree of quality but VA emphasises that there will be no problems as long as the quality is confirmed. Activities are underway to introduce a testing laboratory for COCOM standards and German standards. The institute has contracts in the United States, Japan and Austria, and he is negotiating with Germany. The solution is not joint ventures, but the sale of know-how and production to the various industrial companies. The problem is new equipment, but there is no money.

Old equipment may be used, VA underlines, but to achieve new results modern quality equipment is necessary. The pilot production of the institute has been turned into civil production. Still there are military orders for scientific research. A third of his people are working in pilot production, two-thirds in research. The Russian Academy has, during the past year, lost a third of its employees, he says. Some have gone abroad, others have started their own business, and some have gone to small enterprises. It is particularly the men who are leaving; the women stay. And there are a number of women in scientific work, particularly in book-keeping, planning and what in Russia is called micro-structure laboratory analysis. 'It is good to have women at the microscopes, they have patience', he says. Despite the difficulties, the institute has survived and is developing its contacts abroad.

The third time I meet VA is in April 1997. We talk mostly about philosophy. What is going on and why? His assessment is that, if the State will not restructure, there is no future. According to him, the State has become a fire department. It is trying to keep the enterprises and to pay the salaries in order for people not to take to the streets. But conversion needs structural change, new equipment and new specialists.

VA is still worried about the equipment. It is now at least five years old. There are problems with financing although the institute receives some money from the educational system and state military orders. Contacts to Japan, Austria and the United States are still in operation and the Japanese contracts have resulted in some patents. The institute has been halved since Perestroika, although the structure has not been changed. There is a problem with patenting abroad. The problem with Russian patents has been solved.

VA seems to have one great desire: to live in a normal society with normal enterprises and normal people, not a society of people who steal. He does not want to hear the word 'democracy'; it is difficult to talk about. He is worried about solidarity and about those who are badly off. How is a woman with a child going to survive? Earlier there was at least a possibility to write to the Central Committee. You could complain. Today there is nowhere to turn. The individual is totally without protection, and he adds, 'the State should be for ordinary people'. People do not have the money to live and eat, and there are no clothes. For example, he points out that a student receives 83,000 roubles a month as a grant. The institute has started to provide dinners for 4,000 roubles; thus, the students can eat at least ones a day.

'Habits of thought'

In this chapter, focus has been on the more immaterial side of the socio-technical seamless web of Soviet defence innovations and the ways of working of its communities of practice. Invisible, barriers to crossing the divide between the civilian and the military appear as the naturalised objects and ways of working are to be changed.

First, and most importantly, the military scientists and engineers were mobilised for a national task. There was an ideological background for doing what they were doing. They were task-oriented and motivated to achieve what was decided by the Politbureau. In this sense the communities of practice of the US and the Soviet Union worked in a very different atmosphere. While the US scientists and engineers no doubt have been driven by patriotism this was not utilised as a basis for mobilisation. Technological innovation was generated by competition among research institutes and enterprises privately financed and by the rivalry between the armed forces. There was a technology push approach where automation sophistication and intelligent solutions were the focus. The Soviet system was more goal-oriented to achieve tactical or strategic goals. The technical objectives were defined in terms of the world level or the world's best standard, which then were specified in technical terms in documentation and tested on both prototypes and production.

Now, there is no mobilisation and no task. In fact, there is nothing to believe in. On the contrary, the defence ministries are abolished, at least for a while, and the enterprises are supposed to turn their existing experience, know-how and production into new civilian products. There are no requirements or documents for the civilian production. There is no knowledge about what standards commercial products in the West meet. In terms of technology the 'world level' is still the quality mark of any civilian products proposed by the military engineers and scientists. The new ways of doing documentation in terms of business plans are unknown and traditional technical specifications are offered to Western investors attached with a price tag. While the user of the military innovations is well-known, the Defence Ministry, the situation is very unclear in the civilian field. There is no tradition for market research. Furthermore, many of the engineers and scientists have been reluctant to start producing commercial products because they did not carry the same prestige as military products.

'*Technology is society made durable*' is one of the most famous quotes of the social constructivists' understanding of technology. The Soviet missiles, tanks and aircraft were the Cold War made durable. At the same time, they created durable communities of practice with naturalised work processes and the objects of work. Although institutions have been destabilised and a new society is being built, the technology is still there. The naturalised objects do not go away, the practices of work survive.

Could the Russian conversion effort have been channelled in a different way? Could the engineers and scientists have been mobilised for the great national task of creating a market economy and integrating Russia into the world economy and making it a 'normal country'?

The question of conversion and reuse of military resources, know-how, material and equipment could have been posed in a different way – as a new national task requiring sacrifices, effort and hard work – and leading, some time in the future to higher living standards for the individual.

Potentially, the communities' traditional way of doing things, such as imitating innovations from the West, being task- rather than technology-oriented and creating robust and functional designs with few resources, could have given the Russian enterprises a leading edge. But the search for the universal 'world level' has not been a fruitful direction. Furthermore, producing little things, such as knives and forks or tailor-making products to customer specification is not something that the military scientists and engineers are, at least not yet, proud of doing. The pride of the military scientists and engineers was intimately tied, not to military technology as such, but to technological achievements, new equipment and being the best.

The conclusion here is that technology is not only society made durable. Soviet military technology was also the pride of the scientists made durable. Advanced composite materials and new missiles were their patriotism made durable. Although institutes have been destabilised, the quest for self-esteem has not. Maybe I could end with a quote from Torsten Veblen:

> The change is always in the last resort a change in habits of thought: That is true even in case of changes of technical processes within industry.[21]

And, I might add, in case of radical changes in a nation's economic and social life.

Notes

1 Loren Graham's book *The Ghost of the Executed Engineer: Technology and the Fall of the Soviet Union* gives a good picture of the destruction of Soviet engineers through the life story of engineer Palchinsky.
2 The salaries paid by defence-related research institutes were, on an average, one and a half to two times those of other institutes. There was a gradation of the institutes, scientists of pulsed power establishments had 15 percent higher salaries than the average due to the high level of radiation and oxide concentration in the air from high-voltage discharges (Bystritskii, 1995: 27). For defence-industry salaries, see Gonchar, Kuznetzov and Ozhegov (1995). Alexander (1990: 47) claims that the wage and labour picture of the

defence industry is mixed. According to him, some Soviet analysts and managers describe highly paid workers with many additional private privileges, whereas others claim that there were equivalent pay and working conditions, in defence and civilian jobs.

3 Coordinating Committee for Multilateral Export Controls (COCOM). An organisation created in 1949 to prevent the transfer of militarily useful technology to the Communist world. In 1993, the 17 COCOM members agreed to abolish the organisation following the end of the Cold War. In 1995, 28 nations, including many of the former Soviet Union republics, created the post-COCOM Wassenaar Arrangement on Export Controls for Conventional Arms and Dual-Use Goods and Technologies.

4 See for example Leigh Star (1994).

5 Leigh Star (1994: 20).

6 For example, Kosals (1994).

7 Ibid., p. 203.

8 An interview with a high-level scientist in a Moscow research institute (June, 1994).

9 Evangelista (1988).

10 Holloway (1983).

11 Evangelista, 1988.

12 For the details on the debate between the traditionalists and the non-traditionalists, see Parrott (1983).

13 Parrott (1983) shows that every time the traditionalist position becomes stronger the number of scientists visiting the West is curtailed.

14 Morrison and Little (1991: 247).

15 Ibid.

16 Amman and Cooper (1982: 294–354).

17 The Conversion Law is referred to in the SIPRI Yearbook (1993: 362–3).

18 Popper (1990: 19).

19 Ibid., p. 20.

20 Parrott (1983: 280).

21 Veblen (1904: 394).

Chapter 7

Making Weapons Invisible in Everyday Life

'Sociology of the invisible' is a term used by Susan Leigh Star to introduce in the context of grounded theory the concept of social world. The visible and the invisible are inseparable, and work is the link between the two. Invisibilities are not automatically organised into pre-given abstractions. Someone does the ordering. The ordering is in itself anchored in a series of contingencies, and every anchoring is embedded in a pattern that can be viewed theoretically.[1] The task is to study the unstudied, to understand the organisation of 'deleted work' and the articulation work that goes into keeping things secret.

Using 'dying' as an example, she discusses the work involved in the maintenance and the invisible presence of secret knowledge. In hospitals, nurses, doctors and visitors own secret knowledge of dying that often is invisible for the dying person. To do so requires attention and work from the nurses and doctors. Another example of maintenance work is that involved in managing the continuity of identity – in reconstructing pasts, managing presents and constructing futures. The interruption of experience in the discontinuity of identity is seen as the relation between the visible and the invisible.

Interruptions of experience are what the Russians have experienced in all spheres of life. The maintenance work that has gone into maintaining a minimum of coherence in daily life has been enormous, not to talk about the things that have suddenly become visible, such as the horrors of Stalin or environmental problems. Interruptions in experience also mean interruption in the creation of meaning by communities. Finally, there is the concept of articulation work, which is work that gets things back 'on track' in the face of the unexpected. Articulation work modifies action to accommodate unanticipated contingencies.[2]

Epistemology of the Closet is a book by Eve Sedgwick dealing with the relations of the known and the unknown, the explicit and the in-explicit in homo/heterosexual relations. It is about sexual behaviour and about sexual identities. It is about ignorance and about 'coming out'.

According to her, the closet is the defining structure for gay oppression in this century. A metaphor is 'in and out' of the closet of privacy and secrecy manifests itself as the secret of gay men and women. According to her, homophobia is a special kind of oppression built into the epistemological distinctiveness of gay identity and gay situations in our culture (Sedgwick, 1990).

Now what has dying or being gay to do with Russian defence industry? The bridge consists of the sociology of the invisible, the articulation work in the way in which secrecy, silence and ignorance were built into the everyday life of women working in the Russian defence industry. The identity of a person working for a defence industry in Russia is of course different from a gay person in the West. However, they share the closet. It is a different closet, but in both cases, it has implications for identity. I shall particularly explore the costs of coming out of this closet as the Cold War ends. Keeping the work you do secret, disguising it in everyday life, requires what Susan Leigh Star calls articulation work. While Eve Sedgwick has read texts about love between men, I have interviewed Russian women in the defence enterprises of a city in the Urals in Perm.

During 1992–94 I had visited Perm a couple of times a year, interviewed directors of military industries, chief scientists and designers. I knew a lot about the military enterprises of Perm, some of which I had by now visited personally. Outside the official interviews I had met people in the streets, in shops and at dinner parties. Women in buses had told me about their work, which more often than not was directly related to military production. But I had not talked to the workers of the defence enterprises and I was particularly interested in finding out how the women who worked with arms production saw their work. Although there were no official statistics on how many of the employees, scientists and engineers of the military industries were women, women no doubt were working in all the Perm enterprises, also the military. As the Soviet women accounted for 59% of the university and college level education, they also no doubt fulfilled a number of positions in the military enterprises, design bureaux and research institutes. According to some estimates, 40% of the educated workers in R&D laboratories were women.[3]

In January 1995, I again visited Perm. One of the persons I re-interviewed was the director of the design bureau Temp, located on the premises of Perm Technical University. Temp had been the main design bureau for artillery systems. The bureau had a design department and pilot production and had since 1991 tried to find civilian areas of production. Experiments had been made with glass-fibre piping, high-strength poles for sports and different types of civil 'explosives'. The design bureau had also after 1991 tried to design baby food production lines.

When interviewing the director for the third time, I asked him about the women, if any, in his design bureau. He answered that he was trying to get rid of them. Women could not be used in direct production. It was a job for men. He had never had a female designer. I asked if it would be possible for me, in spite of all this, to talk to some women in his design bureau. He willingly consented. In an hour, all the women at the design bureau who were at work at the time had gathered in one of the meeting rooms. There were 18 of them. The director introduced me as a conversion researcher from the West and asked them to be frank with me. I was astonished at the situation, mostly at the fact that there seemed to be nobody to control our discussion.

A woman in the boat is bad for sailing

I told the women, that I had been in Perm several times interviewing about conversion and that now I was interested in hearing about the role of women in the process. But first I would like to know about the situation of women in the design bureau.

The design bureau had employed 100 women. Today there were only 20. I asked where the other 80 were. Some of the women had voluntarily left the bureau. Some had changed jobs and were now in either the new commercial structures (small businesses, share-holding companies and marketing). Some had started a new education. I asked if any of the women were unemployed. The answer was no. However, one of the women pointed out that there were a number of women who were on voluntary leave; that is, they were away from work, but still registered as employed, though they were in fact unemployed. I asked whether many of the women had decided to stay at home. The answer was that there were today a number of young women who would choose to take care of their children. Most of the women who sat around the table no longer had small children at home. The understanding seemed to be that staying at home was a phenomenon that did exist, but which they thought was limited in scope.

In spite of the fact that the director had just said that there were no women designers, the women themselves identified themselves as designers or technicians. Two of the women had previously been designers, but had moved over to accounting. One of them was visibly sorry to have lost her job as a technician. The two who had learned accounting did not have any formal training in it, but had learned it by doing. The women had been educated at Perm Technical University, previously Perm Polytechnical Institute, in different departments. They were proud of their technical education, although they obviously were seen as less well qualified than their male colleagues.

Is there a difference between the men and women on the job? I asked them. A lively discussion followed where several of the women emphasised that the difference was a question of qualifications. When I asked them how the qualifications differed between men and women, they said it is not a question of education. One of them took up the question of time:

> Men have more time for work, women have the home and the responsibility for everything at home. They have less time and they think about something else.

> It is the men who give time for work. Women do everything. Maybe it is also a question of the will to have a career. Women are educated for something softer. But the young women have more interest in a career than I have.

The fact that men have more time for work and a career is taken for granted. A second difference between men and women is, as pointed out by another of the younger women, the difference in the way women and men are:

> Maybe if a woman is more male, she may move up in her career. But if she is a 'woman inside' she will give it less priority.

When I asked whether the women and men had different positions in work, the answer was *yes*. Women, although they were in all departments and workshops, were more dominant in the accounting, financing and planning departments. Women worked more with 'numbers'. Men were more mobile and worked in the assembly. There were women in middle managerial positions. Women were sometimes leaders of control departments. But higher positions were reserved for men. The agreement was that only in cases where a woman was 'male' or did not have a family did she occupy higher positions.

'*Did you feel any discrimination in employment practices?*' I asked.
The difference in the positions of women and men in work did not seem
to be problematic for the women. Women's dominance in some
departments was seen as women's own choice. Women were not
interested in using so much time for work and they do not seek work in
the assembly. One of the women pointed out that it was 'the
atmosphere of the society'. I asked them whether they could remember
any situations where a woman would have been refused a job because
she was a woman. No examples came to mind. One of the women
remembered that the well-known astronaut, Korolev, never involved
women in experiments or flights. He only selected, according to her,
the best specialists, always men. He is known to have said, 'a woman in
the boat is bad for sailing'.

Women in this design bureau felt they were not discriminated
against, on the contrary they had a number of privileges. Before the
collapse of the Soviet Union the women had one day off a week if they
had either several children or small children. They could take an extra
day off, as a rule, Friday. If a woman had older children, she could take
a day off each fortnight or perhaps once a month. One of the women
pointed out that this was a particular advantage in the military
industries. When I asked the director about this afterwards, he
underlined that it was only in his design bureau that women had this
possibility. It was not the general situation. This was 'so that the
women would feel themselves as women', said one of the women.

Weapons as 'products'

The women in the Perm military enterprises produced tanks, engines
for military aircraft and advanced materials for the aerospace industry.
How did these women talk about the weapons they were producing?
What did they talk about when they talked about their work? I posed
the question to the 18 women of the design bureau Temp.

When at work, the women said, they talked about work freely.
Everybody knew about each other in a working community, the
members were well acquainted with the tasks. Outside work, one did
not talk about it. Their work in a design bureau was talked about
outside as *razrabotka nestandartnovo oborudovania*, meaning
'documentation of non-standardised machines or equipment'. The
women, who worked in the pilot production plant, also a part of the
design bureau, talked about *izdelia*. This could be translated as

products, components or hardware. Some of the military experts have explained to me that the word could also mean end products, the result of work.

One of the women emphasised:

> What happened with these 'products' was not of interest. There were some closed departments. One had to have papers and maybe even extra papers to come in, but one didn't get to know what the machines were used for. People live here close to the industry, we have children in the day-care centre and pioneer camps.

Weapons are products or components. You do not talk about these components in detail, what they are used for or how they are made. According to the women, this was a thing for the workplace. When you come home 'you forget'.

> If you are responsible, you forget the whole thing. You hold your tongue, that's all.

It was '*rabota kak rabota*', 'whichever work'. It was not specific work with weapons. It was work with components, sometimes with space, and with civilian products. The integration of civilian production in the plants balanced work with weapons.

In Perm, only one factory produced end products. The rest of the enterprises produced 'parts', which made the relation to war more opaque. Although these products were clearly identifiable, such as components for rockets or artillery systems, they were naturalised (Leigh Star, 1994). They were taken for granted, you did not think about it, you did not talk about them. They lost their specific meaning. The context of use was actively removed.

Perm was a militarised city, where most people depended on military production for their livelihood. But in the Urals it was a typical city, as military production was, during the late phase of the Second World War and immediately afterward actively moved away from the war zone to the Urals. When you live in a city where everyone is in the same situation, where nobody talks about work or discusses the objects they produce, you no doubt become socialised into the sanitary, clean world of arms production. Many women underlined this particular aspect:

Imagine yourself that everybody works for the military industry. You do not talk. Everybody has the same type of work. You have this kind of work. The other one has this kind of work. We do not talk about work. We talk about the cat, about football. Then we talk about Sakharov and the dissidents and we talk about Angela Davis.

In order to be quite sure about what the women are saying, I finally posed the question: '*What do you say to your children when you talk about work?*'

The answer was 'machines'. You tell your children that you work with machines. Also the children live in a militarised city. Many parents have pointed out to me that the children played military games. The culture educated everybody for this.

Articulating ignorance

Susan Leigh Star talks about 'objects of work', which define communities of practice (Leigh Star, 1994). A community of practice co-uses objects which also mediate the community's rules and relationships, including both acceptance and legitimacy. In a community of practice, objects are naturalised and as she points out:

> By naturalisation, I mean stripping the contingencies of an object, its creation and its situated nature. A naturalised object has lost its aura of anthropological strangeness, and is in a sense 'de-situated' in that members have forgotten to locate the nature of the objects, its meaning or the action that go into maintaining and recreating its meaning.[4]

Communities of practice are established by the objects the members of a community of share. Their actions take place in relation to these objects. To become a member and to participate in such a community of practice is a question of acquiring skills in relation to these objects. The process of becoming a member is a question of naturalisation of these objects and those skills that are required. As activity is always mediated by tools and materials arrangements, the process of naturalisation becomes important. According to Susan Leigh Star, it is not predetermined whether an object will ever become naturalised or how long it will remain so. Rather, activity – work – is required to make it so and keep it so.

> The more naturalised an object becomes, the more
> unquestioning the relationship of the community to it; the more
> invisible the contingent and historical circumstances of its
> birth.[5]

'Articulation work' is her term for the work necessary to maintain
silence and to make things invisible. In the Russian military industry, it
was required of the workers not to talk about their work when outside
work. Work on artillery systems was at home disguised as work with
products or documents. The production of rocket launchers was simply
called machines. Although you lived in a neighbourhood where
everybody worked in the same enterprise, even the same factory, you
could not talk about work. You talked about the cat, football or
something else. At work, you could talk about the objects and artefacts
with their real names. You could talk about technical specifications,
tests and assembly methods. But outside work you had to forget. And if
you were a responsible person you also forgot. This kind of 'double
speak' has required a lot of energy, although the women in the design
bureau I interviewed talked about it as obvious and self-evident.

When talking about components or documents the defence industrial
workers, both men and women, articulated a common secret.
Everybody knew. In a military city like Perm everybody had the same
kind of work. Those not working directly in the production of weapons
worked in the day-care centres, hospitals or a restaurant of a defence
enterprise. And if you worked in the city administration or road
construction, someone in your family was no doubt directly involved in
military production in a city like Perm.

The defence industry workers shared a secret known to everybody.
In a way it was a public closet. The epistemology of gay closet was one
of oppression and shame. Here we have a public closet of national
pride. It was a privilege to work for the defence industry. And the
image attached to it was one of defence. The women I talked to stressed
that they worked for the defence of their country, not for war.

> We were supposed, all the time, to defend ourselves against the
> enemy. That is the way we were educated. Everything had to go
> faster and faster. But we did not produce rockets, all we wanted
> was to have peace.

The meaning attached to the components and documents is one of
defence, not of war. The enemy was the Americans, the West and
especially NATO. Everybody had lost someone in the war, and the

memory of those lost in war was kept alive by the ideology of the party. According to this, arms were not produced for war, but for peace. The word '*oborona*', meaning defence, is used by the women when they talk about themselves or the objects of their work. '*Oboronnoe proizvodstvo*'' is defence production, a necessity not questioned.

Eve Sedgwick analyses the closet in terms of binarisms such as masculine/feminine, majority/minority, innocence/initiation, natural/artificial, same/different etc. Here the two binarisms, knowledge/ignorance and majority/minority are of particular interest. If you understand the Soviet economy as a structurally militarised economy everybody, or at least the majority of the people, were in the closet. It was not a closet of oppression, but rather of privilege and pride. However, it was still a closet, a common secret you did not talk about when outside work. It was an open secret structure where everybody went in and out many times a day. While at work you could freely talk about work. When going home you had to reprogramme yourself and talk about something else. When calling your children from work you entered another world. According to one of the defence managers I interviewed there was a sign on the telephones saying 'The enemy may listen to you.'

How do you construct a social world where you sometimes know and sometimes do not? How do you construct a social world where the enemy listens to you, but where you on the other hand share a common secret with everybody else? Although you can be ignorant about some facts outside work and you can forget the type of production you are involved in, how is this forgetting managed in everyday life? The answer is 'papers'.

Practices of secrecy[6]

Perm was a closed city. Not one that was invisible on the map, like some of the nuclear weapon-producing cities, close to Cheliabinsk or Tomsk. Perm was a closed city of restricted access. According to one of the managers I interviewed:

A closed city was a city that had restricted access for those who could potentially be dangerous for the maintenance of government secrets.

The term 'potentially dangerous' applied not only to all foreigners, but also to some Soviet citizens. Work involving government secrets was not allowed to ethnic minorities and criminals. In the Soviet Union everyone had a *propiska*, a passport with a stamp saying where you lived. Movement was controlled although theoretically everybody had a right to go everywhere. If you were on holiday or a meeting for more than a month you had to have a temporary *propiska*. The milits would always know where to find you.

Some cities had what was called a limited access, *ogranichennaia propiska*. For example, you could only move to Moscow if you had a job and housing or if your mother/father/husband/wife lived there. Also the cities of military production had limited access. One of the people I interviewed in Perm pointed out: 'Only good people were allowed in.'

No foreigners were allowed in Perm. Those working in the military industries were not allowed outside the country. In order to meet scientists from abroad or to arrange an international conference you had to do this outside Perm, for example in the Baltic States.

Perm was a closed city until the end of the 1980s. When I started my research on conversion of the defence industry in Perm in 1991, foreigners were still a rarity. In a few years the city experienced a number of American, German and other delegations coming to Perm. The region of Frederiksborg Amt in Denmark had a co-operative agreement with the region of Perm where cultural workers, school children and business managers travelled back and forth freely. But this was not the case during the Soviet time. It must have been a very strange experience for a city of restricted access and with a history of government secret to suddenly become open at all levels. I hope that some day someone will do the research on this topic.

If only good people were let in, who decided who was 'good'? The KGB made the decisions. All working places and institutions had a so-called *pervyi otdel*, the first department. This was a department deciding the workers' level of secrecy. There were three levels. The lowest, the 'secret' level, or the third form, was the simplest. You could travel. The KGB decided case by case. On the second level, or the 'very secret', you were not allowed out. This applied also to the first form, the 'especially secret'. Within the enterprise spaces were graded after the same forms. The same applied to documents. So a person of the second form could come to places classified up to the second form, but not to the first form. The level of secrecy was a question of negotiation. You could apply for a lower level. This happened when the Soviet Union collapsed. A number of scientists and persons working in the military industries applied for lower forms. If you were granted for example the change from the first level to the third you still had to wait five years. After this you could get to the third form, the secret form, and travel abroad.

What you are allowed to do on these secret levels is talked about as 'looking' at secrets, in Russian, *smotret'*. It is the eyes, which see. If you are on the first level, you can look at all government secrets. If you are on the third level, you can look at fewer documents and enter fewer spaces. Some dissertations and scientific documents were open, some closed. Some defence enterprise managers, on the second form, had permission to take anybody on their premises, but on their own responsibility. If you broke the rules, there was a codex of conduct. There was a responsibility and depending on the degree of your crime, you could either lose money, your freedom or your right to work with government secrets.

Most of the scientists interviewed pointed out that they could leave Perm and meet with other researchers at other places. If you were going to make a speech, your text had to be approved, first by the director, and then by the first department. There was even a central censorship placed in Moscow with a representative in Perm. Here was the final approval that could give the stamp: 'accepted for publication'. During the conversion process, there has been a de-classification of some of the closed documents. Even the formerly closed *Journal of Military Economy and Conversion* was opened.

The basic philosophy was that the fewer contacts the less the probability of revealing government secrets. On the other hand, this lack of contact has probably meant that a lot of research was redundant and that the wheel was invented time and time again. The same applies to when you only talk about documents and components. Synergies and new ideas have a more limited space. It is easy to imagine the redundancies in many of the companies having the same exclusive measuring instruments or other equipment bought in the West without knowing of each other. But as this was the way things were done, there seems to have been very little questioning of the way things were.

In practice, the secrecy form was controlled at posts at the borders. As spaces were graded, you had to show papers at the passages. If you worked at a floor with two different degrees of secrecy, each time you passed from one to the other you were controlled. When I asked one of the women how she felt about these papers and this procedure, she looked at me astonished and said:

It was like entering the tram. You have to show your ticket, it is taken for granted. We are used to it.

'The atmosphere of society'

When I have talked in lectures about the language of the women working in the Russian defence industries I have often been asked: what about the men? How did they talk about weapons and armaments in their work and daily life? I never got to talk to men the same way as I did to women in the design bureau Temp. In interview situations, I had the legitimacy of research in innovation and technology assessment giving me access to managers and chief scientists, sometimes to heads of planning or marketing departments. To come in the defence enterprises on the lower technical or worker level was more difficult although I did occasionally interview men who either were or had been working for the defence enterprises in Perm.

These interviews confirm that it was general practice to talk only of products or documents, and that the defence industry workers signed a document in which they agreed not to reveal any details of their work to outsiders. My role as a female researcher gave me access to the women at Temp in a different way that allowed for a longer and a collective discussion of the meaning of the objects they produced. The situation of women in this respect is of special interest as they were the managers of the daily life outside work. Their articulation work and being in a closet while not at work would require special energy and greater effort. However, the women seemed to take the situation for granted. They worked for defence and talked about components and documents.

The women wanted to be seen as designers/engineers and were not willing to leave their professional identity and enter into the world of small businesses and entrepreneurship as many of their male colleagues did or to stay at home which they saw many younger women do. The women, who had left their job as designers and had become accountants, a job in great demand after the economic transition, had not done this voluntarily. They still wanted to be seen as engineers. Their identity was closely linked to defence. Although all the women during the years 1992–95 had been engaged in civilian work – a few had participated in the design of baby-food lines – they preferred defence work. If I as a Western feminist had expected to find enthusiasm for work with products for daily life instead of weapons for war, I had to rethink my own conceptual framework. The gradual opening of the closet was not attractive to these women. They could have left the closet, looked for work in civilian production either within the design bureau, or outside. But they stayed.

One explanation is that the women prefer to do what they are used to do. They did not want to change, take risks and profit from the new possibilities. The director was trying to get rid of them, but they wanted to stay. They wanted to have things as they were. They had had four years of experience of life in the new Russia and did not like what they saw. The emerging market economy with its new threats and possibilities did not seem attractive compared to the old privileges. There could be another explanation. The women had had a number of special privileges related to their work as mothers and women. In the new world they were no longer wanted. Men were more attractive to the privatised defence enterprises, the social assets of which were being first dismantled. In 1995 the private sphere was increasingly taking over social services with only a minimal welfare guaranteed by the municipality or the State.

Finally, there is a third explanation, that of pride. Like their male colleagues, the world of which I have described in the previous chapter, they were proud of producing for defence. They shared the pride and the national task and saw their own role as co-workers in this patriotic effort. Even if 'a woman in the boat was bad for sailing', the women had felt they participated as equal partners and shared the joy in celebrations when the experiments went well. They were socialised into the defence world, it was the nature of things, or as expressed by one of women 'the atmosphere of society'.

This atmosphere was now gone. Although a small sign of it was still, in 1995, present. The design bureau had a bakery for freshly baked bread to take home, not only for its present but also for its past workers. This bakery was still in 1995 baking the everyday bread for the Temp workers. The smell of freshly baked bread was everywhere. But special papers were no longer needed to pass from one zone to another.

Notes

1 Leigh Star (1991: 266).
2 Leigh Star (1991: 275).
3 These figures were presented by Tatjana Leontieva at the Second European Feminist Research Conference in Graz, July 1994.
4 Leigh Star (1994: 21).
5 According to Susan Leigh Star, deconstructing this invisibility is one of the major shared projects of ethnomethology, symbolic interaction studies of science and gender and the analyst school of historiography, ibid., p. 21.
6 Secrecy is not only practiced in the defence entreprises of the Soviet Union and Russia. Gusterson (1996) has analyzed the daily practices of secrecy in his book on Nuclear Rites describing these practises of the Lawrence Lirenmore National Laboratory (pp. 68-100).

Chapter 8

Work, Sweet Home

At present 70% of all the unemployed in Russia are women. Women will undoubtedly account for the majority in the new wave of redundancies from the defence industries. It may be predicted that most women with university-level education and especially all of those aged 35 and over will be dismissed. The structural changes caused by the conversion in the defence industry are expected to produce job losses as high as 30–40%, which happens to be the current proportion of women in the workforce. Since in other economic sectors unemployment will also be quite high the chances for these women to find suitable alternative employment will be quite poor.[1]

Two years after the collapse of the Soviet Union in 1994, there were officially 32,000 unemployed workers in Perm; of these, 72% were women. On the other hand, unofficial unemployment (leave, reduced working days etc.) was estimated at the time to be 130,000. By 1997 the official unemployment had doubled and was 60–65,000. At the same time there were about 110,000 who did not work full-time and 150,000 who were still registered as employed but were on leave or otherwise out of work.[2] According to an Employment Office employee:

> Women don't want to be registered as unemployed. It is a disgrace to be unemployed. Therefore women keep their contact with the company even though they are on leave and do not get paid. Officially they are not unemployed. There is also the hope that it is easier to find work through friends and family.

The social glue

At the end of the Cold War a strange thing happens in the defence industrial complex of Russia – strange, that is, for us in the West. Although the amount of defence orders is reduced radically, and civilian production cannot compensate for the production losses, workers are not dismissed. They continue to come to work, even in a situation where there is neither work nor pay. In the US reduced defence orders means reduced workforce. Workers are dismissed at once. No American defence worker would come to work without pay.

The situation demonstrates clearly the role of the workplace for the individual and his/her life. The working place has not only provided work and pay, but also community, vacations and leisure activities. All welfare functions have come from the enterprise, although paid by the State.

Also the enterprise, the employer, accepts that former workers are still registered as employees. For this there are many reasons. One is legal. According to the Soviet labour law, it was not possible to dismiss workers. Another is psychological and dependent on the first. The enterprise managers, particularly the defence enterprise leaders, are used to being responsible for the total welfare of their workers. I have met real feelings of social responsibility. Thirdly, there is an economic motive. If the State still pays for the salaries (which they did before the enterprises were privatised and partly continue to do so even after privatisation), the amount of workers count. The more workers, the more potential State subsidies.

Salary payments by the State have been irregular since 1992. There have been delays. The government owes large sums of money to the enterprises. On the other hand the enterprises have been producing goods without orders and expected the State to pay. Resources allocated by the State to conversion programmes in 1992–94 were to a great extent not used for real conversion projects, but for payments of salary and utilities. In spite of the uncertainty of the situation, to maintain the workforce is beneficial and a normal thing to do both for the individual and for the enterprise.

The maintenance of social welfare in the new situation becomes problematic. Some of the Perm enterprises are able to maintain the social facilities of their workers at least at the start. Vacation homes were the first ones to be closed down, followed by day-care centres. Some of the functions were taken over, in some cases, by the municipalities although they lack resources for the maintenance. Some welfare services are privatised, others not. There seems to be no general rule and no clear solutions.

Women are most dependent on the enterprises' welfare services. Thus if unemployed they are afraid of losing their last weak ties to the system. In addition, they consider unemployment a shame. On the other hand, when the directors of defence enterprises in 1993–94 started to dismiss workers, the women were the first to be dismissed. The Soviet rhetoric of equality changes dramatically in just a few years. So even if formally unemployed many of the women choose to stay – without work or pay. I asked one of the women who no longer was employed, but was still registered as employed and came to work every day, why she did so. Her answer was: 'Where should I go, it is my home.'

What is a home?

This is a question asked by Mary Douglas in her article 'The Idea of Home: A Kind of Space'.[3] According to her, home is not only a kind of space, but also a structure in time with aesthetic and moral dimensions. The home organises space over time, the home has a distinct capacity for memory and anticipation. The home makes its time rhythms in response to outside pressures.[4] Home is, to her, memory institutionalised. It is capable of anticipating future events, a capacity to plan, to allocate materials between now and the future, to anticipate needs.

> The home's capability to allocate space and time and resources over the long term is a legitimate matter for wonder. We are not surprised that the cupboard is often bare: what should amaze us is that it often contains an extraordinary variety of things that are going to be used through the year, mentally ticketed for different kinds of expected events. Even more amazingly they have been stacked so that they can be found at right times..[5]

All resource allocations for everyday life took place at the working place, particularly in the defence enterprises. Food was distributed through the shops at the workplace. Not only sausages and flour but also freshly baked bread as in the design bureau Temp. Access to goods in short supply, such as quality clothes or sewing machines, were a privilege for those working in defence industries. Recreation, ice hockey, and films were also managed by the enterprise in their housing neighbourhoods. Employees were called by the administration to hear where they wanted to spend their vacations. The enterprise was in fact a home allocating time, space and resources.

Mary Douglas introduces the idea of home as a collective good, and claims that it would be possible to compare homes on the basis of how strongly the members are committed to the production of this collective good.

The budget is the main instrument of structuring the collective effort. Through the budget the collectivism lays its finger on every allocation and qualifies every decision. The budget slots make a screen through which every private plan must pass lest individual demands put at risk the resources mentally set aside for the rent, the mortgage, the child's education, the summer holidays, the rainy day. However unformed its goals may be, the home protects its general plan, with mutually adjusted budget slots.[6]

In a sense the whole Soviet military-industrial complex was a collective home. The main instrument for structuring this effort was the defence budget. It not only provided resources for the development of solid fuel, rocket engines or new kinds of explosives but also resources for vacations at the Black Sea and children's education not only in the neighbourhood schools, but also in the Perm Technical University. The collapse of the defence budget and the lack of new orders were thus also a collapse of the home. The question – where shall I go? – is therefore a legitimate expression for post Cold War everyday life in cities like Perm.

The Soviet home – the defence enterprise – is being turned into a Russian hotel where everything follows cost efficiency.[7] By investing their vouchers, the defence enterprise managers, engineers and workers may now become owners of their own 'homes'. Although the employees of the former Soviet defence enterprises have become owners of the houses they work in, they are left without the home. However, those who still come to work without pay are the ones still maintaining the idea of a home, a kind of space.

Firing women

The situation of women in the defence enterprises of Perm changed dramatically from 1992 to 1997. Women either stayed at home or became unemployed. Women with low salaries and a husband who could support them stayed at home. A number of women became unemployed, a phenomenon that was not even known in Perm before 1991. Since then employment services, the Employment Office, have been established based on European models.

The new Employment Office in Perm tried to find jobs for those who were laid off. The director emphasised to me in an interview in 1994 that they were working especially for the more vulnerable groups such as married women with children, women raising children alone, young people without work (and work experience), people with criminal backgrounds and members of the army. The office offered limited retraining services free of charge, sometimes in co-operation with the educational institutions in the Perm region. In his view, there was a particular problem with the women from the military enterprises. They were well educated, had professional pride and had experienced the good collectivism of the military enterprises. Although highly specialised and well educated, they faced unemployment and insecure futures.

Not only unemployment and retraining were on the agenda. The cost of sending a child to a day-care centre also became a new factor for women's work. During the Soviet time everyone was guaranteed child-care, usually provided without pay by the enterprises.

One of the young women I interviewed in 1997 and who had two children mentioned that day-care centres cost 250–500,000 roubles a month. At a time the average salary for a woman academician was 300–500,000 roubles a month, which meant that it was difficult for women to support themselves. Her husband could support her, and she had decided to stay at home. She could, as a teacher, get 300,000 roubles and maybe, if she worked two shifts, 700,000 roubles. On the other hand, just to buy food some milk, chicken and vegetables would easily cost 100,000 a month.

Another woman – let us call her Svetlana – used to work at the Composite Materials Research Institute. She was a chemist and a teacher. She had given birth to two children within five years. Svetlana, when interviewed in 1994, told me that she had been on maternity leave and had been fired the same day she came back to work. Women on maternity leave could not be fired, so she was fired the day she returned to work. According to her, young mothers with children were considered to be especially 'problematic'. They stayed at home when the children were ill. Russian children and children in Perm were often sick. Svetlana's two children were, according to her, sick two months of the year. When laid off, she got one month's salary and the message 'if you apply to the Employment Office, you get two months more'.

I asked her how she solved her day-care problem when she was working. She had no problems, she said, her mother was retired and if the children were sick they could stay with her. Others, if both of their parents worked, had many more problems. She told me that a number of women were fired from her institute. The institute kept some women, but fired older women, young mothers and young people in general.

According to her, the workforce of the institute has been reduced by two-thirds. Only one-third remained (1994). In her old department, there were only six persons left.

What did the fired women do? I asked her. Some, who like Svetlana herself were lucky, found a new job. She now worked as a secretary at a university institute. Some stayed at home. Others sold things on the market. They travelled to Moscow to buy goods and sold them here in Perm. Still others got a new occupation. According to her, this was the most 'popular', since there was no more work in science. What are the main differences between her former and present job, I asked her. The only problem Svetlana had had in working for the military was the long working hours and strict control.

In the military institute where she worked, there was both civilian and military work. She did not feel she worked with weapons, but with cosmos or the space shuttle. Although there were factories with special controls, it was not a question of being critical of military work. When she worked for the military, she was paid two and a half times more than elsewhere (before the children were born). There were free vacations, day-care centres and food stamps.

On the market place

The Business Women's Club in the Regional Centre for Qualifications at Perm Technical University had, in 1994–95, its finger on the pulse of what happened to women in Perm. This was the place where unemployed women came to get advice on what courses to take and how to build a new career. Women also came just to get support and to have someone talk to. I interviewed the secretary of the club, Nadezhda Ivanovna for the first time in 1994. She herself had been dismissed from a chemical design bureau. The design bureau, which had had about 100 employees, half of them women, had started dismissing employees two years before. All the women, with the exception of the receptionist and a telephone operator, had to go. The following is her description of the survival strategies of women dismissed from Perm defence enterprises.

The first alternative for these women, if their husbands were employed, was to stay at home. She had no data on this. But due to the economic situation in the country, this was not a very commonly adopted alternative. The second alternative was to look for a low-paid manual job in the sanitary sector. The pay was low, but it was enough to buy bread. The third option was to start a new career. Here age was an important factor.

Women between 30 and 40 years became accountants. At the beginning of the economic reforms, given the need to establish new financial and market-oriented services within enterprises, there had been a shortage of accountants. This need existed not only in the defence enterprises, but also in the new commercial structures, *malyi bizneses*. In 1994, the market for accountants was, however saturated. For younger women between 20 and 30 years old, the main option was to become a secretary or a correspondent clerk. The club helped these women to find a job. There was a certain market, as new small enterprises needed secretaries. However, the prospects were not good.

Finally, there was the option to become a *biznesman*, a word that has been taken into the Russian language as such. These were the entrepreneurs, the heroes of the new economic reforms. I asked her whether professional women with a defence background became self-employed and started their own commercial enterprises. In her opinion, there were very few examples.

The first barrier was self-confidence. Women were not used to becoming independent. Men made all the decisions. Furthermore, the women had to take care of the home. According to her, the 'general attitude' was that 'men are better entrepreneurs than women are'. Secondly, female entrepreneurs had problems in getting financing because banks were unwilling to give loans to enterprises managed by women. A woman willing to start her own company might end up paying a higher interest rate. Finally, there was the problem of day-care. Day-care centres were being closed down. A woman interested in entrepreneurship had to pay other women to take care of her children, if she had the money. The city had a number of day-care centres, but these were extremely expensive. They were, according to her, only for enterprise employees where the enterprise paid 80% of the costs and the parents only 20%. Small businesses and newly established companies were not able to pay these prices.

In spite of all these barriers, she mentioned some successful examples of new 'businesswomen'. A former programming specialist had started a fur company. She had started only six months earlier, was working full time and already had 15 persons employed. A woman working in the administration of a cultural centre had started a firm which organised parties, celebrations, weddings etc. She had also founded a restaurant. There was a woman who had worked with children's cultural activities. She had organised a fast-food firm in her own neighbourhood. Further examples included a woman who started a private school and another who started a firm for social contacts.

In 1997, when I interviewed her for the second time the situation had changed. In 1994 every fourth or fifth of all unemployed women started their own business; now in 1997 this is only one out of ten. Women who wanted a new career had to go to the marketplace. This meant selling things on one of Perm's open marketplaces. The women either sold for others who had imported goods, or if they had money, they themselves travelled to Cyprus or Poland, bought things and sold them. Also women with a high technical education stood on the market, they were *na rynke*. Engineers became saleswomen. They took a two-week course in the Perm Business Women's Club and then they were ready to 'go to the market'.

Olga Pavlova, one of those who participated in a course, remembers her experience:

> I attended the course. They talked about debit and credit, and I did not understand anything, not even the basic things. Not all women can do this. The people are not ready for it, not psychologically, not economically.

She herself sold boots on the market, standing there in rain and snow. Her view of the work, which since then she has left, was:

> Earlier we had a moral principle. It was a national responsibility. Now we only have to think about our own. It is not so easy to change psychologically, it is not possible. It was terrible on the market place.

According to Nadezhda of the Perm Women's Business Club, women on the market have to pay 15 US$ to register with the administration and to get permission. A further problem is the way this work is seen in society. Previously, marketing was not seen as a job. It was humiliating. She pointed out that women could still come and say, 'I will not sell anything' or 'I will not work with trade'. But, she emphasised, 'They have to change their thoughts if they want to survive.'

Nina, director of a fashion center

In April 1997, I wanted to meet some of the women who had started Prikam'e, the new independent women's movement in Perm, and to meet some of the women who had started new careers. One evening we met at the newly established Institute for Child Toxicology to discuss the situation of women in light of the changes that had taken place. One of the women present let us call her Nina, was the most successful female entrepreneur in Perm. This is her story.

During the Soviet time, Nina had worked as a model and as a consultant for fashion journals. This was not high-status work at that time, a situation that has now totally changed. She was fired. Her husband, who was a middle-level scientist, did not get any salary for his work. Her son had started on his own when he was 21. He went bankrupt and had a loan, which had to be repaid. According to Nina, it was the mafia that ruined her son.

Nina had to create her own working place and started by going to the new employment office. She herself maintains that one of the keys to her success was her good looks. She went to the employment office in a short skirt, pushed her bosom forward and asked for help.

> Every time I contacted the new employment office the staff were abroad. They were in the United States to study how the unemployed is over there. Next time I came, they were in England to study how the British unemployed lived. Next time I came they were in France to study how the French unemployed survived. And the next time I came, the director was on holiday. At least 90% of their time went to everything else but getting work for people. But I decided that I would belong to those receiving support from them. I got a ten-million-rouble loan.

She hired a consultant to help her make a business plan and got an office in her husband's workplace at the end of a corridor. Her plan was to start educating fashion models. There was no money for advertising, but at least she had an office. The fact that she now did not work from home, but was officially acknowledged was important. The furniture came from her home. It was empty at home, but at least she now had a furnished office.

Women participated in a course for models. She received some money and could start advertising. As she herself had been a model for 17 years, she had a good professional background. Her intention was to find courses in which women would learn something they could earn a living from, some kind of practical education. At the time (1997) she had only worked for two years, but was already planning a new programme of education for 'image-makers'. The new Russians, the rich, do not know how to do make-up or how to dress, she pointed out.

It is a question of cosmetology, of style; and the new Russians are willing to pay for it.

There are many women in the defence industries who have always sewn their own dresses. Therefore she has trained them in sewing skills. They could now earn from 100 to 1,000 US$ a month. Many were now working and her point is that 'As you can no longer work with technology, you can start to sew and get a job.' According to her, 50–100 women have already received jobs as seamstresses. She is also thinking of the 40- to 50-year-old women. A possibility would be to start a programme of education for *niania*. There are many women who are taking care of children for others and they need training.

I asked her about her relation to the mafia. Did success not create problems with the mafia? She described vividly how small mafiosi started to come to her office in camelhair coats. She claimed that she had protection from higher up, the so-called *krysha* in Russian. Nina was left in peace. Maybe, she said, this was because her son had been ruined by the mafia. Now she would pay the loans of her son. Another factor could be that enterprises like hers got a lot of attention from decision-makers. Maybe because it was about women and fashion.

Nina is an example of a new entrepreneur, using her own education from the Soviet time. Her success was based on a centre with only four employees and herself. The idea was to help women to help themselves to get jobs. She was looking for new markets – the new Russians and the rich – and finding out what they needed and how women could make a living out of this. Her point was that with the training she offers women, they would not have to stand on the market places selling things in all kinds of weather. Others used her as a good example. But there are very few others like me, she said. An important thing at the beginning, according to her, was support from the Perm Businesswomen's Club. Not so much practical support, but above all human and psychological support.

Rethinking identity

The women of the design bureau Temp were proud of their technical education and of being part of the national task. As members of the defence-industrial complex they had a number of privileges that are now gone. Today they face the choice of coming to work without pay or standing in the rain selling goods from Cyprus. While their male colleagues leave to become entrepreneurs and businessmen this is, for many reasons, not the priority of women, although some examples exist.

Soviet women, particularly those in the defence industries, have had to rethink their identities. The choices of the new market economy presented to them are not necessarily free. Many women were, no doubt, happy to become housewives given that their husbands could afford it. Others with new careers have been trained as accountants or secretaries. Very few have become entrepreneurs, the most prioritised choice of the new Russia. Most of the women, however, are either openly, or in practice unemployed, selling goods on open markets. Some have stayed in the defence enterprises in hope of new orders. The question is, how has all this been possible, given the strong ideological element of women's emancipation in the 70-year history of the Soviet Union?

Already in 1929 Stalin declared that the emancipation of women had been achieved. The women's departments that had existed under the party were therefore discontinued and replaced by women's sections in the propaganda department of the Party Committee. As organs for control and propaganda, their task was to demonstrate that the women's movement had not been abolished by the totalitarian state.[8] Through the 70-year history of the Soviet State the ideology of the party included the working woman. It was the task of the State to take care of children in day-care centres, provide meals in restaurants and clothing produced by the textile industry.

The official ideology was not turned into reality in the way that had been expected. Although the State discontinued the production of sewing machines, as clothes would be produced by the industry, the women of the defence industries know how to sew. Daily meals were still prepared at home, although the Soviet kitchens were small. In fact, they became the place for resistance to the regime. While the kitchen for women's emancipation in the West was considered the space for repression it was the only free space for Russian women. Lissyutkina in her review of Soviet women under Perestroika concludes:

> The Russian kitchen was a front of massive resistance to the totalitarian regime and is perceived with sentimental nostalgia today. Here, for the first time in post-revolutionary history, an alternative lifestyle was formed for many Soviet people. Women, who after the beginning of Perestroika demanded the right to return to the kitchen, to the family, and to the home, were not only tired from the lack of home life and the senseless expenditure of energy in the workplace, but also feared handing

over the care of their children to the community organisation and teachers. Most importantly, they by no means perceive the kitchen, which is rarely larger than 5 m^2, as a narrow corridor cut off from the world.[9]

Perestroika did bring about an ideological change in the situation of women. Already Gorbachev in his book *Perestroika* re-evaluated the situation of women under the title 'On Women and the Family':[10]

> Today the country needs women to be even more integrated into decisions about the economy, culture and social life. It is with this in mind that all over the country councils have been established for women.

He praises the achievements of the Soviet State for equal opportunity and for the possibility women have to educate themselves, to make a career and to participate in social and political activities. But, while working for all these goals:

> We have forgotten to pay attention to the special rights of the woman and her needs to be a mother and a housewife and her irreplaceable responsibility for the education of children.

This has meant, according to him, that women with creative work have not had time to take care of their home and the family welfare. And many behavioural and moral problems in social life and production were related to the weakening of family ties. Therefore, *perestroika* has started a 'passionate' discussion about how we can give the woman 'her real predetermined role'.

Legislation to restrict women's access to the labour market has been considered in the Russian Parliament in order to protect 'family life and children's future'. Also in Perm the regional administration has called for the women to stay at home.

Engineers turn housewives

According to Lissyutkina,[11] Russian people are restoring their crumbled world-view and identity with the help of three alternative cultural-value systems. One is the communist ideology, a response to the chaos and famine of today. The second is the traditional values of pre-Revolutionary Russia, which tie together the past and the future. The third is the import of Western values such as democracy, individualism, private enterprise and private property. The women of the Russian defence enterprises have much to gain from their communist past and much to lose, both from the traditional values of pre-Revolutionary Russia and those of democracy, individualism and private property, at least as they are manifested in the Russian reality in the 1990s.

As the femininity of Soviet women is being reconstructed into Russian femininity, the identity politics of the women in the defence enterprises in Perm is built into the transformation to a market economy. Women are no longer able to see themselves as independent economic subjects, nor are they subjects of any useful mission for the country. The immobility of the older women is in contrast to the mobility of the young, who find a place in new economic structures as secretaries or just stay at home. History's most dramatic large-scale transformation of female scientific and engineering identities, hundreds of thousands of them, is taking place without any protest from the world's engineering organisations. This is taking place at the same time as the Technical Universities in the West, for example my own in Denmark, are struggling to raise the percentage of women interested in engineering and are doing everything to keep the female engineering students in the universities.

The identity politics of the Russian transformation and of the women in the defence industry is not limited to the professional sphere. After 70 years of forced participation in working life, the Russian women now face a new choice, that of becoming a housewife. For women who have worked night shifts, in dangerous laboratories or in mining communities, this choice is no doubt welcome as a symbol of freedom. Given the economic situation of the country, however, this choice only reaches those women whose husbands support them economically. The housewife has become a symbolic asset of the new Russian ('those who have made a fortune out of the economic transformation'). Even though this is only a theoretical choice, the choice may have symbolic meanings also for those Russian women for whom the economic possibility of being a housewife is out of reach.

Notes

1 These figures were presented by Tatiana Leontieva, founder of the Women in Conversion Foundation in Moscow, at the Second European Feminist Research Conference in Graz, July 1994.
2 Employment Office data from Perm in June 1994 and April 1997.
3 Douglas (1991: 287–307).
4 Ibid., p. 294.
5 Ibid., p. 296.
6 Ibid., p. 297.
7 Mary Douglas contrasts the not-for-profit home with the for-profit hotel where similar services (food, lodging) are provided.
8 Voronina (1994: 46).
9 Lissyutkina (1993: 276).
10 Gorbachev (1987: 121–2).
11 Op. cit.

Chapter 9

The Making of a Monster

What happens when you lose an enemy? When the basis for coherence in your actions, beliefs and policies suddenly disappears without very little warning? This is what happened to the West when the Soviet Union collapsed. The effects were particularly adverse for the Cold War 'partner', the US. The military-industrial complex of the US had not only to look for new enemies, but also to redefine its role towards the new 'friend'.

In this chapter, I shall look at the West as an actor in the construction of the Post Communist Russia. However, not in terms of changes in military doctrines, government politics or financial aid programmes of the EU, the US or international institutions. Rather, focus is on the conversion of military technologies and the role Western actors played in this process. The social world of Russian military technology cannot be analysed in isolation of the former enemy's reconstruction of the past. If we want to understand change in Russia, looking at it from the perspective of military technology, the former Cold War partners have to be included.

The main actors have changed. The relationship between the West and Russia is no longer only a relationship between states. Enterprises trying to form joint ventures have entered the arena, although the Departments of Defence still frame their possibilities for doing so. The media also plays a role. One thing is to look at these changes from Washington or Moscow. Another is to see it from the perspective of the formerly closed city of Perm and its defence managers and scientists. These are the managers and scientists who before 1991 had never been allowed to travel abroad, whose primary source of information was the KGB and who had been selected as part of the privileged group to fight the Cold War on the technology arena.

The ambiguous partnership

In 1994 Zbigniew Brzezinski, a former US National Security Adviser to the President, asked the appropriate question in an article titled *The Premature Partnership*: If Russia no longer is an adversary, is it already an ally, a client or merely a defeated foe?[1]

The immediate Russian answer to this question, in 1992, would have been an ally. Partnership between the superpowers was on the agenda and a strategy for partnership has also been implemented by the Clinton administration. According to the above-mentioned article, the goal of the Clinton policy was one in which containment of Soviet expansion is to be replaced by partnership with a democratic Russia. The prospect is a stable and enduring Russian democracy based on a free-market economy.

Brzezinski is more hesitant. He underlines that if not openly imperial, the current objectives of Russian policy are at the very least pseudo-imperial. While Russian policy may not be aiming explicitly at a formal imperial restoration, his thesis is that there is a strong imperial impulse that continues to motivate large segments of the state bureaucracy, especially the military, as well as the public.[2]

He proposes that the strategy of geographical pluralism with the former Soviet Union be based on the promise that Russia defines itself purely as Russia. Russia should not be an empire, but a normal state.

The Russian Foreign Minister, Andrei Kozyrev, responded to Brzezinski in his article 'The Lagging Partnership'.[3] According to him, partnership between Russia and the United States faces problems or fails altogether in some areas. This is not due to a wrong strategy, but to the lack of strategy, although there is co-operation on concrete issues. Partnership could in his view run against the interests of military-industrial groups and fractions of government bureaucracies in both countries. These forces are losing ground after the Cold War. They profit from the inertia of past confrontation and the inevitable difficulties of building a new Russian-American relationship.[4]

Kozyrev claims that the majority of Russian political forces want a strong, independent and prosperous Russia. In his view, the only policy with any chance of success is one that recognises the equal partnership between Russia and the West, and at the same time recognises Russia as a world power.[5]

'We want to be seen as partners' was the hope of the Perm defence managers I interviewed in early 1992. There seemed to be no limits to Russian openness to foreigners. Many a manager would carefully explain to me how his country first needed to know who was the enemy, then how many weapons were needed to defend 'us' and finally, who was going to make them. After this, the rest of the defence enterprises, hopefully also his, would be freed from their mobilisation obligations and could convert to civilian production. The remaining problems would then be solved by Western investments and technology. Now that Russia no longer was an enemy, the West would help rebuild its former foe as it rebuilt Germany and Japan after the Second World War and give Russia 'Marshall aid'.

The Russian defence managers were no doubt naive in their expectations. But they had been educated during 70 years during which the West saw communism and the Soviet Union as a foe. In Perm they had not listened to the Voice of America, but knew about the Marshall Plan and of the US help to its enemies after the Second World War.

Judging by the openness expressed in their willingness to convert military technology and concrete proposals for conversion, they were truly interested in finding Western partners, although methods used were primitive – and maybe naturally so given the background of the planned economy – and reflected a total lack of knowledge of Western business practices.

Some would show me proposals, mostly very technical ones, for the manufacture of glass-fibre pipes, for a production line for artificial leather or for composite-material toys. A price tag of 50 or 100 million dollars was attached to these investment proposals without any further specifications. Others would regret that they had not yet worked out any proposal for co-operation: 'We should have hundreds of proposals, but we do not.' Enterprises were preparing and translating brochures into English for the first time ever. One of the managers even gave me a brochure of their rocket launcher and asked for help with contacts in the West.

There were, no doubt, also managers in 1992, who, when faced with the shock of reduced defence orders, were not eager to convert and who were waiting for the return of old times and new state orders. These 'old generation' managers were no doubt also lobbying for increased defence orders. The general atmosphere in 1992 in Perm was for conversion and co-operation with the West. The Perm managers defined the conversion problem as one of investments and of a need for Western technology.

Partners in technology

To me as a Western researcher, who had learnt about the Russian defence enterprises' easy access to resources and about their high-tech capabilities, this, in 1992, seemed odd. Why would Russian defence enterprises need investments from the West, given their easy access to resources, their privileged status and their vertical integration? Were the Russian defence enterprises not wealthy, at least the wealthiest part of Russian industry? And why this search for technology? The scientists and designers were all working with technology, and they were proud of their achievements. During the Cold War years these defence enterprises had produced one of the world's most advanced weapon arsenals and had successfully, given the Cold War mode of thought, competed with the US in the arms race.

The answer I received to these questions was related to the structure of the enterprises and their relation to the State. The Soviet defence enterprises acquired wealth as owners of cultural facilities, day-care centres, housing neighbourhoods and the like. They had resources tied up as mobilisation capabilities including vast reserves of raw materials, space and equipment. But they had no, or very little, reserve capital in investment funds or bank accounts. They lived from hand to mouth. The state would cover all expenses, provide access to raw materials and pay for building projects and equipment imports. As defence enterprises in 1992, in spite of the lack of state orders, continued to produce what they had always produced, namely weapons, they accumulated tremendous debts.[6]

During 1992–93, defence enterprises survived either by continuing (or increasing) their civilian production, by state subsidies and credits used for salaries and/or by selling material reserves and equipment. Some were, no doubt also engaged in illegal activities and had established small businesses on the side (selling of equipment, materials, know-how). Those who could, exported weapons, but the overall export volume fell drastically from 1990.[7] Consequently, investments were, in fact needed for conversion.

While this explains the need for funds, it does not explain the focus on technology. Most of the Soviet defence enterprises had access to high-level technology, and were vertically integrated and had the best engineering brains in the country. But they did not, according to their own view, have access to mass production know-how and technological know-how that could compete with Western commercial products. As demonstrated by the Perm Auto, conversion prototypes were manually assembled, were of poor quality and bad design.

Seen in retrospect, the Russian expectation of access to Western technology was no doubt naive. Although partners, there was a lack of trust and fear of a return to communism in the West. The Russians argued at official conferences, for example at a NATO conversion conference in May 1993, for the removal of the COCOM regulations. The Cold War had come to an end, the Russian representatives at the meeting claimed. The West remained suspicious. Some saw the whole thing as a Russian plot to get access to technology. According to this view, the Russians were not serious about conversion. They wanted only to strengthen their military. Others saw the situation in Russia as too unstable to warrant technology transfer.

The paradox of the matter is that many scientists both in Moscow and in Perm underlined that the military would always get access to the most advanced Western technology. COCOM regulations prohibiting the export of advanced Western, particularly American, technology to the Soviet Union were a problem mainly for the civilian industries.

Personally, I experienced this ambiguous attitude of the West to this technology partnership during a visit to the US Department of Commerce in late 1992. My objective was to learn about the programmes that were being designed for American-Russian co-operation. The task of the unit of the department I visited was to manage programmes to create contacts with Russian enterprises, to promote co-operation and finance traineeships for Russian managers in American firms. The office had some 20 employees, most of them had the time to come and sit at a meeting with a researcher from a small European country. The office had virtually no other resources. One of the employees crystallised the situation by saying:

> We are trying to create contacts between American and Russian enterprises. Our colleagues next door, the export control people, are trying to prevent them. And they have much more resources than we do.

The joint venture adventure

Joint venture is the key concept to understand, at the concrete technology level, the nature of the social dynamics forming the Russian-Western arena for technology renegotiations after 1991. Western aid and joint ventures with Western companies were the top priority on the Russian agenda in 1992–93.[8] Not only civilian but also military enterprises would create joint ventures with Western partners for mutual advantage. The Western companies would get access to Russian markets. Russia would get technology and know-how. Russia would become integrated in the world economy, which could lead to a 'better life' in Russia.

Already in 1991, representatives of the American/Soviet investment company Battery March visited Soviet defence enterprises and reviewed a number of projects in the defence sector. A few were even financed. Delegations from Japan, the United States, Finland and other European countries visited – even distant areas such as Perm – to look at the potential of the military enterprises. A number of formal programmes for co-operation were designed. US AID sent retired business managers to help restructure defence companies around Russia. The European Bank for Reconstruction and Development had a programme for investments particularly in infrastructure, but also for the restructuring of defence enterprises. The European Commission designed the TACIS (Technical Assistance to the CIS countries) programme to provide funds for Russian transformation, also within the military industries.

Many individual enterprises, particularly multinational corporations, sent their representatives to look at investment objects in search of advanced technologies or new markets. A number of research programmes were designed by universities, peace research institutes and foundations to study the 'conversion' or 'economic transition' problem. In 1992–94 hundreds of seminars both on international and bilateral level took place discussing different aspects of these problems. These meetings were often the first confrontations between Western and Russian specialists, managers and policy-makers.

I remember especially one conference organised by the Norwegian government in Stavanger, in the spring of 1993. The government had invited all the managers and leading scientists of the secret cities, i.e. cities that not only were closed but were also wiped out from the map. They were generally referred to, not by their name, but by the name of a larger town in the vicinity, for example Cheliabinsk, and a number. The seminar would discuss the problems of these towns, the possibilities for joint ventures and other co-operative activities.

The Norwegians had invited not only possible partners from their own country, but also representatives from the US Department of Defence and Western conversion researchers like myself. The problems of these towns were explained by the mayors. There was a lack of everything, but particularly critical was the situation in hospitals. There was an urgent need for medicine and hospital supplies. The nuclear scientists presented the technological potentials of these cities and suggested topics for potential joint ventures. The US government representative proposed the St Louis[9] model as a good example for the Russians to follow.

Researchers from the US were very critical of Russian conversion prospects. The Russians present felt that they were not taken seriously and one of the managers exclaimed: maybe we will be poor, maybe our clothes will be rags, but we are proud of our achievements.

Personally, I remember sitting in the bus beside the mayor of the town Maiak, where one of the facilities for processing atomic waste was located. The town was known to be the site of several accidents and was, no doubt, one of the most dangerous places in the world. The mayor expressed great pleasure, when neighbourhood after neighbourhood passed by our window. He, like all the others, was for the first time in the West. I asked him if he was not afraid to live so close to a place like Maiak. His answer was:

> My father was the mayor of the city, I am the mayor and I expect that also one of my small children will be able to live there.

The bus tour ended up in a salmon cultivation plant at the sea with a restaurant. Here we were served in an informal atmosphere, which stimulated the Russians to make speeches and to sing. The mayors and scientists of the secret towns were good singers and also wanted the US government representative to join in. The evening ended with three of the mayors and the US government representative singing together on a Norwegian salmon farm. It was the most heartbreaking scene symbolising a unique time in search of new identities and relations.

But songs are not so easy to transform into joint commercial activities although they may be the necessary first step in creating trust. In spite of visits, delegations, programmes for aid and research projects, Western enterprises in 1992–93 were not ready to participate in joint ventures with Russian counterparts. Maybe some of the visitors and delegations were not even really interested. Some were no doubt speculators, others just curious. No doubt, many were interested also in intelligence activities given the new Russian openness.

There have been a number of studies on why the West-Russia co-operation did not succeed and why the joint venture discourse remained only post Cold War rhetoric. In their study Chapman and Wittneben[10] interviewed a number of American business leaders and concluded:

> The problem in designing effective programmes is that no one is an expert on the subject and no one knows how to do it well. Conversion is linked to whole networks of other political, military, economic, and social issues that are also difficult to

resolve. Most importantly, no government has ever attempted such a massive conversion effort as the one being contemplated in Russia.

The American managers interviewed in the study believed that they had an important role to play in assisting defence conversion in Russia, but three major obstacles prohibited American companies from taking full advantage of conversion-related business opportunities. These were (1) internal conditions in Russia, (2) US foreign economic policy barriers and (3) American business culture and attitudes.

The unstable business environment in Russia has no doubt prevented Western business leaders from all countries from engaging in defence conversion. Unclear property rights, problems with intellectual property, tax regulations etc. have made engagement in actual production difficult, if not impossible. Furthermore, business cultures in the United States and Russia are different.

'Negotiating with the Russians is like playing chess' is a point made in the report *American Ventures in Russia* (1995).[11] According to this report, Russians have a zero-sum view of negotiating. A loss for one side is a victory for the other. Americans are looking for a 'win–win' situation where both partners gain. Russians do not, according to the report, take contracts as seriously as their American counterparts do. They tend to renegotiate them, especially if they have gained more leverage. American partners view contracts as final agreements. While Americans love to do project planning, Russians tend to act and learn along the way by trial and error. The report concludes that a successful business venture depends on the early establishment of good personal relationships between the partners-to-be. These relationships must be sensitive to Russia's culture.

Enemies turn competitors in joint ventures

Although joint ventures have not played a central role in conversion, this does not mean that joint ventures have not been established at all. They exist, at least on paper. A list of joint ventures of the Perm region in 1994[12] contained 170 joint ventures. While German and American joint ventures dominated, the list also included French, Bulgarian, Hungarian, Chinese and even Maltese joint ventures, mostly within trade and distribution, very few in production. According to the Division of International relations of the Perm Region and Administration, only one production joint venture was established up to 1995, a Spanish-Russian joint venture for cable production.

While the examples of joint ventures in a distant region like Perm may not be representative enough, at Stanford University the Centre for International Security and Arms Control has studied[13] nine American high-tech companies and their activities in Russia. These companies include large defence enterprises, prime contractors, such as Boeing, Rockwell International, United Technologies Corporation/Pratt & Whitney and other smaller companies such as Science Applications International Corporation and Sun Micro Systems. The selected companies were all working in computers, aerospace or advanced materials. All had established activities in Russia.

In the cases studied, the American partner had provided the capital while the Russian contribution was technology, research and development, inventory and/or labour. In most cases the co-operative venture was not a profit centre, but a source of technology or other inputs for the American company. The result was, in fact, the reverse of what the Russians had hoped for. The flow of technology was not from the West to Russia, but the other way around. According to the Stanford report, American companies had an overwhelming preference for contractual work or licensing without ownership. In some cases, joint ventures were being negotiated as successors to the contractual relationship. A report from the workshop at which these case studies were presented concludes:

> Not withstanding this diversity, there was considerable similarity of experience in terms of the methods of doing business and the problems encountered. In some cases today's partners may be tomorrow's competitors, therefore, most companies deemed it wiser to be active participants rather than passive potential competitors. Early entry into the Russian business environment was generally considered important even if the level of investment was modest.[14]

The above reflects the US experience. Seen from Perm the situation looks different. The Perm view of 'the West' was best summarised by a professor at Perm Technical University. According to him, there were four ways, in which the West was interested in co-operating with Russia (in 1995).

The first was improving the extraction of raw materials. The West was interested in raw materials, and therefore would help improve the equipment and production facilities for raw-material exploitation.

Secondly, the West was interested in destroying competitors. This was, according to him, happening in paper production. Russian production was no longer competitive. It had equipment from the 1930s. Instead of co-operation in the modernisation of these paper factories, the West was buying pulp and thus preventing Russian competition in paper production. Thirdly, foreign companies were interested in controlling world markets and dictating the conditions for Russian competition. This was also, in his view, the case for the proposed Pratt & Whitney joint venture with the Perm producers of aircraft engines (see below). Finally, the West was interested in exporting ecologically detrimental production to Russia much in the same way it did to the Third World countries.

The magic partnership

In 1993–94, the name Pratt & Whitney became *the* solution to the conversion 'problem' in Perm. One of the largest enterprises in the city, Perm Motor Works, produces engines for aviation and aerospace. The main design bureaux of the city, Aviadvigatel', designs engines. PAKB, a design bureau, develops guidance systems and Iskra, a former science production association, now a design bureau, specialises in rocket motors and gas generators for aerospace applications. All these form a network with Perm Motor Works. Lack of state orders in 1992 had been a great problem for this local research and production cluster. And there was no demand in civilian aviation.

Already in November 1992 at a Stanford University seminar I had heard about United Technologies Corporation's (Pratt & Whitney's mother company) interest in joint ventures in Russia. A joint venture had at that time been established with the Russian's aerospace complex's flagship enterprise, Energomash, specialising, like United Technologies, in space rocket propulsion and rocket engine design. At the seminar the joint venture was described. It was a win–win situation. Russian know-how was obviously 'world level' and the Americans were truly interested. Pictures were shown in which the directors of these two companies hugged each other as a confirmation of mutual trust. United Technologies was willing to respect Russian culture was the message.

I was therefore not surprised to find in June 1994, when I re-interviewed Iurii Dudkin (see Chapter 4), that plans were underway to establish a joint venture between Perm Motor Works, the above design bureaux and the leading American producer of engines for aviation. Pratt & Whitney had teamed up with Iliushin to produce the IL-96M, a long distance plane expected to compete with the European Airbus A-340 S. The engines of Perm Motor Works PS-90A were to fly the plane, at least inside of Russia. In Perm hopes were high, and everybody, especially the involved managers stressed the importance of this step for the conversion of military engine know-how to civilian uses.

When I again came to Perm in 1997 I was told that the Russian airplane manufacturers had joined forces with McDonnell Douglas and the planes would fly with American engines. Chernomyrdin had signed the order for the foreign engines. There were a lot of bad feelings about this unpatriotic deed. Did the government not want to support Russian products? Were the Perm managers not good enough in their lobby work? The general impression among those interviewed was that the engines had not met international standards.

When visiting Perm in 1999 I was told that the engines had not met international standards *in time*. Therefore the bank involved had cut the funding. While there may also be other explanations, the planes are to fly with foreign engines and there is a general discontent with this fact. The one to blame is Chernomyrdin, i.e. the State.

Technological humiliation

According to Nezavisimaia Gazeta (20/10/92), Mikhail Malei, who at the time was the president's counsellor on conversion, would not have opposed the immediate closing of the defence enterprises in Russia if the West would have promised the Russian government 10 billion dollars a year. The military-industrial complex and its technology were for sale.

This is also one example of the technological humiliation of Russia that has been almost total. The West has refrained from technological co-operation and very little Western technology has been flowing into Russia. The direction has been the opposite. Western investments in advanced joint ventures or licensing agreements have imported Russian technology and know-how. Even American business leaders considered that US foreign policy and restrictions on technological exports were one of the main barriers to economic co-operation with Russia.

For the West, technological co-operation with Russia no doubt has represented a dilemma. On the one hand, the total technological humiliation of the military-industrial sector of Russia, which has housed most of its professional pride and national strength, represented a security risk in terms of social unrest and support for nationalist tendencies. On the other hand, support for conversion through technological aid contained risks for the West. Advanced technologies, for example, microelectronics, might support a further military build-up in Russia. Even if no further military build-up took place and Russia became a partner, it might become an economic competitor faster if access to advanced Western technologies was granted. The only incentive for Western technological co-operation with Russia seems to be either total domination of the world market, as in the case of Pratt & Whitney (aircraft engines), or an expected expansion in the Russian market (aviation).

For the Russians, who were expecting technological Marshall help from the West now that the enemy was gone, the relations to the West were a cold shower. Furthermore, the Western 'wait-and-see' attitude supported arguments in Russia that the West, namely the US, was only interested in destroying Russian military power. Many of my interviews from late 1992–93 express this concern: after the immediate euphoria and dreams of a partnership, what was actually going on? Patriotic scientists and engineers were witnessing the destruction of what had taken decades of sacrifices to build.

The concrete arenas where the Russian technological humiliation took place were seminars and particularly exhibitions. One such example was the big OECD sponsored seminar and exhibition in 1993. The objective was to promote conversion and to present to the West the most advanced results of conversion. The Russian had prepared well. The State had funded participation, and the most advanced parts of the defence complex, such as TsAGI were present. The exhibition included amphibian boats for advanced situations, completely new types of aircraft, high-strength composite materials and aerodynamic testing equipment.

The seminar, where I was also to give a talk on 'Barriers to Conversion in East and West', was opened with an introductory analysis presented by an American consultant specialising in high technology. The consultant firm, based in Washington, were now experts on the Russian market. In his speech the head investigator suggested that the Russian were like wax and advised Western companies to behave well in their contacts with their Russian counterparts. His message to the Russians present was that Russian engineers and scientists should start conversion with 'little things', rather than with ambitious high-tech projects.

Russian scientists present were provoked. They went up to the podium and, underlined that they were high-level professionals, who would not have to beg the West for either technological aid or for advice.

> You underestimate us; do not send us biscuits.[15] We will enter the world market as a high-tech nation. We will come into the market independent of what Western partners think. We don't want to start with simple, little things. [The leader of an aviation firm]

The conference was concluded by Mr Salo, a representative of the Russian government:

> We feel offended. We are not soft wax. The West can come with all their advice, but profit and making money are not the only thing. We are proud to be professionals. We want to demonstrate something which the whole of our society will be proud of.

The exhibition was also a disappointment. The Russian firms had expected to meet Western counterparts and to proceed with concrete negotiations. However, the only people who came to the exhibition were Western defence ministry, civil servants and peace activists. They were not the types of clients the Russian exhibitors had hoped for. The Western participants, including myself, tried to explain the situation. Western commercial firms were not organised in terms of 'conversion'. Each company would have to find its own exhibition in its own specific field. Collective Russian demonstrations of the conversion potential was – at the time – mostly of interest to defence analysts and researchers. However, the exhibition results were reflected in the desperate cry of a Russian manager:

> I cannot understand it. I have a saw that can saw almost anything. And I want to sell this saw, but who comes to the exhibition? Only defence people and journalists. I do not need investments, I have products to sell. I want you to buy our products. Please come and buy my products. I have received the conversion credits for Mr Salo and Mr Telnov.[16] I have no contact with the Ministry of Defence. Please come and see my products.

Distorted message

On Friday, 21 January 1992, I could have made the world news. The
international press was knocking at my door at the Danish Technical
University and the telephone did not stop ringing. The story was as
follows: on my way from the 'Conversion and the Environment'
conference in Perm in November 1991 I had stopped in Moscow to
visit the Centre for Military Economy and Conversion. When I asked
them about the flow of Russian scientists from the military sector to
other countries, one of the researchers mentioned that about 500 people
had left the military-industrial complex to go abroad.

In January 1992 there was a NATO NACC Conference in
Copenhagen. My colleague Anders and I attended this conference.
Anders had in passing mentioned to a Danish journalist present that we
had some figures on how many people had left the defence industry to
go abroad. Early next morning the Danish Radio was on the phone and
wanted an interview. I commented on the problem of unpaid salaries in
the military industry and the fact that research conditions were
deteriorating. Some people were moving to the West; but in general,
Russian scientists wanted to stay where they were, in Russia. The 500
were by no means all nuclear scientists, but rather the total number of
defence industry employees who had moved to the West, not
necessarily permanently.

The Danish Radio presented this interview as the main topic in every
newscast during the day. The Prime Minister was asked to comment.
Pushed into a corner he declared that the Russians would have to bring
this flow of people under control. Denmark would require this as a
precondition for the planned EU aid to Russia. Later that day he had to
withdraw his statement. Of course, Russia needed help.

My research office at the Technical University of Denmark was
flooded by telephone calls from journalists from all over the world. All
wanted to hear the figures directly from me. I tried to explain carefully
that this was by no means only nuclear scientists and that it was a figure
I had received during an interview about conversion. I was able to put
off most of the press, but I had to consent to an interview on Danish
TV. That evening I was the main headline in the TV-news, followed
directly by a Danish intelligence officer's comment on what they were
doing to prevent the emigration of Russian scientists.

I was puzzled. The media was deliberately presenting a distorted
view. From the way the news was presented that day, a listener could
not but get the impression that masses of Soviet bomb-makers were on
their way to hostile countries. I do not doubt that some may have left

and many others may have had the offer. But the reporters were only interested in the numbers. How many? And to get a confirmation that countries hostile to the West were involved. There was no interest in the context, such as lack of pay, deteriorating research conditions and a very insecure future for those employed in the military research complex.

Maybe a more relevant question would have been why were so many staying? Why do researchers stay, when they for the first time in their life had a chance to travel abroad? Why do they stay, when they are not paid? In 1991–92 some 5,000 scientists (in all) and by 1994 some 280,000 scientists had left to work more or less permanently abroad.[17] Why did the rest, about 700,000 decide to stay?

The incident alerted me to the picture the media were giving about Russia. There was a need to report on Russia. Fear sold well. Reports dealt not only with nuclear scientists moving to countries like Libya, but also with the millions of unemployed, the freezing cold winters and Zhirinovskii. There was a period when anything Zhirinovskii said or did was reported in the Western media, totally out of proportion, if you compare with the attention the same news received in Russia. He became, in a way, a Western construction.

Vibeke Sperling is one of the most experienced journalists in Denmark when it comes to the past conditions in the Soviet Union and those of present-day Russia. She was, since the collapse of the Soviet Union, the Danish Radio's voice in Moscow (until 1997). When asked about the stories journalists do *not* write, she wrote in an article:

> One would wish there would be space for a tradition for in the hard core of news for more background horizon and that the journalist set more of the agenda herself. The question is how do you, when chasing news, give more space for nuances and conclusions that do not fall into one or the other fallacies. As a news journalist, one is locked into a specific way of working with news, a way that does not tell the whole story. The accidents I report do take place, but Russian reality is not the sum of these accidents.[18]

Recreating otherness

As the communist Soviet 'other' disappeared there was in the West an obvious need to construct a Russian 'other'. The collapse of the military system, mafia, unstable business environment and a chaotic political life all support this Russian otherness. Bad news is good news and a lot of people in Russia today are hungry. But as Vibeke Sperling points out, life is more than the sum of all the accidents. All the problems are there, but everyday life does go on. People want to lead normal lives and one of the most used Russian sayings is '*vse normal'no*', everything is 'normal'. This is the Russian answer to the simple question, how are you?

While I shall discuss the political consequences of Russian 'otherness' in the final chapter my point here is that the West has been an active partner in constructing Russia as a monster. Support for economic reforms and crash programmes for achieving macro-economic change have produced consequences for Russian everyday life, maybe unintended, that will be with us for a long time to come.

The Western arena for the negotiations of Russian otherness has consisted of the delegations that have visited Russia, the seminars/exhibitions that have taken place, the media reporting, the concrete proposals for partnerships with enterprises, the US Department of Commerce's export promotion and control activities as well as of international institutions, such as the International Monetary Fund.

This unique encounter between two worlds might have produced not only a monster, but also understanding and mutual reflection on the future of this planet. Instead, it has produced a totally humiliated former empire that no doubt will work for the restoration of its dignity in ways we in the West are unable to understand and even less to participate in. Iver Neumann, who has studied the East in European identity formation concludes in his book *Uses of the Other*[19] how Russia has constantly been the 'European other' although this no longer manifests in the danger of communism. The 'barbaric' has replaced the image of a communist enemy:

> The representations of Europe have been sundry and various as have representations of Russia, but what one has here is not a case of simple leaving out. No matter which social practices a period has foregrounded, be they religious, bodily, intellectual, social, military, political, economic, or otherwise, Russia has consistently been seen as an irregularity.

Notes

1 Brzezinski (1994).
2 Ibid., p. 76.
3 A. Kozyrev (1994: 59–71).
4 Ibid., p. 60.
5 Ibid., p. 61.
6 According to Mikhail Malei, the military industry's debt was 3 trillion rubles by mid 1992 due to the fact that industries had produced without orders, sent their products to their former clients and written the cost down as debt. Later, in 1994, debts occur because the Ministry of Defence fails to make on-time payments to defence companies. According to Rouvez, 1995, the debt of the Ministry of Defence to the companies has reached 2.4 trillion rubles with another 700 billion rubles in unpaid advances.
7 The Russian expectations for military exports as means to fund conversion never materialised. By 1991, the Soviet Union had exported about four billion USD worth of arms, a decline from the 9.7 billion the year before (SIPRI Yearbook, 1992). In 1992, according to the Chairman of the Russian Committee for Defence Industries, Victor Glukhikh, arms exports were also worth four billion USD (SIPRI Yearbook 1993). The decline in Soviet, and then Russian, arms exports can be attributed to several factors. From an all-time high of 23 billion USD in 1989 (SIPRI Yearbook 1993), arms exports in Russia were down to the magnitude of 3–4 billion USD. This was due to factors such as the prolonged economic crisis, the fact that Soviet allies used to receive weapons free of charge or at nominal prices, and the collapse of the Warsaw Pact. According to BICC (1997: 65) arms exports in 1997 amounted to USD 2.3 billion. Arms exports have been gradually rising and a post-Soviet record of 4.4 billion USD woth of esports is expected for 2001. (http://www.cast.ru/english/publish/2001/nov-dec/preliminary.html)
8 Technical aid is provided for defence conversion through the European Union's Tacis programme (particularly for industrial restructuring, Rouvez, 1995), NATO and OECD (1994). The US has a programme Nunn-Lugar for weapons destruction and defence industry conversion (900 million USD in 1992–95, Conversion, 1995) to the former CIS. Direct Western involvement in the Russian military sector has been limited. By late 1992 there were 180 joint ventures, of which about 50 were in the Russian aircraft industry (Anthony, 1994: 94). The EBRD, which was expected to fund conversion, has not done so and has a policy of concentrating investment mainly in the private sector (Mesjasz, 1994).
9 This model has in detail been discussed in Cronberg *et al.* (1995).
10 Chapman and Wittneben (1992: iii).
11 Baev *et al.* (1995: 5).

12 Passport to the Perm Region, Perm (1994).

13 See Bernstein (1997).

14 Ibid., p. 19.

15 At this time the West was sending humanitarian aid to Russia under intense media coverage.

16 Mr Salo and Mr Telnov were high-level representatives of the Ministry of Economy at the seminar.

17 Estimates of how many Russian specialists have left the country differ. According to data presented at the NATO Advanced Research seminar on Defence Conversion Strategies in Pitlochry, Scotland, in July 1995, 13,000 researchers (scientists with advanced education from institutes and enterprises) from the Ural area were working in the United States, Canada and Europe. During 1991–92, some 5,000 scientists left more or less permanently to work abroad and at this time the total number of those staying abroad for longer periods of time was estimated to be about 220,000. (Formin *et al.*, 1993; Kügel, 1993, both cited in Kaukonen, 1994). According to the OECD study of science, technology and innovation policies from 1994, some 280,000 people were estimated to have left the R&D institutions of the former Soviet Union. However, according to OECD, R&D staffs are still considered to be oversized and will continue to drop from 1 million to the level of 300,000 scientists and engineers, which is only 30 % of the original number.

18 The Danish magazine *Månedsbladet*, no. 110, January 1995.

19 Neumann (1999:110).

Chapter 10

Renegotiating 'Defence' Technologies

The Cold War in the US ended with a technological handshake. This handshake was also on the logo of the Technology Reinvestment Project, TRP, of the Department of Defence.[1] It symbolised the future co-operation between the military and civilian sectors and technologies, which were to be developed with both military and civilian applications. In the handshake, military security (an officer's hand) meets economic security (a businessman's hand) in a future where military technology is no longer isolated. The discourse is about dual-use.

What is this handshake about? In the US since the beginning of the 1990s there have been many interpretations. One possible interpretation is that it is a new way of legitimating expenditure in military technology. Military technology was supposed to pay off in spin-offs. A dollar spent on military technology would give advances to commercial technology. Now that this paradigm is no longer valued,[2] a new concept has to be invented. The dual-use paradigm is attractive. Research money will be spent on basic research where innovations and applications for both the military and the civilian field are foreseen. Examples include new materials, sensors or advanced instruments. The US dual-use programme has already produced a number of catalogues and examples of potential dual-use technologies.[3]

A second explanation, and a more plausible one, is that the dual-use concept will make it easier for the military to access advanced commercial technologies. This has been a problem in the United States for a long time, as commercial technology, particularly electronics, has become more and more advanced, while the military's computers – although this may be difficult to believe – have been lagging behind. The new dual-use concept is simply about more effective defence technology, although access to commercial technologies may also raise problems, particularly, if they are of foreign origin. How to replace parts in wartime?

A third interpretation concerns industrial policy. State expenditure on research and development for the military has been the way the US government created a national technology base. In a country where industrial policy and state intervention in the affairs of commercial companies are not accepted, military technology has been a way to go around this sensitive theme. Military research and development has constituted the industrial policy of the US, the very nature of the spin-off paradigm bears witness to this. The dual-use handshake is simply a new way of defining industrial policy. It is legitimate for the government to spend money on R&D, as this will also have military implications.

Finally, there is a social constructivist interpretation. After the Cold War, the black box of military technology has been opened, and technology is being renegotiated. Commercial and military actors form new networks and shake hands. They agree on new forms for research activities. They become partners. The government saves money, the military becomes more efficient and the commercial sector gets access to more R&D.

Although the dual-use discourse was at the time seen as a way to cross the border between the military and the business environments a number of warnings have been issued.[4] These views stress that there are both conflicting goals and technological divergence in military and civilian R&D. Commercial conditions for use are more predictable while military products have to be designed for a range of conditions. Military strength and international competitiveness are not necessarily compatible.

Despite this criticism, the 'dual-use' discourse has dominated technology policy debate in the US in the 1990s and has enrolled most of the actors. More traditional views on military production and military R&D are pushed aside, as in this comment:

> Should defence prove unable to work with the commercial sector, it would be forced to retreat into a specialised ghetto, with the military technology focused on specialised requirements pursued by a few private firms or by dedicated government arsenals. With little access to commercial technologies, components and subsystems, costs would rise and capabilities shrink. In the extreme, this scenario ends in collapse – a debilitated and isolated enclave.[5]

A similar dual-use handshake would never be able to symbolise the technological future of Russia, for the simple reason that there is no hand to shake. There were no civilian technologies which were more advanced than the military; in fact, there was hardly any high-tech civilian technology to speak of. Although much of the dual-use rhetoric is also present in the Russian discourse on new technology policies the preconditions for dual-use are very different.[6] Therefore, the negotiations concerning the future technological base for Russia are much more complicated than the 'after-the-Cold-War dual-use consensus' of the United States. Let us look at one example, pulsed power.

The case of pulsed power

Pulsed power is the process of transforming mechanical, electrical or other types of energy into electromagnetic energy. It is a question of storing this energy, compressing it in time and delivering it in short electromagnetic pulses. The pulses thus produced may be used in weapons programmes to investigate the interaction between targets and directed energy flows. The technology can be used in testing military hardware and electronics in conditions simulating nuclear explosions. It can contribute to underground nuclear tests, substituting for regular full-scale testing of weapons.

In short, pulsed power provides extremely high pulsed pressure and temperature as well as high intensity of the electromagnetic pulse, x-rays and neutron fluxes, which in certain aspects simulate the conditions in atomic explosions.[7] This is one of the technologies where the Soviet Union had a leading edge.

A number of research institutes all around the country have worked with pulsed power. Of the Soviet studies conducted with pulsed power, 70% were funded by the Military-Industrial Commission and the Soviet Academy of Sciences. By 1991 the Academy of Science had budgeted an estimated $25 million on pulsed power programmes, while the Military-Industrial Commission had funded $120 million worth of research.[8] The institutes working with pulsed power include the Kurchatov Institute of Atomic Energy in Moscow as well as institutes in secret cities, such as the Institute of Experimental Physics in Arzamaz 16.

Vitalii Bystritskii from the Institute of Electro-Physics in Tomsk has studied the possibilities of converting pulsed power to civilian applications. I met him at a NATO Conference on Defence Conversion Strategies in 1995, at a time when he had already established contacts with the University of California and was building a link between American and Russian science.

According to Bystritskii, the possibilities for civilian application of pulsed power were many, such as photolithography, laser welding or epoxy-resin curing. It could be used in the sterilisation of medical instruments or in cleaning slush water. He had studied how the pulsed power institutes were coping with their problems in conversion and what was the level of the international assistance to research and development in pulsed power. His conclusion from these studies was:

> Unfortunately, large-scale technological programmes require high level of funding. This necessarily includes state funding, which will not be forthcoming in the near future. This is why big-scale pulsed power applications are still more likely to be found in new directions within Military-Industrial Commission and related R&D establishments. Considering the existing conditions, it is unlikely that large numbers of commercial spin-offs will soon be formed or that the commercial will be a large part of the near future of pulsed power research in Russia.[9]

The future of pulsed power conversion would ultimately depend on the future market for high-tech products. Some of the institutes, for example the High-Current Electronic Institute in Tomsk, had established co-operatives for commercial activities. They are in logging and trade with the Japanese, in fabrication of new products for plasma coating of electronics and metal parts. In the first case, the co-operative traded local timber for computers from Japan. In the second, the co-operative tried to find markets inside the region. The advanced research institute in this field has formed spin-off co-operatives, which by now are commercial shareholding companies. They are not working with pulsed power.

Contacts have also been formed between the Russian pulsed-power facilities and national US laboratories such as the pulsed power division of Sandia and the technology division of Los Alamos. The Department of Defence has had a Nunn-Lugar programme funding Russian scientists, as has the International Science and Technology Centre in Moscow, which is funded by US, Japan and European Community funds. The NATO Science Programme and co-operation partners have provided a platform for collaboration between Russian pulsed-power centres and corresponding institutes in Germany and France.

At the NATO conference Vitalii Bystritskii summarised his findings: If pulsed power finds something the society needs, then there will be funding.

The technological imperative

There is a lot of boundary work to do. Maybe pulsed power will never cross the line and will always remain in the military sphere. But it makes visible some of the problems facing Russian science. Although state centres have been established for the best research facilities, and some additional research funding has been forthcoming for the most advanced institutes, Russian science during the past ten years has been in a state of flux. The 'scientific-technological revolution', the key to the orthodox-Marxist understanding of social change, has collapsed dramatically leaving hundreds of thousands of scientists without either faith or monthly pay. Some have found work as taxi drivers, others have tried to find a job on the side selling their knowledge to private interests or even attempted to find jobs in the West. Young people were no longer attracted by the prospect of working for science, but rather chose to become economists or lawyers.

The rhetoric of Russian conversion is about how to safeguard the high-tech capabilities of the defence industries. If conversion is to take place, this should be a high-tech to high-tech conversion, i.e. advanced technologies from the military sector are to be transformed to civilian uses, preferably on an equal technological level. This national goal is reflected in the national conversion programmes. The regional plans for defence conversion restate the goals of safeguarding the technology base of the region.

A high-tech to high-tech conversion is not unproblematic in the Russian context. I have in Chapter 3 discussed the resource divide, which separates the military and the civilian sectors and technologies. The technology gap due to this resource divide creates an effective barrier to conversion on a high-tech to high-tech level. Engineers, scientists and managers are aware of this gap and try to bridge it in their conversion proposals. Technical specifications are developed that raise the technological level of the civilian production for example, through advanced materials or new instrumentation. However, the civilian enterprises are not willing or able to pay, or else they prefer to buy foreign products. So, for example in 1994, the city of Perm was buying foreign-made plastic pipes from Italy, even though one of its converting enterprises was producing similar pipes. It is not easy to cross boundaries when foreign products are both better and cheaper. Boundary objects do not result automatically from the high-technology base of the military. Boundary crossings became complex processes and not just a question of good intentions and defined goals.

Consequently, the dual-use discourse has very little meaning in the Russian context. Time and again during the 1990s the Russian government has launched federal programmes for the development of the national technological base. Following the US example, lists of critical technologies have been drafted. High-technology projects are to be stimulated in cases that both enhance military security and facilitate commercial economic growth. So for example in the beginning of the 1990s the government launched a programme identifying 14 priority areas for technology development for the period 1995–2005. Due to lack of funding these programmes, however, remain good intentions.

At the end of the 1990s, with at least a preliminary result available, we can conclude that although the Russian military-civilian technology divide based on resources has collapsed, very few boundary crossings have taken place. As indicated in previous chapters there are areas where joint ventures have been established with foreign companies, often to exploit Russian technology. There are also examples even in Perm where there has been domestic demand for defence technology. One of these is the Gasprom initiated commercial development of gas-pumping stations from technologies developed for jet engines. But there seems to be only one broader avenue where Russian defence technologies may have a leading edge, namely the commercialisation of space.

Commercialisation of space

In September 1997, the US space shuttle Atlantis had just docked successfully with Station Mir, the 11-year-old Russian space station. The shuttle brought a crew who would spend four months on the station trying to repair the problems besetting it. Problems such as a series of fires, a collision, and computer failures had troubled the Russian-American crew for months. One of the American scientists commented upon arrival that the Mir mission was 'like a crystal ball, looking into a future eight, ten, twelve years into the life of our next space station'.[10]

Commercialisation of space may be seen as the only chance that could save Russian high-tech science. The Cold War aerospace technologies cannot easily be transferred into civilian products as the pulsed power example demonstrates so well. There are very few needs for such advanced solutions, and if the needs do exist, the technology is too expensive. Only in space would there seem to be commercial possibilities, as performance is important and money is not the issue.

However, space exploration is a risky business; and if scientists, as in Russia, have to work for months without pay, it may be hard to keep up the motivation.

Russia is trying to preserve a full-scale programme of space exploration. Although it may reflect nostalgia from the old days, it is still the pride of the country. US–Russian co-operation in space is taking place; and the Russian engines and vehicles are presumably simpler, more reliable and cheaper than their Western counterparts. Many of the American companies have exploited Russian technology, particularly liquid-fuel-rocket engines. Cost-effective vehicles are using Russian parts or Russian design; and for example, Aerojet of Sacramento, California is marketing a Russian rocket engine NK-33.[11]

The following is an extract from a *Herald Tribune* article under the title, 'The Russians are Winning in Space':[12]

> The Russians lost the Cold War, but they are starting to win the international race to fire hundreds of new satellites and spacecraft into the heavens, challenging Western rocket scientists and companies for launching jobs worth billions of dollars.
>
> The rise of Russia as a commercial space power is based on engines and vehicles that are simple, reliable, and cheap yet often fly circles around their Western counterparts. Eager for an edge, many American companies are adopting the foreign gear and forming East–West alliances meant to exploit tons of thundering Russian metal.
>
> 'They put more into it,' Charles Vick, an expert on the Russian space program at the Federation of American Scientists, a private group in Washington, said of the Russians. 'They made so many more varieties.'

The article goes on to describe how Moscow perfected possibly ten times as many kinds of liquid fuel rocket engines as Washington did. As cost effectiveness is also entering into the space race, Russian designs have shown a competitive edge. According to the *Herald Tribune* article reverse engineering is taking place this time in opposite direction:

> Jan Monk, chief engineer for advanced transportation at the Marshall Space Flight Center of the National Aeronautics and

Space Administration, has repeatedly travelled overseas to inspect the Russian gear. In an interview, he noted how the Russians had mastered the stratagem of routing kerosene fuel around hot rocket nozzles to cool them, improving efficiency.
'We just never thought of that,' Mr. Monk said, clearly impressed. 'It was outside our way of thinking.'

A similar example is the co-operation between the leading Russian design and manufacturing company for space rocket propulsion Energomash and United Technologies/Pratt & Whitney in the US. The US company markets Russian products, such as the liquid propelled engine RD-180 both for commercial customers and the US Airforce. Lockheed Martin is expected to buy at least one hundred RD-180 engines at a total cost of one billion USD. This joint venture is based in Florida with Pratt & Whitney's Florida facilities working as subcontractors. The companies equally share equity and the board of directors. The largest customer, Lockheed Martin, has a non-voting seat on the board.[13]

Given the legacy of the first Sputnik in orbit in 1957 and the first man in space in 1961 the commercialisation of space would seem to be an ideal task for the former military-industrial complex of the Soviet Union.

But can a country live or even survive on the commercialisation of space? Costly space programmes provide very little welfare, even though a few more scientists may survive. Soviet liquid fuel engines may be better than the Western solid counterparts, but how many of them are to be produced and sold a year? And is it feasible in a country where teachers do not get their salaries, where the army lives in tents and where the retired are starving to support a costly high-tech venture, which is not failure-free, as has been shown by problems of the Station Mir.

On the other hand, Mir has been in space for eleven years. The United States has bought time on MIR and scientists have no doubt learnt a great deal about the physiological effects of weightlessness, not to mention knowledge about changes in body fluids, bones and the heart. Plants like wheat can be cultivated over successive generations in space; and the problems with computers, power or fires have been solved. The *Herald Tribune* editorial that urges 'do not laugh at Mir' may have a point.[14]

New dangers, new defences

Military technologies are about 'defence'. Dual-use technologies are about commercial technologies entering into the sphere of defence. In the US this happens through allowing commercial specifications to be used in the military and by giving the military access to advanced commercial technologies. Is there also in Russia a penetration of commercial and civilian technologies into the sphere of the military?

After the Cold War, new borders and threats are being constructed requiring new kinds of defences and consequently new kinds of defence technologies. Defence against most attacks or crisis management will not be carried out by the weapon systems of the arms race.

Campbell, in his book *Writing Security*, argues that the Cold War was not primarily about anti-communism as otherness, nor about the Soviet Union as a military threat. Rather it was about the difference between the civilian and the barbaric, i.e. those with undesirable qualities. According to him:

> The international should be approached as an arena of practice in which some subjects emerge with the status of actors, who are sustained by a variety of practices that establish the boundaries of legitimate meaning and naturalise a particular order.[15]

According to Mary Douglas,[16] danger is always present at the border. It may involve threats at external boundaries or a violation of internal boundaries. It might be located in the margins of the boundary or it might arise from contradictions within. According to her, where there are no borders there would be no danger. Danger is a part of all our relationships with the world. How do we orient ourselves to danger, particularly at a historical juncture in which many novel dangers seem to abound? Can we do more than simply extend the old register of security to cover the new domains?[17]

To understand the new construction of 'defence' technologies I would like to focus on a few of the micro level histories about new securities and insecurities in Russia. Risk and insurance are also an issue in the Russian security environment. But they no longer exist only at the State borders. They are no longer part of the need to defend the country from forces beyond the sea. They lie in the life on the streets and constitute the enemy within.

The official Russian discourse about security may be about the expansion of NATO, about Salt Treaties and about destruction of existing weapons. There may be frustration among nuclear scientists and defence-industry managers over the fact that the Americans won the Cold War and that they have now destroyed the Russian military power and weapon industries. But the security concerns of individuals, also those participating in the social world of military technology, are now different. Danger is present at new borders close to one's body, the home. If the enemy from within is the threat, from which you need protection, protection involves new technologies, new products, new solutions. The emergence of a new security environment is partly built on the foundations of the old one, military technologies are negotiated into these new defences. At the same time civilian technologies and products become defence components. Protection is no longer a task for the State but one for the individual or the family. Security is being privatised.

Doors and frames

'I hate living in a metal box', said Ksenia. We were sitting in a restaurant in Kiel, in 1995, summarising our impressions of a conference on conversion in the Baltic Sea region. Ksenia is a specialist on Russian conversion. Formerly employed by the Russian Academy of Sciences, IMEMO Institute, as a military economist, she is extremely knowledgeable about the Russian military industry. She is working as a consultant mediating between Western businessmen and consultants who come to Russia to give advice on conversion and Russian enterprise managers, economists and engineers. She is in the middle of the hotchpotch between Western advice and Russian reality.

Having steadfastly resisted all offers by the EU and the OECD to move to the West, she is still living in Moscow. She had recently been robbed, late one evening on her way home from work. The experience had left scars, and her family has installed a metal door to protect the home and the family.

Is it the metal that makes you feel safe? [I asked her.]

No, it is not the metal. It is the frames. You know how in the old Soviet doors the frames were not really fastened to the wall. Anybody could kick them in. Today, when you install a metal door, the frames are also changed and they are really fastened in the wall.

So anybody could come in through the old door?

Yes, but nobody did. It was not necessary to protect yourself in
the house. But now it is, it is necessary. And it makes me feel
that in am living in a metal box.

Today the production of metal doors is a lucrative business. Russians
who can afford it, have replaced their old padded doors with frames that
were not properly fastened to the wall by a metal door with strong
frames well bolted into the wall. In fact, you can tell the difference
between the rich and the poor by the material of their door. Especially
elderly people and elderly women in particular are afraid, and many of
them cannot afford metal doors.

Perm in the western Urals is far from Moscow. But also here metal
doors and frames have replaced plastic-coated, padded-frame
constructions. Criminality has increased gradually. In November 1991
there were no problems for a foreigner like myself walking on the street
or living in a Perm hotel. In 1992 I had no problems taking the bus
alone from the city to Perm Technical University. Since 1993 the
situation has changed. From then on I have always been accompanied
by my hosts, taken by the hand from one interview to another. The
house of my hosts, a home close to Perm Technical University,
beautifully located on the outskirts of the university facing the forest on
the other side, has become more and more barred. Window bars
appeared first on the windows of the first floor, then also on the second
floor. In January 1995, the balcony of my room had been barred in.
Ella, the mother of the house, was, like Ksenia, irritated by having to
live behind bars and locks, defending her home.

During the Cold War it was the military enterprises of Perm that had
barred windows and barbed-wire fences surrounding them. Today it is
the private homes that are being fenced in protecting us on the inside
from those on the outside. A new image of the enemy is not only
emerging globally, but also within Russia. The enemy is no longer on
the other side of the borders of the nation. It is inside, attacking the
boundaries of the family home. A new kind of home is being fenced in,
that of the nuclear family, rather than the nation and the enterprise.
Danger is no longer present at the State borders but at the front door.
Doors are being reconstructed so that the frames are well bolted and
prohibit the foe from entering. Risk is present. A metal door is an
insurance policy.

Kirassa enterprise

The family home is protected by metal doors. The body is also being threatened. During the Soviet period the streets were calm and quiet. This is a thing of the past. Armed hold-ups occur, people are robbed on the streets, and businessmen and bankers are being shot in the street. If small businesses do not pay protection to the mafia, their directors are in danger and their facilities may be bombed or burnt. A new kind of risk environment has emerged, focused on the body.

In 1995 I asked the Perm Regional Administration about the most successful small business in the region. I wanted not only to visit the large defence companies with their distressing stories about failures in conversion but also to see some successful examples of the emerging small enterprises, if possible, with roots in the military enterprises. At the time, the most successful small enterprise in the Perm area was Kirassa, a small private joint-stock company producing bulletproof vests.

In February 1995, I received permission to visit Kirassa and to talk to its director about their business development and the secret of its success. My guide from the regional administration took me to a housing area, which looked distressed in the February morning with snow, gravel and poorly maintained streets. We parked the car, walked over to the entrance to the apartment house and entered. Inside, the whole staircase had been reconstructed into small offices, among them the offices of Kirassa. On the third floor, I met with the director in a two-room apartment. He was busy but had consented to an interview. The first thing he showed me was a new brochure in English about Kirassa's products.

The brochure proudly displayed the armoured protection jackets, in all colours and sizes. Some of the jackets would provide protection only against cold steel and stabbing weapons, others also against bullets of specified calibre and even against fragments of these bullets. A colourful special version provided protection for the neck against sliding stabs. Modifications were available for users such as the police, detective agents, businessmen and escorts. A further option was a secret-wear modification, and a light version to be worn under normal clothing.

After studying the brochure, my first question to the director was about the market. Who needed Kirassa's products? According to the director, bulletproof vests were in demand by the armed forces, by the Ministry of Interior and by private persons. Of a total of 1.5 million bulletproof vests produced in Russia in 1995, 100,000 were produced by Kirassa in Perm. Of these, 90% went to government clients, the army or troops and the Ministry of the Interior. The rest were bought by private customers such as businessmen, their escorts and the like. In reality the private market was bound to be much larger. It was only since 1992 that private persons have been able to buy bulletproof vests. Until 1992, they were considered to be weapons. The sale of weapons to private individuals, the director emphasised, was still prohibited in Russia.

The director then told the story of how the idea was born. He used to work at the Ural Branch of the Composite Materials Research Institute in Perm. He and some of his colleagues decided, already during the late Gorbachev years, to use their knowledge of materials in order to earn some money. In the institute, they had worked under the system of *khozraschet*.[18] In short, this meant that they had not received budget money from the company, but had created their own activities within the framework of the Composite Materials Research Institute. He himself had spent a lot of time travelling, creating networks and making contacts with other companies. Under *khozraschet* it was possible to create some autonomy within the enterprise, at least for the pool of money the ministry had allowed to be used for the so-called 'performance-oriented activities'. Not all contracts went through the ministries, and there was some economic space for direct activities between enterprises, a space providing for a socialist 'market' and a 'profit'.

Around 1989 he and his colleagues wanted to start a small firm in order to use their experience of composite materials for the creation of better bulletproof vests than those produced by the military industry. The Composite Materials Research Institute did not like the idea of creating a small enterprise within the Institute, at least not at that time. The director of Kirassa was visibly critical of his experiences within the Institute:

> All its lifetime the Institute has had the task of creating expensive products and new productions. This was what we could do, we could create productions. But we could not trade. This was not seen as having perspectives. What we knew how to do was to produce.

Due to the lack of co-operation with the mother institute, the group decided to establish its own firm in 1990. At this time a so-called *maloe*

predpriiatie (a special legal form for a small business) was established
which in 1991 was turned into a joint-stock company, Kirassa. Already
in 1992 there were State orders for bulletproof vests. The idea was to
start development of other new products, to test the ideas through
feasibility studies, prototype production and market analysis. Today the
group consists of seven different production companies, one of which is
producing bulletproof vests. Kirassa is centrally placed in terms of state
orders and has good relations to the new state bureaucracy. According
to the director, the company has been close to its customers, working
closely to define both demand and product quality.

To my question about whether the director has been able to use some
of his knowledge and experience from the materials research institute
and the defence industry, he willingly admitted that he had. Knowledge
of composite materials and materials in general has been crucial for the
success of Kirassa's products. He worked 20 years in the defence
industry and was very familiar with quality control, due to contract
research and development activities with outside contractors. Most of
his working life he had been travelling. His friends and colleagues
around the country have created the network necessary for Kirassa's
success.

Furthermore, as former employees of the military enterprises, the
group was able to rent production facilities and equipment more easily
from their old enterprise or its partners than outsiders could. This made
it possible to begin production without large-scale investments. In fact,
in 1990 Kirassa started with a starting capital of only 20,000 roubles.
But, the director emphasises that the products are new. The institute has
no intellectual property rights to them, in spite of the useful background
knowledge and contacts gained there.

'What about competition?' I asked the director, as we were ready to
leave. Although there are 20 firms, also one large state firm, producing
bulletproof vests, competition is not the problem, he answers. The
market is expanding rapidly and Kirassa has good contacts right up to
the Ministry of Defence. Although a successful company, Kirassa had
no problems with the mafia. This is, the director underlines, due to
Kirassa's contacts with the Ministries of Defence and Interior.

The defence of the body

Metal doors and bulletproof vests are two products symbolising the
new technologies of defence. These provide a boundary to danger and
protect against threats to the body. The boundary zone of danger is
getting closer. State borders are being replaced, and the disease is

beginning to attack the body. Visual surveillance of the person ringing the door-bell has replaced – or at least complemented – satellite surveillance of the enemy. The foreign is no longer outside the State borders. The 'foreign' is within.

Is it a question of civilisation versus the barbaric, of the ordinary citizen against the mafia, the criminals and perhaps even a corrupt police force? Or is the difference between those who are becoming poor and those who are getting rich, those to be protected and those who represent a threat? The new boundary-producing political practices create new kinds of differences, which cut across previous lines of solidarity and create new kinds of alliances.

The new object of attack is the body. The boundary between NATO and the Warsaw Pact is no longer producing the difference between *us* and *them*. If meaning and identity are, as defined by Campbell, always the consequence of a

> relationship between the self and the other which emerges through the imposition of an interpretation, rather than being a product of uncovering an exclusive domain with its own pre-established identity.

What kind of interpretation is needed to understand this change? If foreign policy produces boundaries between states, what kind of policies produce boundaries within a state? Are we here dealing with a globalisation of contingency with increasing tendencies towards ambiguity and indetermination creating insecure subjects and ultimately insecure bodies? Is the body the ultimate border where post-Cold War protection against the foreign is to be built up?

The body and the State have often been interrelated. The State has been represented by a body where the prince occupies the place of the head, the Senate the place of the heart and the officials and soldiers the hands.[19] This understanding of the State as a body reflects a hierarchy, an understanding of the body as a hierarchical relationship between those determining (the prince) and those being determined (the soldiers). The hierarchical understanding of the body (and perhaps also the State?) has given way to a more organic understanding represented, for example, by Donna Haraway.[20] She uses the term 'cyborg' to denote the combination of the technological and the organic, the body. It is a military metaphor, a cybernetic organism, where the technological becomes so intertwined with the human that separation no longer is possible. Identities are constructed with technology and everyone is built into this process.

The new disorder is not created merely by the end of the Cold War, the collapse of its boundaries, but rather by the transformation to a new economic system, by the insecurities about how this system is to be constructed with rights for the individual and the means of protection of these rights. It is also about faith in the government and its ability to deal with the problem, faith in the police and its credibility and about wars within the borders, such as Chechnya.

In the US the administrative divide between the military and civilian is bridged by the discourse of dual-use technologies. Military technologies are expected to provide a more effective military. Dual-use in the Russian context is only possible in situations where price is not an issue, such as in the future commercialisation of space. This reflects the resource divide and the technology gap between the military and civilian productions. However, negotiation of Russian defence technologies is not only a question of crossing this divide, but also a question of new defences. Conversion of military technology in Russia does not take place in a vacuum. It takes place in a situation where boundaries and defences are being reconstructed, not only at the national borders.

Notes

1 The front page of ARPA (1993).
2 Alic *et al.* (1992: 10).
3 The Technology Reinvestment Project, ARPA.
4 Critical views have been expressed in Alic *et al.* (1992); Marcussen and Yudken (1992).
5 Alic *et al.*, 1992:363.
6 I have dealt with the questions of Russian technology policy in more detail in Cronberg *et al.* (1996); Cronberg (1996).
7 Bystritskii (1995: 5).
8 Ibid., p.17.
9 Ibid., p. 343.
10 *International Herald Tribune*, 29 September 1997.
11 *International Herald Tribune*, 30 October 1996 (The Russians are Winning in Space).
12 Ibid.
13 BICC (1999: 75).
14 *International Herald Tribune*, 28 August 1997 (editorial: Don't laugh at Mir).

15 Ibid., p. 45.

16 Here Campbell quotes M. Douglas, *Purity and Danger: An Analysis of the Concept of Pollution and Taboo*, London (1984: 122).

17 Ibid., p. 92.

18 This was a form of socialist profit; where an enterprise acquired more independence and had less contact with the bureaucrats. The enterprise could, in certain ways, dispose of its 'profit', which, however, was closely defined as all prices were regulated.

19 Campbell (1992: 88).

20 Haraway (1989: 14).

Chapter 11

Welfare in Warfare

The deconstruction of the seamless web of military technology and its social dynamics in a situation where radical changes are taking place enables us to understand the way technology becomes embedded into society. The invisible becomes visible, and taken for granted practices form straitjackets counteracting necessary reforms. By using concepts from grounded theory such as awareness, boundary work, arenas and social worlds, I hope that I have been able to show the patterns for how military technology was built into the Soviet Union and the way it still affects the Russian way of thinking, the communities of practice in the military industry and the meanings attached to technology. My claim is that we are able to understand Russia and the pain involved in the process of change by looking at those who are losing their former privileges. The reshaping of Soviet military technology becomes a cornerstone in building a new Russian society.

This chapter ties together the fragments presented in the previous chapters. As such, it becomes a test on whether grounded theory can facilitate better understanding of Russia and its transformation. I started this book by criticising my own previous approaches to Russian conversion such as innovation economics and the sociology of technology. I will conclude by stating that the following analysis could not have been written as the result of such lines of approach.

The military and the rest

The Soviet Union was a dual society. In spite of all the egalitarian rhetoric, there was a difference. This difference was not only about a privileged elite as analysed in many Western sociological studies, and nor was it one of education or qualifications. The Soviet modernisation process, the project of bridging the gap between Tsarist Russia and the industrialised West, had a different duality built into it. On the one hand, there was the military production, industries and technology. On the other hand, there was the rest, the non-military, the civilian, the production and technologies not intended for war or defence. This duality was constructed in multiple ways, some more visible than others.

There were material privileges. Those working in military industries, from the director to the workers, had salaries which were two or three times higher than the rest. Other privileges were also built into military work. When the brightest students were recruited, they could expect to get housing earlier than others. Waiting for a car of one's own took less time. Everyday life was easier. When others queued hours for food, food products were distributed by the institutes and enterprises belonging to the military-industrial complex. While many other working places also distributed products, the best quality was always reserved for the military enterprises. As the enterprises were also the source of social welfare, their employees frequented the best vacation spots, best doctors and the best ice-hockey fields.

The material benefits were important, but not decisive. Equally important were the prospects for challenging work. A young person interested in science could have access to equipment, materials and books, not available to others. Working for military research was in many ways different from civilian research. The defence ministries channelled money through the universities for those interested in working for defence. One of my interviewees also pointed out that to defend a civilian dissertation was a lot of work. In military research, for example when working for Sputnik or other prestige projects, it was not even necessary to have a dissertation. You could become a leading general designer or receive high academic awards without the sweat and tears of the civilian field. The daily frustrations of civilian industries such as poor quality of components and materials were less in the military enterprises. Components were stamped 'good enough for military use'. A consequence of this was that poor quality products accumulated in civilian production. The working communities were disciplined and committed as opposed to the rest of the society. It was only natural that the scientists and engineers of the military-industrial complex also socialised with others belonging to this privileged group.

The most important factor in the social construction of difference was, however, respect. Everybody else looked up to those working for the military. The task of defending the country was the first priority. Those working in defence research institutes, design bureaux and production enterprises demonstrated their love for the country and were highly respected. Respect in the Russian society is important. I have been told that before the Revolution banks and people in trade bought respect by giving money to charity. The University of Perm was built this way. The whole system functioned under this respect for the military. Films, radio and TV promoted the members of the military-industrial complex as examples to follow and to respect. They received honours of the Soviet Union and were the heroes decorated with medals and orders. Stalin personally received scientists and engineers from the military industries and research establishments, an honour not available to others.

One can wonder how the military-industrial complex, the government secret, could be so respected and at the same time so invisible. No one was supposed to know who was working for the military. Officially, they worked only with documents and products. No one was supposed to know where the most respected specialists working with nuclear weapons were located. But everybody knew. Maybe this mystery surrounding the military-industrial complex was part of its attraction. Maybe it was an important part of the construction of the difference between the one important task, that of defending the country, and other less important tasks. Those who were decorated were called heroes of 'unknown achievements'.

My conclusion is that pride and respect are the key to understand this constructed duality, the construction of difference between those who were subjects of this pride and others. When everything in society builds up to your privileged status from small details of everyday life to having challenging work, identity becomes dependent on this respect. High technology, military high technology, becomes a part of this construction. 'They master high technology' was a saying reflecting the admiration for those working for the military enterprises. High technology becomes mystified as a symbol of doing something important, of being respected by others and of having a privileged status in society. This pride was not only a feeling belonging to the scientists and engineers at the top. It was a collective feeling that everybody shared.

In this context, it is easier to understand the Russian policies of clinging desperately to the technology of the defence enterprises. To insist on a high-tech to high-tech conversion and to try to preserve the high-tech capabilities of the military industry and to reject restructuring of the enterprises became a sign of survival in this difference, in this pride. All this may be understood – as many in the West have done – as an indication of the imperialist Russia trying to retain its military power or as a preparation for a new arms race. But it may also be understood as a conscious effort of trying to maintain some fundamental structures and cultures in the Russian society, or at least as an effort to protect the society from total collapse.

In 1991–92 a collective destruction of self-images took place in
Russia. This happened almost overnight and almost without warning
although the Gorbachev conversion effort had taken place. A scientist
once pointed out to me in an interview that 'when a weak person gets ill
it is not so problematic, but when a strong person becomes ill it
becomes dangerous'.

Problems and programmes

> A strong wind blows on the taiga, the top moves, nothing
> happens at the bottom.[1]

The first aid to this ailing patient, the Russian defence industry, was to
be Western technology. Problems of conversion would be solved by
more technology, this time from the West. In a way, this faith in
technology as expressed in 1992–93 by Russian scientists and engineers
reflects the Marxist idea of technology as the driving force in society. It
is a symbol of progress, of the scientific-technological revolution and of
the linear world view, where Russia is to catch up with the West. In
fact, the Soviet Union and its industrial revolution was a step in this
direction. Russia would now, after the collapse of the Soviet Union
finally be integrated into the world economy through Western
technology.

The first advice the Western experts gave was to separate welfare
from warfare. The enterprises that had provided for all aspects of life of
their workers should, according to the Western view get rid of their
housing units, hospitals and vacation centres. While the Russians
offered technical specifications, the objects of their pride, the Western
specialist talked about business plans. Many of the words used carried
different meanings. How to understand marketing when your
background is in a socialist plan economy? How to understand
intellectual property rights when you have no tradition in competition
between companies? The foreigners came, looked and left.

The West could not solve the Russian conversion problem, nor its
economic transformation and integration to the world market. What
was achieved, in addition to a few joint ventures, was an encounter and
an arena for interaction. The numerous visits have no doubt given the
Russian managers and engineers knowledge about the West they never
had before. It has given them experience in trying to manage business
in a Western way although the transfer of management methods and
theories in themselves has been unsuccessful. The results are very
moderate, if not modest, given the high expectations.

Although the image of Pratt & Whitney on the Perm scene is still very positive, no one any longer hopes that they will be able to solve the problems of Perm Motor Works. Although the liquid rocket engines of Russian design are giving Western companies something to think about, the export of Russian technology is not enough to feed the country. One would have to have a mega-scale commercialisation for Russian space technology to provide welfare and feed the whole country. I remember that one of the defence managers in 1992, when the West was sending humanitarian aid to Russia asked me, 'How many tons of butter do you think the West would have to send each day to feed Russia?'

While foreign experts have not been able to cross the divide from the military to the civilian economy, the role of the State could have been reconstructed in the transformation process. Traditionally, a strong actor, it could have played a decisive role in crossing the divide. However, this was not seen as a central problem in the reforms. The economic reforms focused on creation of new enterprises and the military industries were left to convert on their own, although a number of conversion programmes were designed. The State's confusion about its role in relation to the military enterprises is best reflected in the continuous changes through the 1990s related to the place of the military institutes, design bureaux and production enterprises in the state structure. When the nine defence ministries in 1991 were abolished, military production and technology become a part of the Russian Ministry of Industry. This reflected the new equal status with the rest of the industry. However, this did not work out and in the beginning of 1993 the Ministry of Industry was replaced by the State Committee for Industrial Policy and the State Committee for Defence Industry. The latter was to work closely with the Ministry of Defence thus again giving the defence industries a special role. It still needed special attention given its role in the economy and the prospects for high-tech conversion. For a short time, the Ministry of Defence Industry reappears just to become later reorganised into a department under the Ministry of Economy. Since 2000, five separate agencies, almost in the same way as past ministries, have organised specific types of defence productions, such as aerospace, shipbuilding or conventional weapons. These agencies are co-ordinated by the State Commission on Military-Industrial Affairs, a commission much like the past Soviet VPK although without the same power to command the industry.

Furthermore, the new Ministry of Industry, Science and Technology also exercises influence over the defence enterprises (see p. 27).

The same confusion is reflected in a number of conversion plans. Since the Gorbachev plan for conversion in 1990–91 failed, the Russian government has drafted a number of conversion programmes. Lists of critical sectors to be supported or of critical technologies to be strengthened have been drafted. The funds that have been distributed under the heading of conversion have been used mainly for salaries, social assets and utilities in the enterprises. In the defence enterprises of Perm, there are very few traces of any government proposals for conversion although some of the companies did receive state subsidies. From 1999, the government's official policy has not been to support enterprises, but to support infrastructure.

Restructuring of the enterprises of the military-industrial complex has been one of the key questions. This is a sore point for the ruling political elite, as nobody wants to close down objects of national pride. The last programme 'Conception for the restructuring of the military-industrial complex of the Russian federation' was approved in August 1997 and differs from its predecessors, not only in its use of words such as diversification and consolidation from the US conversion discourse, but also in the fact that it is available through the Internet (www@vpk.ru).

The restructuring programme was in a way an effort to increase State control of the defence enterprises. However, the State lacks the financial means and maybe even the managers to implement its plans. At the heart of the problem is not only the strong lobby of the defence enterprises, but also a conflict related to the role of the State. The companies still see the State as a guarantee against loss-making. The regions, particularly those depending on the military enterprises, are afraid of losing their production potential. While the Russian state needs to adjust its defence industry to the new situation, it is too weak to do so.[2]

The above may give the impression that no real changes have taken place in the military-industrial complex. This impression is not quite true. Privatisation has had a great impact. The Russian privatisation programme, much criticised for distributing wealth to the former political elite, criminals and enterprise managers, has also been implemented in the military-industrial complex. Companies like Pratt & Whitney have shareholder interests in the military-industrial complex of Russia. The former research institutes, design bureaux and military enterprises of the Soviet Union represent today a manifold of ownership models. In the Perm area there are enterprises that still belong to the State structure. Others have been corporatised but the State still has the majority of the shares. Others had been privatised either totally or with the State maintaining a golden share. Depending on the model of privatisation, a number of conflicts are mounting in the horizon.

First, there is the conflict between the State and the shareholders. Some of the new owners try to transfer the losses to the State (payments of salaries), at the same time maintaining the shareholders' right to profits. Secondly, there is a conflict between Moscow and the regions. Some of the new shareholders, for example of Perm enterprises, are from Moscow while the enterprise has its activities in the Perm region. The representatives of the region are afraid that the Moscow partners are only interested in profits and not in the needs of the local economy. Although in Perm there are no examples of riots where workers protest against new owners or against international takeovers, examples are known from other locations.[3]

In summary, institutions both within and outside the military enterprises have been fundamentally destabilised. The actors who might have been able to create networks and alliances for new awareness structures – the foreign investors/experts and the State – have failed to do so. Maybe the Western restructuring concepts such as diversification, consolidation and dual-use do not work in the Russian context. Nevertheless, some restructuring has taken place, and in 1997–98 there was an increase in the civilian production of selected enterprises,[4] although these activities are not necessarily the results of the conversion programmes of the state. Nor have these changes achieved the objectives of conversion, namely to integrate Russia in the world economy as a high-tech nation or to guarantee the welfare of the people. Due to the duality of the society, explanations have to be sought in the way the social world of the military was structured. In the Soviet Union and now in Russia enterprise restructuring is not only a question of restructuring the enterprise, but of much more.

Restructuring social worlds

A good master builds a new home before he destroys the old one. They (the government) have destroyed the old one without building a new.

In the social world of Russian military technology, high morals and challenging work were combined with the smell of freshly baked bread and vacations at the Black Sea. It was a complex whole where at the centre there was the enterprise surrounded by all the facilities that satisfied the individual's everyday needs. The individual lived all his or her life in this world providing both with stability and challenges. The individual was recruited directly from school to the important task of defending the nation. And although 'a woman in the boat was bad for sailing', even the women of this social world preferred to design artillery systems rather than lines of baby food.

For those who were inside, the system was in fact not a world of work, but a world of home. Ultimately, the boundaries of this home were those of the nation. The defence of these boundaries was a moral task, a value shared by the whole society. Or in the words of one of the women I interviewed, 'this was the way we were educated'. If the defence of the home was the most important task, then the production of weapons was a necessary, important task. It was not a question of killing children, but of protecting children. It was a question of keeping pace with the technological advances of the US.

Creative destruction is a concept used by Schumpeter to underline that the old has to disappear before the new can be built. The destruction of the social world of the military technology, the socio-technical ensemble, where the social has been seamlessly interwoven with the technical, started by reorganising the social. The social facilities built into the structures of the military enterprises, such as day-care centres, vacation homes and health care facilities, were sold, closed down or moved to the care of the local administration. This was a spontaneous process in 1992 when the military enterprises did not receive orders and were short of funding. It was also a process promoted by Western experts trying to streamline Russian companies after the Western model.

This process of destruction of welfare built into warfare was probably one of the worst mistakes of both the transformation to the market economy and the crossing of the divide between the military to the civilian. It was a separation of the technical from the social, of welfare from warfare. The local administrations were not prepared for this task as the social facilities were handed over to them. And they had no money for taking care of the maintenance. In cases where child care services such as day-care centres were privatised, only a very few people – and no single mothers – could pay for them. Some of the services were simply discontinued as vacation homes were sold to private interests.

Employees of the military-industrial complex are not only losing their social welfare. They are also losing work. Some of the best people leave the social world of the military to enter commercial structures. These are mostly men, often high-level scientists or well-qualified workers. The enterprises themselves are creating small companies on the side in order to survive economically. Unemployment is gradually increasing although not reflecting the actual reduced production levels of the enterprises. Some women, if their husbands can afford it, stay at home, while others take on two or three jobs in order to be able to support their unemployed husbands and sons. Women who have been proud of their working communities and of their technical education have to reconstruct their world-views.

The social world of the military technology has started to crumble. Science and technology have gradually lost their previous privileged position; and professions such as economist, accountant and lawyer have become more popular. Research institutes of the former military-industrial complex barely survive, some with connections to the US, others by allowing their employees to work on private contracts on the side. Production facilities stand still as the slowly emerging small-scale production enterprises import machinery and equipment from abroad. The scientific-technical revolution has come to a standstill. There are a number of loss-making enterprises.

The atmosphere of secrecy has gradually disappeared and people can freely talk about the objects of their work such as rocket launchers and missiles. New kinds of secrets have emerged, now related to competition on the market. The brief phase of total openness has become more and more closed as company secrets and internationally competitive innovations have to be protected. As the structures of society have collapsed, criminality and the mafia have taken over.

The transition glue

Russian reforms have been about change, about new concepts such as investment or new ways of doing things such as joint ventures. Very little attention has been paid to continuity, stability and time for adaptation.

If I were to assign one role for the military industry and its technology during the ten years of transformation it would be one of transition glue. In a society where everything else has collapsed, been destabilised or replaced by something else, military technology and the efforts to convert it have actually provided a dimension of stability. Although the institutions of military technology, both the state structures and the relationship among enterprises, have been fundamentally destabilised, technology has turned out to be more resilient to change than institutions. Translated into constructivist terms, this means that collapsing institutions do not necessarily mean collapsing technologies. When the black box of Cold War was opened, renegotiations around technologies took place. But the technologies were not indefinitely renegotiable. There is a hard core, seeming to survive macro-level institutional instability.

The meanings attached to military technology were those of pride and achievement. This was something to save, to take care of, to convert on a high-tech level. It was not something to be abandoned, to be thrown out as something without value. Energies were directed towards conversion work, towards civilian uses and new product development and new technical specifications, however naïve when seen from the Western viewpoint. Making business plans, marketing, the ways of working in Western enterprises were not learnt in a vacuum, but rather in the context of the things that had been done before. In trying to convert technological achievements, the engineers and scientists probably understood more about the nature of the Soviet military technology than they would have from working in a small company making civilian products. Learning is more effective in trying to change something you already know rather than by starting from scratch. When the Perm engineers and scientists constructed the Perm Auto, in spite of its failure as a car they learned a number of fundamental things about automobile design, technical requirements and production.

Although the Soviet Union collapsed, the military enterprises stayed. They were not closed down and people continued to come to work although there were no orders. Instead of going out on to the street, demonstrating and challenging the existing order, the workers, engineers and scientists continued to come to work without pay. The enterprise provided continuity during a time of crisis, which is difficult for outsiders to understand. The dismantling of the military-industrial complex did not result in social unrest as might have been expected. It did not result in large-scale demonstrations against the government. Although crime rates have increased and corruption is widespread, the creation of a new Russia was a peaceful transformation although not totally without bloodshed.

The gradual transformation of the Russian society towards market economy has been less violent with hopes attached to the military enterprises and their high tech civilian futures than would otherwise have been the case. In this sense the military sector has been an asset not a burden. Although gradual disillusionment and increasing discontent has been attached to the process of converting military technologies to civilian uses, this process has provided the best part of the Russian workforce with meaning and hope, in spite of the fact that military production has gone down dramatically during the past ten years without corresponding increases in civilian production either within the military industry or outside. Although today we may judge Russian conversion as a failure, at least in the context of a retooling approach and turning the existing enterprises into civilian production, our children may look at the transition with different eyes. The gradual reforms and changes that have taken place may have been chaotic and unplanned, but the social order has been maintained and a new one is emerging.

Future fears

The task of defending one's home is no longer consistent with national mobilisation and commitment to defending the borders. The borders move closer. The defence of home is now based on metal doors and window bars. The protection of one's body, against the enemy from within, requires bulletproof vests.

The questions of security and threats have become much more complex than they were during the Cold War, although no immediate external enemy seems to be threatening Russian security. In fact, an authoritative panel of political analysts convened to discuss Russia's national interests and security agenda in 1996 found it virtually impossible to formulate Russia's national and security interests other than as a political declaration.[5]

While thinking on security is still dominated by issues such as the NATO enlargement, disputes over the Black Sea Fleet or the deployment of Russian troops and bases in the 'near abroad', non-traditional security issues are also entering the new military doctrine. Here threats to domestic stability such as illegal armed groups, organised crime, corruption, illicit profilation of weapons, drug trade and attacks on the facilities of nuclear, chemical and biological industries were taken up. A post-Soviet debate about non-traditional security issues is gradually emerging.[6]

There seem to be very few types of non-traditional security risks not present on the Russian arena. Even the income gap is a social risk with possible consequences such as social unrest and chaos. Likewise environmental pollution, industrial and technological accidents, and procession and disposal of radioactive and toxic materials are included in security risks.[7] In Perm, not only the production of rockets to defend the nation took place. Today the destruction of these same rockets is an environmental hazard for the city.

Amid all these security risks, the fear that was most strongly expressed by the defence scientists and managers I interviewed was that of becoming a Third World country. For those who built the support structures of the Cold War and participated in the arms race as a partner with the other superpower of the world, a future as a Third World country is a nightmare – this in a country that has been proud of its technological and scientific progress.

There are many indications that Russia may, in fact, be on its way to realising this nightmare. After 1991 the decline in life expectancy accelerated steeply and by 1994 had reached the level of the 1950s. After a short upward trend, life expectancy has stabilised to almost exactly the same level as that of 1984.[8] Tuberculosis, a disease most clearly associated with poor living conditions, is endemic in Russia. Notification rates have risen from 34 per 100,000 population in 1991 to 76 per 100,000 population in 1998. In general, health indicators are declining and the rates of infectious diseases as well as sexually transmitted diseases are rising.[9] Organised crime and corruption find their ways deep into the state structures. According to some sources, there are more than 6000 criminal groups and about 150 criminal societies in Russia.[10] According to the Russian Ministry of Interior organised crime groups spent up to 50% of their income on bribing state officials.[11] Russia's organised crime is estimated to be in control of over 40.000 economic entities, including 400 banks and 1500 state sector enterprises.[12] It is therefore not surprising that the entire population, not only enterprise managers and scientists, are losing confidence in a Western type democracy.

Could it have been otherwise?

The critical question of social constructivists is: could it have been otherwise? The constructivist answer is always yes. History is not predetermined, there are no given paths. It all depends. Could it have been otherwise in relation to the conversion of military technology? Could there have been another path and a less painful process for the transition from a communist society to a market economy? As a constructivist, my answer is also yes. Macro-economic reforms, no doubt, were necessary. It was necessary to cut military orders and to try to turn the existing technological potential to commercial production. But a lot of other things could have been different. The direction of things could have been different in a process where new meanings and values would have been negotiated from the bottom-up, rather than from the top-down. While, of course, there are no given answers, the diffractions in this book demonstrate some of the things that could have been otherwise.

In many an interview the interviewee has expressed distress over the fact that there was only destruction, and no construction work: scientists, engineers and workers in the military industries were used to build for destruction, and have now been mobilised to destroy their own achievements.

The deconstruction of welfare in warfare should have been the first focus. The mental images of the social sphere both of the workers and the management were intimately linked to the enterprise. There were no other models. In a centralised plan economy the local and regional administrations have had very little to say. Suddenly, they are to take over, according to the Western model, the welfare services of the enterprises. There was no preparation for this and there were no resources. Maybe the West should have sent, instead of retired business executives, retired social service managers to every local community to discuss Western welfare models, in order to create some kind of consensus among the population on how the welfare of the future should be provided. The transfer of the social assets led to the destruction of an organic whole which, in turn, led to fear, insecurity and political instability. An indication of how linked the enterprises and the social services were is the example of one of the design bureaux in Perm. Although the company has formally transferred its social facilities such as housing to the municipality the utilities (water, sewage, electricity) still link the housing units to the enterprise.

Maybe the Western model for social services was not the best one in the Russian context. However, a new home should have been built before the old one was destroyed. In the new home there should also have been room for single working mothers and retired women. There should have been space for both day care and health care in a way the population could afford.

In a centrally planned economy the State has been the almighty father who has given resources, paid salaries and distributed welfare in a way that penetrated all spheres of everyday life. Western researchers have rightly taken up the problem of the civil society, the lack of independent civil organisations to carry a dialogue with the State. (For example the women in Perm were organised in a state-governed organisation. The first independent women's movement was created in Perm only in 1996.) Even when the defence enterprises have been privatised the State is supposed to have its protective hand over them. Some directors are still fighting for the State to take the responsibility for loss-making companies, even if they are privatised. What is the role of the State in a post communist society turning towards the market and carrying out economic reforms?

Western specialists came with solutions, they knew the answers. But they were not sensitive to the way everything depended on everything else. A few bottom-up examples of restructuring might have shown the companies in Perm, how to create new forms of economic activities and the social services. Instead there were the top-down macro-economic reforms which were difficult if not impossible for the Russians to understand. For a woman in Perm formerly employed in the defence industry market economy became equal to standing in the rain and selling boots.

Russian privatisation in the mid 1990s was probably the largest example anywhere in the world of redistribution of wealth in a short period. Under the cover of vouchers to the people an ownership class of criminals, former members of the Soviet ruling elite and enterprise managers emerged in Russia. I will always remember, in 1999, when I revisited Perm, and passed through the hall of the regional administration building. In one corner there was a group of elderly women and some men protesting against something. I asked my companion what was going on. He said that these were the people who had lost their money through an investment company. They were now protesting and wanted the government or the regional administration to take responsibility. Somehow, I tend to agree.

Economic reforms were carried out in the hopes of preventing the communists from returning. Everything was to be carried out fast. Progress was to be irreversible so that the old times would never return. The reforms might have prepared the people better to the changes necessary and prevented some of the anarchy and corruption prevailing today. Building a civil society takes time, and so does changing the old habits of thought and the mental images that have guided social thinking. Maybe the pace of the process has in fact been counterproductive. It may be leading exactly to what it was supposed to prevent: if not to the restoration of the communist society, to some anti-Western, spiritual version of authoritarian rule. Russia will no doubt seek to restore its respect and pride. Given the threats of the future this will not be an easy task. But of course, it all depends.

Notes

1 *Taiga* is a Russian word meaning 'old forest'.
2 Late 2001 a new restructuring and conversion programme has been adopted. This is a new effort to scale down the defence complex, improve the government control and make it more commercially oriented. Maybe this time the government is strong enough to implement the programme.
3 See for example the business section of *Herald Tribune*, Friday, 5 November 1999.
4 According to BICC (1999: 74) this growth has been mainly financed by arms export activities and profits from a few liquid domestic markets.
5 The meeting was convened at the Institute of the World Economy and International Relations. The results were published as *Kontseptsiia natsional' nykh interesov* (1996). For further discussion, see Medvedev (1998).
6 For a more detailed analysis of the issues, see *Basic Provisions of the Military Doctrine of Russian Federation* (1994) and Belaia Kniga (1996).
7 Ibid.
8 *The Lancet* 357, 24 March 2001, 917–21.
9 *The Lancet* 358, 11 August 2001, 445–9.
10 See Olga Kryshtonovskaya's article (Russia's Illegal Structures) in *Post Soviet Puzzles* (1995: 591–614).
11 Belaia Kniga (1996:113).
12 Medvedev (1998); Handelman (1994).

Bibliography

Accordino, John J. (2000) *Captives of the Cold War Economy: The Struggle for Defense Conversion in American Communities.* Westport, CT: Praeger.

Adams, Gordon (1984) 'Undoing the Iron Triangle: Conversion and the 'Black Box' of Policies', in Suzanne Gordon & Dave McFadden (eds.), *Economic Conversion: Revitalizing America's Economy.* Cambridge, MA: Ballinger.

Adjusting to the Drawdown (1992) Report of the Defence Conversion Commission, December 31 1992. Washington D.C.: Department of Defence Conversion Commission.

Aeroe, Anders (1992) *Coping with Reduced Defence Spending: Conversion within the U.S. Military Industrial Complex in the 1990s.* Lyngby: Unit of Technology Assessment. Technical University of Denmark. (Technology Assessment Text No. 7).

Albrecht, Ulrich (1988) 'Spin-off: a Fundamentalist Approach', in P. Gummett & J. Reppy (eds.), *The Relations between Defence and Civil Technologies.* Dordrecht: Kluwer.

Alexander, Arthur J. (1992) *Perspectives on Russian Defence Industry Conversion.* Paper presented at the conference on 'Industrial Demilitarization, Privatisation, Economic Reform, and Investment in Russia', Stanford University, Center for International Security and Arms control, Palo Alto, CA., December 1-2, 1992.

Alexander, Arthur J. (1991) *Some Considerations for Foreign Investment in Soviet Military and Civilian Industry.* Washington D.C.: Japan Economic Institute of America. (Unpublished).

Alexander, Arthur J. (1991) *Recent Events in the Former Soviet Union and Implications for Foreign Investment.* Washington D.C.: Japan Economic Institute of America. (Unpublished).

Alexander, Arthur J. (1991) *The Soviet Defence-Industrial Complex and Defence Conversion in Transition: Testimony before the United States Senate Committee on Armed Services, September 19, 1991.* Washington D.C.: Japan Economic Institute of America. (Unpublished).

Alexander, Arthur J. (1990) *National Experiences in the Field of Conversion: A Comparative Analysis.* Paper presented at the United

Nations Conference on 'Conversion: Economic Adjustments in an Era of Arms Reductions', in Moscow, 13-17 August 1990.

Alexander, Arthur J. (1990) *Perestroika and Change in Soviet Weapons Acquisition*. USA: Rand Corporation, June Issue.

Alic, John; Lewis M. Branscomb, Harvey Brooks, Aston Carters & Gerald Epstein (1992) *Beyond Spinoff: Military and Commercial Technologies in a Changing World*. Boston: Harvard Business School Press.

Amann, Robert & Julian Cooper (1986) *Technical Progress and Soviet Economic Development*. London: Basil Blackwell.

Anderson Marion (1988) 'The Impact of the Military Budget on Employment of Women', in E. Isaksson (ed.), *Women and the Military System*. New York: Harvester & Wheatsheaf.

Anthony, Ian (1994) *The Future of the Defence: Industries in Central and Eastern Europe*. Stockholm: SIPRI.

ARPA (1995) *The Technology Reinvestment Project: Dual Use Innovation for a Stronger Defence*. Washington D.C.

ARPA (1993) *Programme Information Package for Defence Technology Conversion, Reinvestment and Transition Assistance*. Washington D.C.

Baev, Andrei; Mathew J. Von Benche, David Bernstein, Jeffrey Lehrer & Elaine Nangle (1995) *American Ventures in Russia*. Center for International Security. Stanford: Stanford University.

Ballentine, Katherine (1991) *Soviet Defence Industry Reform: The Problems of Conversion in an Unconverted Economy*. Canadian Institute for International Peace and Security: Background Paper, July 1991.

'Basic Provisions of the Military Doctrine of the Russian Federation', (1994). *Jane's Intelligence Review*. Special Report, January.

Bauman, Zygmunt (1992) *Intimations of Post-Modernity*. London: Routledge.

Belaia Kniga rossiiskikh spetssluzhb, (1996) (White Book of Russia's Security Series). Moscow: Informatsionno – izdatels'skoe agentstvo "Obozrevatel".

Bernstein, David (ed.) (1997) *Cooperative Business Ventures between US Companies and Rusian Defence Enterprises*. Centre for International Security and Arms Control. Palo Alto, CA.: Stanford University.

Bernstein, David (1999) *Commercialization of Russian Technology in Cooperation with American Companies*. Stanford, CA: CISAC. Stanford University

Bernstein, David (1994) *Defence Industry Restructuring in Russia: Case Study and Analysis.* Centre for International Security and Arms Control. Palo Alto, CA: Stanford University.

Bernstein, David & J. Lehrer (1995) 'Restructioning of Research Technology in Russia: The Case of the Central Aerohydro-dynamic Research Institute', in J. Di Chiano (ed.), *Conversion of the Defense Industry in Russia and Eastern Europe.*

Bernstein, David & W.J. Perry (1992) *Defence Conversion: A Strategic Imperative for Russia.* Palo Alto, CA: Stanford University.

Bijker, Wiebe E. (1995) *Of Bicycles, Bakelites, and Bulbs: Toward a Theory of Sociotechnical Change.* Boston: MIT Press.

Bijker, Wiebe E. & J. Law (eds.) (1992) *Shaping Technology/Building Society: Studies in Sociotechnical Change.* Cambridge, MA: MIT Press.

Bonn International Center for Conversion (1999) *Conversion Survey 1999.* Baden-Baden: Nomos Verlagsgesellschaft.

Bonn International Center for Conversion (2002) *Conversion Survey 2002: Global Disarmament Demilitarization and Demobilization.* Baden-Baden: Nomos Verlagsgesellschaft.

Borisov, L.P. (1996) Politologiya. Uchebnoe posobie. Moscow: Izdatel'stvo Belye alvy.

Braidotti, Rosi (1990) Keynote address at the seminar: 'Women's Studies and the Social Position of Women in Eastern and Western Europe'. *European Network for Women's Studies.* The Hague. 22-27 November.

Branscomb, Lewis M. (1994) *Targeting Critical Technologies.* Paris: OECD. (Science Technology Industry Review no. 14).

Branscomb, Lewis M. (1993) *Empowering Technology: Implementing a U.S. Strategy.* Cambridge, MA: MIT Press.

Brzezinski, Zbigniev (1994) 'The Premature Partnership', in *Foreign Affairs,* March/April: 67-82.

Brzezinski, Zbigniev (ed.) (1969) *Dilemmas of Change in Soviet Politics.* New York: Columbia University Press.

Bytstritskii, Vitaly (1995) *Converting Pulsed Power to Civilian Applications in Russia: Problems and Promise.* Centre for International Security and Arms Control. Palo Alto, CA: Stanford University.

Callon, Michel (1992) 'The Dynamics of Techno-economic Networks', in Rod Coombs; Paolo Saviotti & Vivien Walsh (eds.),

Technological Change and Company Strategies. London: Harcourt Brace Jovanovich Publishers.

Callon, Michel (1987) 'Society in the Making: The Study of Technology as a Tool for Sociological Analysis', in W. Bijker, T. Hughes & T. Pinch (eds.), *The Social Construction of Large Technological Systems.* Cambridge, MA: MIT Press.

Campbell, David (1992) *Writing Security: United States Foreign Policy and the Politics of Identity.* Manchester: Manchester University Press.

Centre for International Security and Arms Control (1995) *Conversion, 1995: A Report on Russia's Defence Industry.* Palo Alto, CA: Stanford University.

Chapman, K. & K. Wittneben (1992) *American Business Involvement in Defence Conversion in the former Soviet Union: Opportunities, Constraints, and Recommendations.* American Committee on U.S. - C.I.S. Relations. December.

Chernyshov, S. (ed.) (1995) *Inoe: Khrestomatiya novovo rossiiskovo samosoznaniya* [The Other: Anthology of the New Russia's Self-consciousness]. Moscow: Argus.

Clarke, Adele (1991) 'Social Worlds/Arenas Theory', in D. Morries (ed.), *Social Organization and Social Social Processes: Essays in Honour of Anselm Strauss.* New York: Aldine de Gruyter.

Cohn, Carol (1988) 'A Feminist Spy in the House of Death: Unravelling the Language of Strategic Analysis', in Eva Isaksson, (ed.), *Women and the Military System.* New York: Harvester & Wheatsheaf.

Committee for Economic Development. Research and Policy Committee (1991) *The Economy and National Defense: Adjusting to Military Cutbacks in the Post-Cold War Era.*

Cooper, Julian (1995) 'Conversion is Dead, Long Live Conversion', in *Journal of Peace Research* 32 (2):129-32.

Cooper, Julian (1994) 'The Soviet Defence Industry Heritage and the Economic Restructuring in Russia', in *The Post Soviet Military Industrial Complex, FOA Symposium.* Stockholm: Swedish National Defence Research Establishment, October 20.

Cooper, Julian (1991) *The Soviet Defence Industry: Conversion and Reform.* London: Pinter.

Cronberg, Tarja (1997) 'The Feeling of Home: Russian Women in the Defense Industry and the Transformation of Their Identities', in *European Journal of Women Studies*, 4 (3):263-281.

Cronberg, Tarja (1996) 'Concepts of Military Technology: Contesting the Boundaries Between the Civilian and the Military', in Philip Gummett; Mikhail Boutousov, Janos Farkas & Arie Rip, *Military R&D after the Cold War: Conversion and Technology Transfer in Eastern and Western Europe*. Dordrecht: Kluwer. (NATO ASI Series).

Cronberg, Tarja; Anders Aeroe & Erik Seem (1996) *Technological Powers in Transition: Defence Conversion in Russia and the US 1991-1995*. Copenhagen: Akademisk Forlag.

Cronberg, Tarja (1996) 'Destabilizing Institutions - Restabilizing Technologies: The Politics of Institutionalized Practices of Russian military Conversion', in Martin Grundman (ed.), *Transformation and Arms Conversion in the Baltic Sea Region and in Russia*. Münster: Lit Publishers.

Cronberg, Tarja (1996) 'A Technological Power in Transformation. Negotiating Russian High Technology Future', in John Campbell & Ove K. Petersen (eds.), *Legacies of Change: Transformations of Post-Communist European Economies*. New York: Aldine de Gruyter.

Cronberg, Tarja (1995), 'Conversion in the Perm Region of Russia', A paper presented at the *NATO Advanced Research Institute Seminar on Defense Conversion Strategies*. Pitlochry, Scotland, July 1-14.

Cronberg, Tarja (1995) 'The Entrenchment of Military Technologies: Patriotism, Professional Pride and Everyday Life in Russian Military Conversion 1992-1994', in Joe Dichiaro (ed.), *Conversion of the Defence Industry in Russia and Eastern Europe*. Bonn: Bonn International Centre for Conversion. (Report 3).

Cronberg, Tarja (1994) 'Enterprise Strategies to Cope with Reduced Defence Spending: The Experience of the Perm Region', in Michael McFaul & Tova Perlmutter (eds.), *Privatisation, Conversion and Enterprise Reform in Russia*. Boulder, CO: Westview Press.

Cronberg, Tarja (1994) 'Civil Reconstructions of Military Technology United States and Russia', in *Journal of Peace Research*, 31 (2):205-218.

Cronberg, Tarja (1992) 'The Social Reconstruction of Military Technology: With Special Reference to the Environment', in Niels Petter Gleditsch (ed.), *Conversion and the Environment*. Oslo: PRIO.

Douglas, Mary (1991) 'The Idea of a Home: A Kind of Space', in *Social Research* 58 (1).

Douglas, Mary (1984) *Purity and Danger: An Analysis of the Concept of Pollution and Taboo*. London: Taylor & Francis.

Edwards, V.; G. Polonsky & A. Polonsky (2000) *The Russian Province after Communism: Enterprise Continuity and Change*. Basingstoke: Palgrave Macmillan.

Enloe, Cynthia (1993) *The Morning After: Sexual Politics at the End of the Cold War*. Berkeley, CA: University of California Press.

Enloe, Cynthia (1988) 'Beyond 'Rank', Women and the Varieties of Militarized Masculinity', in E. Isaksson (ed.), *Women and the Military System*. New York: Harvester & Wheatsheaf.

Enloe, Cynthia (1983) *Does Khaki Become You? The Militarization of Women's Lives*. London: Pluto Press.

Enserink, B., W.A. Smit & B. Elzen (1990) 'Assessments and the B-1 Bomber Network', in *Project Appraisal*, 5 (4):235-254.

Evangelista, M. (1988) *Innovation and the Arms Race: How the United States and the Soviet Union Develop New Military Technologies*. New York: Cornell University Press.

Fujimura, Joan (1991) 'The Sociology of Science: Where Do We Stand?', in D. Morries (ed.), Social Organization and Social Social Processes: Essays in Honour of Anselm Strauss. New York: Aldine de Gruyter.

'Future Relations between Defence and Civil Science and Technology' (1991) prepared by the DRC/SPSG Defence Science and Technology Policy Team for the Parliamentary Office of Science and Technology. London: *SPSG Review*. (Paper No. 2).

Gansler, Jacques (1995) *Defense Conversion: Transforming the Arsenal of Democracy*. Cambridge, MA: MIT Press.

Gansler, Jacques (1988) 'Integrating Civilian and Military Industry: The Segregation of the Defense and Commercial Economies is Hurting Both, and Only Government Can Break Down the Barriers to Cooperation', in *Issues in Science and Technology*, (5):68-73.

Genin, Vladimir; E. Perry & J. William (eds.) (2001) *The Anatomy of Russian Defense Conversion*. Walnut Creek, CA: Vega Press.

Gimpelson, Vladimir (1993) *Labour Market and Employment in Russia: Beginning of Changes*. NATO Collegium.

Gonchar, K.; Y. Kuznetsov & A. Uzhegov (1995) *Conversion of the Post-Soviet Defence Industry: Implications for Russian Economic Development*. Bonn: Bonn International Centre for Conversion. (Brief 1).

Gonchar, Ksenia (2000) *Russia's Defense Industry at the Turn of the Century*. Bonn: Bonn International Center for Conversion. (Brief 17).

Gorbachev, Mihail (1987) *Perestroika*. New York: Harper & Row.

Goskomstat CCCR (1991) Statisticheskie materialy. Moskva.

Graham, Loren (1993) *The Ghost of the Executed Engineer: Technology and the Fall of the Soviet Union*. Cambridge, MA: Harvard University Press.

Green, Alex E.S. (ed.) (1995) *Defense Conversion, a Critical East-West Experiment*. With former Soviet Union perspectives by Victor V. Chernyy. Hampton, VA: Deepak.

Gummett, Philip et al. (ed.) (1996) *Military R&D after the Cold War. Conversion and Technology Transfer in Eastern and Western Europe*. Dordrecht: Kluwer. (NATO ASI Series).

Gusterson, Hugh (1996) *Nuclear Rites: A Weapons Laboratory at the End of the Cold War*. Berkeley, CA: University of California Press.

Handelman, S. (1994) *Comrade Criminal: The Theft of the Second Russian Revolution*. London: Michael Joseph.

Harvey, J.R.; C. Brikley, A. Black & R. Burke (1995) *A Common-Science Approach to High-Technology Export Controls: A Report of the International Security and Arms Control*. Palo Alto, CA: Stanford University.

Haraway, Donna (1989) 'The Biopolitics of Post-modern Bodies: Determination of Self in Immune System Discourse', in *Differences*, 1 (1):3-44.

Haraway, Donna (1996) 'Modest Witness: Feminist Diffractions in Science Studies', in P. Galison & D. Stump (eds.), *The Disunity of Science*. Palo Alto, CA: Stanford University Press.

Haraway, Donna (1991) 'Cyborg Manifesto: Science, Technology and Socialist - Feminism in the Late Twentieth Century', in *Similars, Cyborgs and Women: The Elimination of Nature*. New York: Routledge.

Harbor, B. (1990) 'Arms Conversion and Military-Civilian Technological Synergy', in *Science and Public Policy*, 17 (3):194-200.

Hill, Catherine et al. (1991) *Converting the Military Industrial Economy: The Experience of Six Communities*. Piscataway: Centre for Urban Policy Research, Rutgers - The State University. (Working Paper No. 24).

Holloway, David et al. (2000) *The Anatomy of Russian Defense Conversion*. Walnut Creek, CA: Vega Press.

Holloway, David (1983) *The Soviet Union and the Arms Race*. New Haven, CT: Yale University Press.

Horne, Mari (1995) 'Political Origins of Corporatists Order; the Politics of Enterprise Reform', in Michael McFaul & Tova Perlmutter (eds.), *Privatisation, Conversion and Enterprise Reform in Russia*. Boulder, CO: Westview Press.

Horrigan, Brenda (1992) 'How Many People Worked in the Soviet Defense Industry?', *RFE/RL: Research Report,* 21 August:33-39.

Hughes, Thomas (1994) 'Technological Momentum', in Merritt RoeSmith & Leo Marx (eds.), *Does Technology Drive History? The Dilemma of Technological Determinism*. Cambridge, MA: MIT Press.

Hughes, Thomas (1986) 'The Seamless Web: Technology, Science, et cetera, et cetera', in *Social Studies of Science*, 16:281-292.

Inbar, Efraim & Benzion Zilberfarb (1998) *The Politics and Economics of Defence Industries*. London: Frank Cass.

Isaksson, Eva (ed.) (1988) *Women and the Military System*. New York: Harvester & Wheatsheaf.

Iziumov, Alexei; Leonid Kosals & Rozalina Rijvkina (1995) 'The Shock of Independence' in Joseph DiChiaro (ed.), *Conversion of the Defence Industry in Russia and Eastern Europe*. Bonn: Bonn International Centre for Conversion.

Iziumov, Alexei (1990) The National Experience of the USSR. Proceedings of the United Nations Conference on Conversion: Economic Adjustment in an Era of Arms Reduction. Moscow, 13-17 August.

Kaldor, Mary (1982) *The Baroque Arsenal*. London: Sphere Books.

Kapstein, Ethan B. & C. Marshall Mills (1995) *Defence Conversion in Russian Regions*. The OECD Observer, February/March.

Kaukonen, Erkki (1994) 'Science and Technology in Russia: Collapse or new dynamics?' in *Science Studies*, (2).

Khotkina, Zoya (1994) 'Women in the Labour Market: Yesterday, Today and Tomorrow', in P. Posadskaya (ed.), *Women in Russia: A new Era of Russian Feminism*. Moscow: Verso.

Kontseptsiia razvitiia promyshlennosti permskoi oblasti na period 1999-2002 gg. Orientiry bydyshchevo, 1999. Perm: Haychnoe izdanie. (Seriia: Promyshlennost Primkam'ia b XXI veke).

Kosals, Leonid (1994) *Why Doesn't Russian Industry Work?* London: I.B. Tauris.

Kozyrev, Andrei (1994) 'The Lagging Partnership', in *Foreign Affairs,* 73 (3):59-71.

Krasiltsnchikov, V.A.; V.P. Gutnik, V.I. Kuznetsov, A.R. Belonisov & A.N. Klepatsh (1994) Modernizatsija: zapybezhnyi opyt i Rossija. [Modernisation: the foreign experience in Russia]. Moscow: Rossiski nezavisimyi institut satsialnyh i natsionalnyh problem.

Latour, Bruno (1991) 'Technology in society made durable', in John Law (ed.), *The Sociology of Monsters.* London: Routledge.

Lissyutkina L. (1993) 'Soviet Women at the Crossroads of Perestroika', in N. Funk & M. Müeller (eds.), *Gender Politics and Post-Communism: Reflections from Eastern Europe and the Former Soviet Union.* London: Routledge.

Lorentzi, Jakob & Magnus Nilsson (1994) *Spin-Off, Dual-Use and Conversion: Fashion or Reality.* Collingdale, PA: DIANE Publishing.

Luckman, T. & A. Schutz (1974) *The Structures of the Life-world.* London: Heinemann.

Lynch, John E. (ed.) (1987) *Economic Adjustment and Conversion of Defence Industries.* Boulder, CO: Westview Press.

MacKenzie, Donald (1990) *Inventing Accuracy: A Historical Sociology of Nuclear Missile Guidance.* Cambridge, MA: MIT Press

Markova, Vera D. (1993) *Conversion and Marketing. Novosibirsk: The Russian Academy of Science, Sibirian Branch.* Novosibirsk: Institute of Economics and Industrial Engineering. (Preprint 89).

Markussen, Ann & Joel Yudken (1992) *Dismantling the Cold War Economy.* New York: Basic Books.

Matjeva, S.J. (ed.) (1994) *Modernizatsija v Rossiia i konflikt tsennostej* [Modernisation in Russia and the conflict of values]. Moscow: Institut filosofii RAN.

Melman, Seymour (1988) *The Demilitarized Society: Disarmament and Conversion.* Montreal: Harvest House.

Medvedev, Sergei (1998) *After Socialism: 'New Security' Threats in the Former Soviet Union.* Helsinki: The Finnish Institute for International Affairs. (Working Paper 8).

Medvedev, Sergei (1998) *Democracy, Federation and Representation: Russian Elections in Retrospect.* Helsinki: The Finnish Institute for International Affairs.

Melman, Seymour (1986) 'Swords into Ploughshares: Converting from Military to Civilian Production', in *Technology Review,* 89 (1):62-71.

Melman, Seymour (1983) *Profits Without Production*. New York: Alfred A. Knopf.

Melman, Seymour (1981) 'The Conversion of Economics - Possible Means and Inpacts of Converting Industrial Resources from Military to Civilian Service in Israel, Egypt and India', in *New Outlook - Middle East Monthly*, (April):5-11.

Mihailov, B.V. (ed.) (1994) *Grazhdanskoje obshtshestvo i perspektivy demokratii v Rossii* [The Civil Society in the Perspective of Russian Democracy]. Moscow: Rossijski Nautshnyi Fond.

Miller J. (1987) *Politics, Work and Daily Life in the USSR*. Cambridge: Cambridge University Press.

Morrison, D. & S. Little (1991) 'Technological Cultures of Weapon Designs', in *Science as Culture*, 2, Part 2 (11):227-258.

OECD (1994) Regional Adjustment of Defence Dependent Regions in the Post-Cold War Era. GD (94) 34.

Office of Technology Assessment (OTA). US Congress (1994) *Assessing the Potential for Civil-Military Integration: Technologies Processes and Practices*. Washington D.C.: US Governmental Office. (OTA-ISS-611).

Office of Technology Assessment (OTA), US Congress (1991) *Redesigning Defence: Planning the Transition to the Future US Defence Industrial Base*. Washington D.C.: US Government Printing Office. (OTA-ISC-500).

Office of Technology Assessment (OTA), US Congress (1991) *Adjusting to a New Security Environment: The Defence Technology and Industrial Base Challenge*. Washington D.C.: US Government Printing Office.

O'Prey, Kevin P. (1995) *A Farewell to Arms? Russia's Struggles with DefenseConversion*. New York: Twentieth Century Fund Press. (A Twentieth Century Fund report, Russia in transition).

Parkhalina, T.G. (1995) *Problemy global'noi bezopasnosti: materialy seminarov v ramkakh nautshno-isslegovatel'skoi i informatrionnoi programmy* [Global Security Issues: Proceedings of the seminar]. Moscow: INION RAN.

Parrot, B. (1983) *Politics and Technology in the Soviet Union*. Cambridge, MA: MIT Press.

Passport to the New World (1994). Moscow: Passport International. (July-August).

Passport to the Perm Region. Perm: Division of International and Foreign Economic Relations of Perm Regional Administration.

Patomaki, Heikki & Christer Pursiainen (1998) *Against the State, With(in) the State or a Transnational Creation: Russian Civil Society in the making?* Helsinki: The Finnish Institute of International Affairs. (Working Papers 4).

Perlmutter, Tova (1994) 'Reorganization of Social Sciences', in D. Bernstein (ed.), *Defence Industry Restructuring in Russia, Case Studies and Analysis.* Palo Alto, Ca.: Centre for International Security and Arms Control.

Perry, William (1994) *Acquisition Reform, A Mandate for Change.* Secretary of Defence. February 9.

Pistor, Katharina (1995) 'Privatisation and Corporate Governance in Russia: An Empirical Study', in Michael McFaul & Tova Perlmutter (eds.), *Privatisation, Conversion and Enterprise Reform in Russia.*

Popper, Stere W. (1990) *The Prospects for Modernizing Soviet Industry.* Santa Monica: Rand.

Posadskaya, A. (ed.) (1994) *Women in Russia: A new Era of Russian Feminism.* London: Verso.

Puppe, W.G. et al. (1997) *Conversion of Military Enterprises: A Practical Approach of Industry and Science.* Dordrecht: Kluwer. (NATO ASI Series. Series 4: Science and Technology Policy).

Pursiainen, Christer (1998) *Venajan idea, utopia ja missio* [The Idea, Utopia and Mission of Russia]. Helsinki: Gaudeamus.

Rabinow, P. (1984) *The Foucault Reader.* New York: Pantium Books.

'Regional Resilience and Defense Conversion in the United States', (1997) in *Research in Urban Economics*, 11. Greenwich, CO: JAI Press.

Salieva T. (1991) *Characteristics of Women's Movement in the USSR during Perestroika. A paper on Women in a Changing Europe. European Feminist Re-search Conference.* August 18-22, Aalborg.

Samuels, Richard (1994) *Rich Nation - Strong Army.* Boston: MIT Press.

Schweitzer, Glenn E. (2000) *Swords into the Market Shares: Technology, Economics, and Security in the new Russia.* Washington D.C.: John Henry Press.

Segbers, K. & S. de Speigeleire (1995) *Post-Soviet Puzzles: Mapping the Political Economy of the Former Soviet Union.* Baden-Baden: Nomos Verlagsgesellschaft.

Senghaas, D. (1990) 'Arms Race Dynamics and Arms Control', in Niels Petter Gleditsch & O. Njølstad, *Arms Races: Technological and Political Dynamics.* Oslo: PRIO and Sage Publications.

Sergounin, Alexander A. (1993) *Regional Conversion in Russia: Case Study of Nizhny Novgorod*. Copenhagen: Centre for Peace and Conflict Research. (Working Papers 12).

Shaping Actors, Shaping Factors in Russia, (1997) Brussels: Forward Studies Unit. European Commission. (Working Document No. 1482).

Shlykov, Vitaly (1995) 'Economic Readjustment within the Russian Defence-Industrial Complex', in *Security Dialogue*, 26 (1): 19-34.

SIPRI Yearbook, (1993) Stockholm International Peace Research Institute. Oxford: Oxford University Press.

SIPRI Yearbook, (2001) Stockholm International Peace Research Institute. Oxford: Oxford University Press.

Star, Susan Leigh (1994) *Misplaced Concretism and Concrete Situations: Feminism, Method and Information Technology. Gender-Nature-Culture-Feminist Research Network*. Odense, DK: Odense University. (Working Paper no. 11).

Star, Susan Leigh (1991) 'The Sociology of the Invisible: The Primacy of Work in the Writings of Anselm Strauss', in D. Morries (ed.), *Social Organization and Social Social Processes: Essays in Honour of Anselm Strauss*. New York: Aldine de Gruyter. Hawthorne.

Southwood, Peter (1991) *Disarming Military Industries: Turning an Outbreak of Peace into an Enduring Legacy*. Basingstoke: Palgrave Macmillan.

Stowsky, J. (1986) *Beating Our Ploughshares into Double-Edged Swords: The Impact of Pentagon Policies on the Commercialization of Advanced Technologies*. The Berkeley Roundtable on the International Economy. Berkeley: University of California. (Working Paper 17).

Strauss, Anselm L. (1987) *Qualitative Analysis for Social Scientists*. Cambridge: Cambridge University Press.

Strauss, Anselm L. (1959) *Mirrors and Masks: The Search for Identity*. New York: Free Press.

Susman, G.I. & S. O'Keefe (eds.) (1998) *The Defense Industry in the Post-Cold War Era: Corporate Strategies and Public Policy Perspectives*. Oxford, UK: Pergamon.

Udis, Bernhard (1978) *From Guns to Butter: Technology, Organizations and Reduced Military Spending in Western Europe*. Cambridge, MA: Ballinger.

United Nations, Department of Economic and Social Affairs (DESA), UNDP (China), China Association for Peaceful Use of Military Industrial Technology (CAPMIT) (1999) *Restructuring and reform:*

Business Development: Opportunities in Military Industry: Conversion to Civilian Markets. New York: United Nations.

US Department of Defense (1990) *Soviet Military Power.* Washington D.C.

Wallensteen, Peter (ed.) (1978) *Experiences in Disarmament, on Conversion o Military Industry and Closing of Military Bases.* Uppsala University, Dept. of Peace and Conflict Research. (Report no. 19).

van Opstal, Debra (1991) *Integrating Commercial and Military Technologies for National Strength: An Agenda for Change.* Washington, DC: The Centre for Strategic and International Studies.

Veblen, Torsten (1904) *The Theory of Business Enterprise.* New York: Augustus M. Kelley Publishers. (Clifton reedition 1995).

Voprosyi Ekonomiki i konversi (1991).

Voronina, O. (1994) 'The Mythology of Women's Emancipation in the USSR as the Foundation for a Policy for Discrimination', in P. Posadskaya. (ed.), *Women in Russia: A new Era of Russian Feminism.* Moscow: Verso.

Wainwright H. (1983) 'Women Who Wine', in Dorothy Thompson (ed.), *Over Our Dead Bodies: Women Against the Bomb.* London: Virago.

Walker W.; M. Graham & B. Harbor (1987) 'From Components to Integrated Systems: Technological Diversity and Integration between the Military and Civilian Sectors', in Philip Gummett. & J. Reppy, *The Relations between Defence and Civil Technologies.* Dordrecht: Kluwer.

Waters E. (1993) 'Finding A Voice: The Emergence of a Women's Movement', in N. Funk & M. Müeller (eds.), *Gender Politics and Post-Communism: Reflections from Eastern Europe and the Former Soviet Union.* London: Routledge.

Weber, Rachel Nicole (2001) *Swords into Dow Shares: Governing the Decline of the Military-Industrial Complex.* Boulder, CO: Westview Press.

Yudken, Joel S. & Michael Black (1991) 'Towards a New National Needs Agenda for Science and Technology Policy: The Prospects of Democratic Science and Technology Policy Making', in Gregory A. Bischak (ed.), *Towards a Peace Economy in the United States: Essays on Military Industry, Disarmament and Economic Conversion.* London: Macmillan.

Zaichenko, A. (1988) 'Risk and Independence of Innovative Activity', in *Voprosy Ekonomiki*, (1, January):41-51 and in *Soviet Union Economic Affairs*, (May 12):27-33.

Appendix

Output Dynamics of Russian Defence Industry 1991-2000.

Table 1
Performance and Structural Indicators of the Russian Defence Industry as of 1991-2000

	1991	1992	1993	1994	1995	1996	1997	1998	1999	2000
Military output as % from 1991	100	62	43	26	21	17	13	14	20	28
Civilian output as % from 1991	100	93	83	56	49	41	40	37	48	58

Source: Gonchar K., 2000. Brief 17. Russia's Defense Industry at the Turn of the Century. Bonn International Center for Conversion, Bonn. pp. 44 and 45. 2000 data from Bonn International Center for Conversion 2002, Conversion Survey 2002: Global Disarmament, Demilitarization and Demobilization. Nomos Verlagsgesellschaft. Baden-Baden. p. 56 and Ksenia Gonchar, Bonn International Center for Conversion (interview, June 2002).

Table 2
Output Dynamics of Russian Defence Industry Sectors
(Percentage 2000/1991)

	Military	Civilian
Aircraft	23,4	40,4
Armaments	-	-
Ammunition	21,4	19,2
Shipbuilding	61,5	43,3
Radio	44,2	39,6
Communications	13,0	20,3
Electronics	10,4	30,2
Space	47,2	87,9

Source: Gonchar K., 2000. Brief 17. Russia's Defense Industry at the Turn of the Century. Bonn International Center for Conversion, Bonn. pp. 44 and 45. 2000 data from Bonn International Center for Conversion 2002, Conversion Survey 2002: Global Disarmament, Demilitarization and Demobilization. Nomos Verlagsgesellschaft. Baden-Baden. p. 56 and Ksenia Gonchar, Bonn International Center for Conversion (interview, June 2002).

The above tables give a rough idea of the production dynamics of the Russian defence industry. Uncertainty with respect to data-gathering methods, changes in the sectoral structure of the defence complex and the fact that the State Statistical Agency stopped publishing data on military production of the defence complex render any comparison difficult. When several figures (for example for 1999) are available the higher has been selected. In spite these reservations the data gives the order of magnitude of defence production in relation to 1991, makes the trends in civilian and military production explicit and gives an indication of how the sectors have performed in relation to each other using 1991 as a base. For the sectors the total military output in 2000 of all the industries belonging to this sector is compared with the total military output in 1991. The same for the total civilian output of each of the defence sectors (including not only 'aircraft' for civilian purposes but all civilian production of this defence sector).

Preliminary figures for 2001 (www.vpk.ru) indicate a total growth of the output of the defence complex by 4.5 %. Highest growth rates are in aviation (17.1 %) and electronics (15.7 %), worst off is shipbuilding (-

35.4 %). The growth of the civilian output is estimated to 11.8 %. This would imply a reduction of the military output of the defence complex in spite of the fact the arms exports in 2001 increased considerably.

For the Perm region corresponding figures are not available (according to the Regional Administration in June, 2002). An analysis of the Perm industry from 1999 (Kontseptsiia razvitiia promyshlennosti, 1999) indicates the following relationship between civilian and military production for any given year (p. 32). According to the Perm Regional Administration the relations have been stable in 1999-2001 with military production of 8.5-10%.

Table 3
Military/Civilian Production of the Perm Defence Industry.

	1990	1991	1992	1993	1994	1995	1996	1997	1998
Total	100	100	100	100	100	100	100	100	100
Military	30	25	14	10	10	9	10	11	10,5
Civilian	70	75	86	90	90	91	90	89	89,5

These figures do not allow for comparison to the 1991 levels of production. In relation to the national figures in Table 1 Perm is on the one hand not a privileged area (only a few enterprises have been selected as prime contractors by the federal government). On the other hand Perm has a large proportion of aviation which is performing well.

www.ingramcontent.com/pod-product-compliance
Lightning Source LLC
Chambersburg PA
CBHW050437280326
41932CB00013BA/2150